In the Realm of

MIRACLES
&
VISIONS

In the Realm of

MIRACLES
&
VISIONS

E. Randall Floyd

HARBOR
HOUSE
Augusta

In the Realm of Miracles and Visions
By E. Randall Floyd
A Harbor House Book/2006

Harbor House
111 Tenth St.
Augusta, GA 30901
www.harborhousebooks.com

Book design by Nathan Elliott

Library of Congress Cataloging-in-Publication Data
Floyd, E. Randall.
  In the realm of miracles and visions / E. Randall Floyd.
    p. cm.
  ISBN 1-891799-64-9
  1. Miracles. 2. Supernatural. 3. Visions. I. Title.
  BT97.3.F56 2006
  202'.117--dc22
                                        2006028627

Printed in the U.S.A.

10 9 8 7 6 5 4 3 2 1

OTHER TITLES
BY
E. RANDALL FLOYD

100 of the World's Greatest Mysteries:
Strange Secrets of the Past Revealed

The Good, the Bad & the Mad:
Weird People in American History

Deep in the Heart

In The Realm of Ghost & Hauntings

Contents

To my beautiful wife, Anne

> *"Miracles are not contrary*
> *to nature, but only contrary to*
> *what we know about nature."*
> —St. Augustine

DO YOU BELIEVE IN MIRACLES?

MIRACLE: *"an event that appears unexplainable by the laws of nature and so is held to be supernatural in origin or an act of God."*

—American Heritage Dictionary

The subject of this book is miracles.

Whenever something out of the ordinary happens—a hail-Mary pass that scores the winning touchdown, an unexpected windfall of cash, a phone call from a long-lost friend, a biopsy that comes back negative—we say it's a miracle.

In recent years it has become customary to refer to any unexpected daily occurrence as a miracle—a promotion at work, birth of a normal baby, even beating a traffic light.

Consider the following:

• An autistic basketball player enters the game for the very first time in his career—with only four minutes left—and scores 20 straight points to help win the game...

• A police officer shot by an armed robber survives without injury when the bullet strikes a metal coin in his pocket...

• A young co-ed motoring alone through an Arizona desert runs out of gas but manages to drive 60 miles to safety on an empty tank...

• A toddler falls from an eighth-story window in New York City and survives without a scratch...

• A crippled woman throws away her crutches and walks free

after being touched on the forehead by a Texas evangelist...

• A white buffalo—sacred to Native American tribes—is born in Wisconsin.

Were these miracles?

While skeptics argue that miraculous happenings are nothing more than mere coincidence, religious people say miracles are the work of God. How else can we explain the above stories—or the ability of a young mother to move a two-ton automobile to free her trapped child, or how a British airman survived falling 18,000 feet from his burning aircraft with hardly more than a scratch?

Belief in miracles has come a long way since Moses parted the Reed (formerly "Red") Sea in biblical times and ecstatic saints and nuns secluded in remote caves and monasteries communed with angels and demons. Today, images of Christ have been spotted in pieces of sheet metal, in smoke from the *Challenger* explosion and on the side of doublewide trailers. He's been seen hobnobbing with homeless people in places like Miami and Cairo, while paintings and icons of the Virgin Mary are said to shed tears of blood.

As if to inspire the faithful and taunt the skeptics, glowing "crosses of light" have appeared in the windows of churches and bathrooms from the Philippines to Philadelphia. The Indian government was shut down not long ago when police couldn't control mobs cramming into temples to see religious idols lapping up milk from spoons and bowls.

In Mexico, millions of sick and lame people sip water from a muddy well and are miraculously healed. In Dusseldorf, Germany, leading newspapers run headlines about people who say they have been cured of cancer, obesity, baldness and other ailments just by drinking water flowing out of a dark cave.

Until a couple of years ago, the Immaculate Virgin appeared regularly on a windswept Georgia hillside to offer messages of hope and peace to millions of pilgrims. In fact, a vision of Mother Mary, often accompanied by angels and saints, has become the most commonly reported miracle in our modern age.

Clearly, something out of the ordinary seems to be going

on—but what?

While most of these phenomena are easily dismissed as illusions, hallucinations or, in a few cases, outright fraud, many remain inexplicable. During the past 175 years, for example, the Catholic Church has authenticated at least 14 apparitions as "worthy of pious belief"—findings that leave Catholics free to believe or disbelieve as they wish.

In July 1991, *Life* magazine's cover story asked "Do you believe in miracles?" and reported that the vast majority of people embrace the notion that supernatural events do occur— quite often, in fact.

"There's been a rash of sacred apparitions all over the world," said editor Peter Bonventre. "It's one of the greatest stories of our time."

Four years later, in April 1995, *Time* magazine featured an eight-page spread on miracles and concluded, "People are hungry for signs."

Do these occurrences mean God is sending signals to us?

Hardly, says William Dinges, religion professor at the Catholic University of America in Washington, D.C. "You go looking for a miracle, and you see a miracle," he summarized in a *U.S. News* report.

Skeptics argue that miracles are nothing more than wishful thinking and blind luck. Famed English philosopher David Hume dismisses the very idea of miracles as humbug, describing them as "transgressions of the laws of nature," while pointing out that only barbaric and the least educated people believe in miracles.

Religious thinkers, on the other hand, maintain that miracles are the work of God. Lisa Schwebel, who approaches miraculous apparitions analytically in her book *Apparitions, Healings and Weeping Madonnas*, insists there is no reason to deny the spiritual validity in apparitions and other wonders.

"Within the created order," she writes, "human beings are not merely biological, nor is nature merely natural. Matter and spirit are open to one another. This is the real miracle."

Since earliest times, miracles and rumors of miracles have been part of religious dogma from one corner of the world to the next. Sent by God, they are seen as mystical reminders that the Almighty cares about the members of His flock enough to occasionally intercede on their behalf.

In prehistoric times, witch doctors drove away demons by performing miracles. Similarly, the magi of ancient Mesopotamia divined miracles to foretell the future. The Christian Bible is full of stories linking God to miraculous events—the parting of the Reed Sea, Ezekiel's wheel, Jesus feeding the multitudes, and accounts of how He raised Lazarus from the dead.

Miracles were common during the Middle Ages as church leaders sought to offer hope, comfort and meaning in a world gone mad with war, death, disease and despair. Monarchs, emperors and popes looked to cosmic signs and consulted visionary prophets before embarking on military crusades or planning political strategy.

Even today, with AIDS and bird flu epidemics on the rampage and the civilized world struggling against global terrorism, newspapers regularly headline front page stories about Marian apparitions, stigmata, visions, crop circles and weeping icons.

And it doesn't end there.

Television and radio programming proclaim "miracle cures" for everything from balding to obesity. Garage door systems are described as "miraculous inventions," while movies about ice hockey games invoke the word *miracle* in the title. And who can forget the "miracle catch" made by Franco Harris of the Pittsburgh Steelers two decades ago?

In ages past, the term *miracle* was usually reserved for truly extraordinary events—comets lighting up the night sky, an invading army suddenly withdrawing from a besieged city, a blind man regaining his sight. These were miracles that transformed lives, won wars, sparked revolutions and, in some cases, changed the course of history.

Did Joshua's trumpet blast not bring down the walls at Jericho? Would Constantine have been victorious at Milvian Bridge had he not seen the sign of the Cross before launching his forces into battle? How different would the world be today had a certain young Austrian named Adolf Hitler not gone ga-ga over an ancient spear thought to possess special powers—the same spear that supposedly penetrated Christ's side while nailed to the cross?

Believers insist these miraculous events and notions were prompted by divine intervention—sometimes by good forces, sometimes by evil. But they are all seen as miracles, miracles that—in these cases at least—changed the course of history.

While belief in miracles is at the core of certain Charismatic and Pentecostal faiths, the Roman Catholic Church, taking a more cautious view than Protestant denominations, implemented a codified system of determining what is and what is not a miracle.

Outside the shadow of Rome, miracles have enjoyed something of a renaissance in recent years, thanks to new outbreaks of religious wars, millennial anxiety, the resurgence of Islamic fundamentalism and cultural shifts in society. In her book, *The Power of Miracles*, *New York Times* reporter Joan Anderson argues that miracles have become everyday occurrences in American life.

"It is clear that people everywhere are becoming more fascinated with religion, are searching more for spiritual connection, and are longing for signs of God's guidance and protection," she writes. "Today, people crave and believe in miracles more than ever before."

Hardly a week goes by, she notes, without reports somewhere in America of a "celestial vision, unexpected healing, inexplicable protection and many other signs and wonders."

To be sure, some religious leaders warn against "false miracles" being performed in the name of God. They remind us of Paul's admonition that evil powers often cast miracles in the name of Satan and his unholy angels. Beware of phony miracles and miracle-makers, the Bible seems to be saying, for they might be nothing more than "darkness disguised as light" for the benefit of Satan.

Amid all the theological debate and media hoopla, most of us still pray for miracles. We search for "signs and wonders," comforting reminders that we are not alone in the universe, that we walk in the graceful presence of angels, that a Higher Power is up there looking after us.

We know that because He sends us miracles.

*"There are only two ways to live your life.
One is as though nothing is a miracle. The other
is as though everything is a miracle."*
—Albert Einstein

WHAT IS A MIRACLE?

The story is told about a boy who comes home from school one day, and his father asks him what he learned in religion class.

"It was awesome," the boy replies. "We were studying about miracles in the Bible when we got to the part about Hebrew slaves trying to escape the Pharaoh's army."

"What happened?" the father asks.

"They were trapped. The Reed Sea was in front of them, Pharaoh's men closing in fast behind them. They were facing certain doom."

"Then what happened?"

"Like I said, Dad, it was a miracle," the boy answers. "Suddenly, out of nowhere the Israeli army and air force appeared with F-16 jets and tanks and blew the Pharaoh's army to smithereens."

Each year, tens of thousands of people around the world experience what they believe to be miracles. While these modern-day miracles might not be as dramatic as the sudden intervention of the Israeli military, many are perceived as life-altering events. Most of these miracles rarely make news, but let an apparition of the Virgin Mary suddenly appear on a country hillside or the face of Jesus appear in a bowl of Corn Flakes and it's the lead story on CNN.

Sacred miracles and visions are among the oldest phenomena in the world, and they appear to be on the rise as populations struggle to deal with social decay, rising fuel prices, plagues and global terrorism. World wide, people who claim to have experienced miraculous phenomena number in the millions.

Images of Jesus have been seen floating in the clouds, on the side of houses, on tree stumps, in windows—even on a tortilla. Crosses of light have been spotted on mountaintops, on bedroom walls, in glasses of milk. By far, images of the Virgin Mary are most numerous, with reports flooding in from all parts of the world.

Believers say miracles like these are God's way of reassuring an increasingly secular world that He has not forgotten His people. Miracles, they explain, are simply reminders that God's grace is only a prayer away.

There are generally two kinds of miracles—private and public. Private miracles are smaller and more personal—an unexpected letter from a long-lost friend, finding a misplaced wedding ring after 20 years, the underdog team winning the game at the buzzer.

Public miracles happen on a much grander scale. These miracles are astounding and undeniable—usually brought about by supernatural forces intervening with the established laws of nature. When thousands of people gathered on a hilltop claim to see the Virgin Mary, or when the body of a centuries-old saint lies as fresh and uncorrupted as the day she died, these occurrences are seen as major miracles.

In an age of hip-hop, Blackberries and plasma big screens, why would anyone want to write a book about miracles and visions? Weeping statues, wooden icons that bleed and ooze oil and levitating saints seem so un-cool, not the kind of things to get excited about on Spring Break.

But recent studies suggest that growing numbers of people of all age groups are yearning to know more about supernatural phenomena, particularly the interaction of miracles and visions in their lives. A *Newsweek* poll shows that 84 percent of adult Americans say they believe God performs miracles, and 48 percent report they have experienced or witnessed one.

Most people who believe in miracles are religious. After all, Jesus healed the sick and raised the dead. The Roman Catholic Church honors miracle-makers by granting many of them sainthood. Protestants, on the other hand, generally reject the "cult of the saints" but still believe God works in mysterious ways to reward the faithful through miracles.

Today, three-fourths of all Catholics say they've prayed to God or a saint for a miracle at least once. The number of Evangelicals is much higher—81 percent—while 54 percent of other Protestants believe God can, and does, answer prayers occasionally with a miracle. Pentecostals accept miracles as an everyday part of life.

Some theologians say this resurging interest in miracles reflects an increasing nostalgia for a simpler time, a "purer and safer era" when rosary recitations, novenas and benedictions— largely abandoned by many churches in the 1960s—were commonplace.

Whatever the cause, miracles apparently have become a permanent fixture on the contemporary cultural landscape. Even before the turn of the new millennium, indications were strong that increasing numbers of Americans were turning to spiritual values in record numbers—perhaps as a reaction to the anarchic days of the 1960s and 1970s and the excesses of the last two decades of the twentieth century.

With the fall of communism, there also appears to be a resurgence of the spirit in Eastern European countries, as well as Asia, Africa and South America. Since the 1980s, the number of miracles being reported and documented has grown so fast that church leaders and scientists are working overtime to keep up with the flood of signs—weeping icons, bleeding statues, encounters with angels and other visions—reported each year in the media and in confessional booths.

While religious leaders usually see miracles as a blessing and proof of a divine power, many say there is a dark side of these occurrences that must not be overlooked. Moses, for example, warned the Israelites that evil forces can also produce miracle works.

"One should be very careful in accepting miracles as proof of Jesus Christ or God the Father," said scholar and author Ernest L. Martin. "Only if the signs and wonders are manifested within the righteous standards shown in the Holy Bible can any credence be afforded them. Simply because a miracle is performed in the name of God or Christ is no guarantee that the source is the true God."

Miracles can even be dangerous things in the minds of some believers because Satan and demons occasionally produce miracles and visions to deceive and otherwise create confusion among the faithful.

In recent years, serious efforts have been made to validate reported miracles. The Marian shrine at Lourdes, France—where the first miraculous cures were accepted in 1862—had only 67 of 6,000 healing claims authenticated by its medical boards. In Iran, the Jamkaran Holy Mosque—which has been attracting pilgrims for more than a thousand years—has validated eight miracles out of more than 300 claims.

Doubters will always deny the validity of mystical phenomena, while believers—whether snake-handling Pentecostals in the piney backwoods of Tennessee or robed Catholic clerics in the marbled halls of the Vatican—will continue to interpret miracles as the work of a strange but, mighty and benevolent, God.

"I do not think our successes can compete with those of Lourdes. There are so many more people who believe in the miracles of the Blessed Virgin than in the existence of the unconscious."
—Sigmund Freud

APPARITIONS

While meditating alone in a cave on the Greek island of Patmos, a man named John had a dream. And in that dream Christ appeared to him, standing tall in the midst of seven candlesticks, and commanded him to write down what he saw and heard.

The result, as every Sunday School child knows, was the New Testament Book of Revelation—or The Apocalypse—in which John recorded the many harrowing visions given to him by Christ, including the end of the world.

John's apocalyptic vision was not the first recorded in the Bible, nor would it be the last. In the Book of Genesis, God appeared to Adam and Eve in the Garden of Eden and issued various instructions. Moses "went up to the mountain" and received commands from the burning bush. Jesus Christ returned from the dead and wandered among his living disciples 40 days before ascending to heaven.

According to St. Paul: "He (Jesus) appeared to Peter, and then to the Twelve Disciples. After that, he appeared to more than five hundred of the brothers at the same time."

Besides visions of Christ, Paul tells of many other apparitions he encountered, most notably along the road to Damascus where he saw a "heavenly vision" and heard the voice of the Lord.

The whole Bible is replete with apparitions, dreams, visions, prophecies and miracles that continue to be studied and taught at churches, temples and synagogues throughout the world. Even secular schools teach about Emperor Constantine's mystical revelation at Milvian Bridge, and about Joan of Arc, the Maid of

Orleans, who received numerous visions through which she was urged to lead the French army to victory against the English.

Angels count among the numerous apparitions mentioned in the Bible. Some scholars list as many as 140 angel sightings scattered throughout the Old and New Testaments, including the archangel Gabriel. Jesus, too, had visions of angels, as did other noted men and women in the Scriptures, including Jacob who even wrestled with a winged being. Famous saints are among the manifestations experienced by visionaries, usually accompanying the Virgin Mary.

Darker angels have been known to make their presence known as well, including the Devil who often transforms himself into an angel of light in order to seduce souls. Throughout history many of the Christian mystics who have received divine apparitions also experienced various kinds of demonic attacks.

The Catholic Church generally recognizes two kinds of apparitions—those considered "Not Worthy of Belief" and those "Worthy of Belief." Those considered Not Worthy have been proved to be false, while those deemed Worthy of Belief show signs of authenticity and are therefore recognized and declared authentic by the Church.

Millions of Americans say they've experienced religious visions. These apparitions occur more frequently during or shortly after long periods of fasting, meditating, prayer or great stress or anxiety. While religious people generally believe these apparitions are real manifestations of their deity, skeptics say they're more likely the result of various natural causes.

Recent medical studies have linked the mystical experiences of St. Paul, Moses and other famous religious leaders in ancient times to temporal lobe brain disorders. In his controversial book, *The Origin of Consciousness in the Breakdown of the Bicameral Brain*, Princeton psychologist Julian Jaynes argues that the brain activity of ancient people—those living roughly 3,500 years ago, prior to early evidence of consciousness such as logic, reason and ethics—would have resembled that of modern schizophrenics.

"They heard voices, summoned up visions and lacked the

sense of metaphor and individual identity that characterizes a more advanced mind," Jaynes writes. "Some of these ancestral synaptic leftovers are buried deep in the modern brain, which would explain many of our present-day sensations of God or spirituality."

Gregory Holmes, a pediatric neurologist at Dartmouth Medical School, believes that Ellen White, founder of the Seventh- day Adventists movement, suffered from temporal lobe epilepsy. During her life, White received hundreds of dramatic religious visions considered key to the establishment of her church, which today boasts more than 12 million followers.

According to Dr. Holmes, White suffered a severe blow to the head at the age of nine and never returned to school. During long periods confined to bed, she became "highly religious" and began to experience powerful visions.

"Her whole clinical course, to me, suggested the high probability that she had temporal lobe epilepsy," concludes Holmes. "This would indicate to me that the spiritual visions she was having would not be genuine, but due to the seizures."

Daniel Giang, a neurologist and spokesman for the Seventh-day Adventists, disagrees with Holmes' findings. He insists the visions began too long after the accident to have been caused by it.

"Ellen's visions lasted from 15 minutes to three hours or more," Dr. Giang says. "She never apparently had any briefer visions. That's quite unusual for seizures."

While the studies continue, so do the visions. For the faithful, these apparitions are nothing less than holy manifestations from God, and no amount of laboratory experimentation or scientific research can alter their fundamental belief that what they've experienced is real and genuine.

Apparitions, unlike ghosts and phantoms of popular lore, rarely intend to frighten or harm recipients. They come bearing good news or to issue instructions and appear in a variety of locations, from scenic hilltops and lakeshores to bedrooms and jail cells. Most make themselves apparent while the recipient is in a state of ecstasy, a trance-like condition either induced spontaneously or brought on by intense prayer, meditation or fasting.

Religious people, especially Christians, still believe that God grants miracles and visions to the righteous. All they have to do is look—and believe.

Angels in Blue and Gray
Virginia

HEAVENLY VISITATIONS are nothing new.

Since earliest times, stories have been told about angels and other spirit-like beings descending from the clouds to interact with humans. Ezekiel's encounter with a flaming wheel and Jacob's courageous wrestling match with a winged angel are among the many biblical accounts of angelic intervention on Earth.

It is one thing to engage a solitary angel, as did Jacob—but quite another to encounter an entire army of angelic beings, as did a group of Virginians during the American Civil War. The miraculous event came at the height of the conflict, while battles raged across Greenbriar County in the western part of the state.

The date was Oct. 1, 1863. The place: a small valley several miles west of Lewisburg. Around 3 p.m., a mysterious army of phantom soldiers suddenly appeared in the sky, marching directly overhead in a westerly direction.

Hundreds of eyewitnesses supposedly watched the eerie procession as it continued across the hazy blue sky, finally vanishing in a puff of green-tinged smoke beyond a low line of hills.

Moses Dwyer, a prominent local planter, was sitting on his front porch listening to the roar of distant musket-fire when he saw "thousands upon thousands" of strange aerial beings floating into view. He described them as "grim and weary," marching in step to a muffled drumbeat.

"They were traveling in the same direction," Dwyer told a newspaper reporter. "They were marching double-quick, some 30 or 40 men in depth as they crossed the valley and ascended the almost insurmountable hills opposite."

Dwyer and other witnesses said the eerie army of cloud-borne marchers "seemed to stoop, as if carrying a heavy load up a steep mountain."

Another witness said, "The men were of great variety and size. Some were extremely large while others were very small in stature. As they marched, their arms, heads and legs could be seen distinctly moving. They observed military discipline with no stragglers breaking ranks."

Some witnesses claimed that a multitude of other objects also appeared to be edged in a light-blue glow.

"All of the soldiers wore a uniform outfit—white shirts and white pants," commented another observer.

Although most witnesses described the marchers as militaristic, one gave the following account: "They were not armed with guns, swords or anything that would give the indication of men marching off to war. They continued through the valley, over a steep road, up the hills and finally, in approximately an hour, disappeared from sight."

News of the apparition spread fast. So did reports of other sightings of similar but less spectacular armies in surrounding counties.

Had God sent an army of angels to warn both sides to end the bloody conflict?

Some clergymen thought so, while certain newspaper editors and generals interpreted the vision as a positive sign that they should continue the struggle, that God was on their side. Throughout history, from Milvian Bridge to Remagen, success in battle had been attributed by many leaders to divine intervention.

So it was in Greenbriar County in October 1863, with witnesses on both sides speculating that the "miracle at Greenbriar" was a sign from God.

Two weeks after the initial sighting, on Oct. 14, a remarkably similar vision was observed by Confederate pickets at nearby Runger's Mill. A number of locals confirmed the second spectacle, claiming that it lasted more than an hour.

More attempts were made to explain the pair of phenomena, none to the satisfaction of eyewitnesses or the legions of others who have studied the incidents. One editorial writer stressed that these were more "angelic armies" sent into battle on the Confederate side because God favored the South.

Another writer disagreed with that assessment, arguing instead that the ghostly soldiers were Northern reinforcements sent down from a "tear-stained Heaven."

Eventually, the bloody business of war diverted attention from the miraculous incident. For years, however, folks in the region continued to gossip about the day the angels came down to Virginia.

Marian Miracles

WHILE STORIES ABOUT ANGELS figure prominently in religious and literary texts, the most famous and most frequently sighted sacred apparition is Mary, the Mother of Jesus. According to the Catholic Church, Mary never actually died but was instead taken bodily into heaven in an event called the Assumption.

Ever since, Mary—also known as the Immaculate Virgin, Blessed Virgin, Blessed Mother and Holy Mother—has been returning to earth periodically to comfort the sick and poor, council the faithful, offer cryptic instructions and occasionally issue dire warnings of global consequences. Mostly she comes solo, but sometimes she's accompanied by her son, Jesus Christ, and an assorted host of angels.

Mary usually appears in a pure white light, clad in a long robe and head covering or veil. She speaks in a language familiar to those present, usually foretelling apocalyptic disasters and urging people to repent, pray and do penance.

Marian sightings have been documented since the fifth century, but the twentieth century has been called the "Era of Mary" because more than four hundred were documented during this period alone, mostly in Europe and the Americas. These modern apparitions usually occurred to large numbers of people and, unlike in earlier centuries, groups of children seemed to be the preferred audience.

Apparitions are often accompanied by other miracles—rosaries changing colors, the sun spinning and twisting, bizarre cloud formations and considerable thunder and lightning. Devotees also comment about "tingling sensations" when in the presence of an alleged apparition. Objects are known to glow or radiate heat. Angels and other divine beings, including the Baby Jesus, are also often seen descending from the heavens with Mary.

Not all religious people and organizations are open to or welcome such visions. The Special Assembly of America of the Synod of Bishops claims that all apparitions, and Marian apparitions especially, tend to cause division with local churches.

"Within the church community, the multiplication of supposed apparitions or visions is sowing confusion and reveals a certain lack of a solid basis to the faith and Christian life among her members," it said in a paper.

In a recent interview at Fatima, Portugal, site of the famous mid-nineteenth century Marian sighting, Cardinal Joseph Ratziner said, "To all curious people, I would say I am certain the Virgin does not engage in sensationalism; she does not act in order to instigate fear. She does not present apocalyptic visions, but guides people to her Son. And this is what is essential."

Hints are offered throughout the Bible urging readers to ignore fake miracles and visions. In John 20:29, Christ says, "Have you come to believe because you have seen me? Blessed are those who have not seen and have believed."

Marian apparitions are said to occur most often during times of great turmoil and stress—war, famine or natural disaster. Her reasons for appearing vary, but usually she appears to urge people to pray and seek peace.

Since the time of St. Francis of Assisi, the Holy Mother has made appearances to people from all walks of life—saints, priests, nuns, housewives, airplane pilots, construction workers, soldiers on the battlefield.

Whether a devout Catholic, an atheist or simply a die-hard skeptic unwilling to accept the notion of a 2,000-year-old virginal Holy Mother roaming the earth, one can't help but appreciate the following stories about miraculous events that touched—and, in some cases, changed—the lives of millions of people around the world.

Our Lady of Fatima
Portugal

IT WAS THE SUMMER OF 1917, and the "war to end all wars" was raging across northern Europe. In a poor, remote corner of central Portugal, far removed from the bloody battlefields of France, miraculous events were about to unfold that would change the lives of countless millions of people around the world.

On May 13 of that year, a lady "brighter than the sun" appeared in a ball of light to three children quietly tending their sheep in a place called the Cova da Iria, near Fatima, a small village about 90 miles from Lisbon.

The apparition said she was from heaven and asked them to return to this same spot for the next six months—and always on the thirteenth day of the month. Before gradually fading away, the radiant lady told them she had a message of vital importance to share with them, an apocalyptic message for the entire world.

"Do not be afraid," she reassured the three children—Lucia, 10, and her two cousins, Jacinta, 7, and Francisco, 9. "I will not harm you....You are going to have much to suffer, but the grace of God will be your comfort."

Terrified, yet exhilarated by their mystical encounter, the children ran home crying and told their parents about the strange vision from the skies. They were accused of "telling lies" and were punished with a thrashing. Still, on June 13, the children—accompanied by some 50 inquisitive villagers—trekked back out to the lonely hillside for their noonday rendezvous with the mysterious lady.

Kneeling on the rocky ground and clutching their rosaries, the children looked up and saw the radiant glow—just like before. At this point, the children began to suspect this "glowing messenger from God" was actually the Virgin Mary. No one else saw anything, except some peasants who noticed inexplicable movement in the clouds.

At one point, Lucia begged the Lady to take them to heaven. "Francisco and Jacinta will be taken soon, but you are to stay here some time longer," the Lady replied. "Jesus wishes to make use of you to make me known and loved. He wants to establish in the world devotion to my Immaculate Heart."

A month later the children returned to the site, accompanied by some 5,000 people. This time the luminous apparition warned of a coming catastrophe that would be even greater than the current war in Europe, one that would destroy the world.

The first sign of the disaster would be seen in the heavens— "a bright, unknown light which will be God's sign that He is about to punish the people of the world for their crimes."

The lady also gave them a grim vision of Hell, described as a "vast sea of fire within the earth, full of lost souls like black animals, tumbling in pain, burning within and without, shrieking horribly."

Again, nobody else saw the vision or heard anything unusual—and once again, the children were given a beating for lying.

The miraculous events taking place at Fatima coincided with attempts by the Roman Catholic Church to halt the spread of Bolshevism. Frustrated after years of appealing for world peace, Pope Benedict XV finally asked the Virgin Mother to intercede for peace on the planet.

Many thinkers in and outside the church saw Russia and the specter of communism as evil, the work of Satan. If atheism triumphed, the Catholic Church in Europe and elsewhere around the world would be in peril.

Amid this backdrop of war and the dark cloud of communism, church leaders saw in the Fatima miracle a chance to reinvigorate the church, to bring people back to God and away from the holocaust at hand.

On Oct. 13, a rainy, miserable day, a crowd of 70,000 people accompanied the children back to the hillside to look for the apparitions. This time the shining lady, again invisible to all but the children, announced her identity: she was none other that Our Lady of the Rosary, and she told them three "secrets" about the future.

Then something quite shocking happened.

The black clouds suddenly parted and the sun came out. At first it seemed to start spinning, and then it began to plunge crazily toward the earth. The crowd was terrified. After a few moments of this, the sun returned to its normal position and then, twice more, repeated the same maneuver.

One of the witnesses, Maria Carriera, testified to the spectacular nature of the solar miracle. "It turned everything different colors—yellow, blue, white—and it shook and trembled," she said. "It seemed like a wheel of fire which was going to fall on the people. They cried out, 'We shall all be killed, we shall all be killed!' At last the sun stopped moving and we all breathed a sigh of relief. We were still alive and the miracle which the children had foretold had taken place."

Later, people found that their clothing, which had been soaked in the downpour, was quite dry.

As the Lady had foretold, the two younger children, Francisco and Jacinta, died during the influenza epidemic of 1918-19. And as a result of her experiences—and to escape from the publicity that was turning her into a sideshow freak—Lucia became a nun and learned to read and write so she could record the "secrets" the lady had told her. The first was the vision of hell, previously described, and the reference to what many believe was World War II.

In 1927, Sister Marie das Dores—as Lucia now called herself—claimed that Christ himself had visited her and that He had asked her to be ready for "the Lady's final and most momentous message of all"—which would be imparted to her sometime in the year 1960.

That year, 1960—the year Lucia said she would get the

Virgin's final message—she joined the convent of Coimbra. Thousands of Catholics throughout the world demanded to know what the Madonna had said to her, but Lucia, now 53, refused to talk. She did not reveal her secret until 1967, and then only to Pope Paul VI.

In 1930, church officials concluded an official investigation of the Fatima events and formally pronounced them "worthy of belief." Such formal declarations about miraculous events are extremely rare. Six successive Popes have also proclaimed their belief in Fatima.

Pope *John Paul II* went much farther, crediting Our Lady of Fatima with saving him from an assassin's bullet. He personally visited Fatima three times, the last time in the year 2000.

Meanwhile, all manner of theories circulated in the Church about the long-awaited "third secret." Some claimed it spoke of nuclear war or of the deposition or assassination of a pope. Finally, during a trip to Portugal for the beatification of the visionaries Francisco and Jacinta, Pope John Paul II made a startling announcement: he planned to release the text of the third secret.

A few months later, the Vatican officially released the text.

In part, here is what it says:

"...We saw an angel with a flaming sword in his left hand; flashing, it gave out flames that looked as though they would set the world on fire; but they died out in contact with the splendor that Our Lady radiated toward him from her right hand; pointing to the earth with his right hand, the Angel cried out in a loud voice: 'Penance, Penance, Penance!'

"And we saw in an immense light that is God something similar to how people appear in a mirror when they pass in front of it: a Bishop dressed in White, we had the impression that it was the Holy Father. Other bishops, priests, men and women religious going up a steep mountain, at the top of which there was a big Cross of rough-hewn trunks as of a cork-tree with the bark; before reaching there the Holy Father passed through a big city half in ruins and half trembling with a halting step, afflicted with pain and sorrow, he prayed for the souls of the corpses he met on his way; having reached the top of the mountain, on his knees at the foot of the big Cross he was killed by a group of soldiers who fired bullets and arrows at him, and in the same way there died one after another of the other Bishops, Priests, men and women Religious, and various lay people of different ranks and positions. Beneath the two arms of the Cross there were two Angels, each with a crystal aspersorium in his hand, in which they gathered up the blood of the Martyrs and with it sprinkled the souls that were making their way to God."

It is said that Pope John Paul II believed the text refers to the failed attempt by Mehmet Ali Agca to assassinate him on May 13, 1981—the anniversary of the first vision at Fatima. After the attack, the pope said he kept concentrating on the Holy Mother, and believed that the Virgin Mary spared him from death.

"It was the motherly hand that guided the bullet's path," he said.

At least one high-ranking church official—Bishop Paul M. Hnilica—thinks the third secret was something else. In one conversation with the pope, he said the pope told him: "…I have come to understand that the only solution to all the problems of the world, the deliverance from war, the deliverance from atheism, and from the defection from God is the conversion of Russia. The conversion of Russia is the content and meaning of the message of Fatima. Not until then will the triumph of Mary come."

Many scholars and theologians do not believe the released text is the real third secret. In 1957, Sister Lucia herself hinted that "the devil is in the mood for engaging in a decisive battle against the Blessed Virgin…and the devil knows what it is that most offends God and which in a short space of time will gain for him the greatest number of souls. Thus, the devil does everything to overcome souls consecrated to God, because in this way, the devil will succeed in leaving souls of the faithful abandoned by their leaders, thereby the more easily will he seize them."

In 1984, Cardinal Joseph Ratzinger—later to become Pope Benedict XVI—said the Third Secret pertained to "…the dangers threatening the faith and the life of the Christian, and therefore of the world...."

The Bishop of Fatima, Cosme do Amaral, said in 1984: "Its content concerns only our faith. To identify the Third Secret with catastrophic announcements or with a nuclear holocaust is to deform the meaning of the message...."

In 1980, Pope John Paul II went on record saying his predecessors did not release the secret "so as not to encourage the world power of Communism to make certain moves."

"Mother Mary Comes to Me"
Conyers, Ga.

THEY CAME FROM as far away as Australia, Russia, Germany and China, tens of thousands of men, women, and children, braving the October chill to participate in one of the most celebrated mystical experiences in American history—a farewell message from Mary, the Blessed Mother of Jesus Christ.

Arriving by pickup trucks, tractors, SUVs and caravans of buses, the faithful gathered on a hilly farm outside Conyers. Ga., a bedroom community 30 miles east of Atlanta, to listen reverently while a middle-aged housewife named Nancy Fowler imparted what was promised to be the Virgin Mother's final message—at least in this part of Georgia.

Clutching rosaries and with tear-stained faces and camcorders scanning the skies, they sang, chanted and prayed, hoping to record the flickering of the sun or perhaps the opening of the door to heaven. Some raised icons, crucifixes and other holy items skyward in hopes they would be blessed by her holy presence.

Finally, the moment arrived—and out onto the porch stepped Fowler. Bleary-eyed and in a soft, almost childlike voice, she intoned over a loudspeaker: "Today my Lady has come for the last time in this way. We will not be able to see Our Lady again in this way until we are in Heaven."

Many of the faithful snapped photos of the sun as Fowler

spoke. In some of the pictures, the sun seemed to change color; in others it seemed to spin in slow circles and cast off strange plumes of fire.

Paul Ault of Dayton, Ohio, displayed two Polaroid photographs he said were taken while the Virgin Mary was speaking with Fowler. The photos both showed the blue sky with billowing clouds. To one side was a vertical cloud shaped like a Madonna image wearing a white robe and long grey mantle.

"I've never seen anything like this," Ault noted. "I took both of these shots and, look, you can see her in one and you can't in the other."

In the end, after Fowler bade the crowd farewell for the last time, the multitude packed up their cameras and sleeping bags and left. Many went away convinced they had beheld miracles that day—rosaries turning gold, the sun spinning and changing colors, and the scent of rose petals filling the air.

The date was Oct. 13, 1998, eight years to the day since Mary had first appeared to Fowler, the ex-wife of an Air Force officer, and relayed messages through her to the world. Ranging from admonitions to prayers, to warnings of war, the messages had always come to Fowler on the same day each year—Oct. 13—and always while alone in her "Apparition Room" at the farmhouse.

Each time she received a message, the former nurse and Cambridge, Mass., native would go outside and announce over a loudspeaker what she had been told to the anxious multitudes gathered around her farmhouse.

Fowler often spoke of Mary's "ever so gentle smile" and tears that flowed with "so much love for her children." She once warned of a "war greater than man has ever known." She frequently delivered messages against abortion and told of prophetic visions—that a ship would sink and that, somewhere beneath a building, the "ground will crack."

"The future holds no concern to those who truly seek God and truly love Him and remain in His favor," she once revealed.

Doctors who attached electrodes to Fowler said they

found unusual brain wave patterns during visions. One neurophysiologist, Dr. Ricardo Castanon of La Paz, Bolivia, said the visionary's heart rate dropped to minimal levels and her brain produced delta waves similar to those experienced in deep sleep.

From the beginning, the official position of the Roman Catholic Church was one of skepticism. A spokesman for the Archdiocese of Atlanta said the Church was reluctant to conduct an investigation of the Conyers apparitions for fear it would only add fuel to the wave of Marian sightings popping up across the United States during the decade of the 1990s.

On the one hand, said Monsignor Peter A. Dora, "This shows a legitimate hunger on the part of many people for spiritual matters, and that we applaud. On the other hand, there's always the possibility that this could turn out to be inauthentic and therefore a scandal to those who have placed credence in it."

Jesus first came to Nancy Fowler in February 1987. Recently divorced and in despair, she said her life changed dramatically after Christ visited her one night in a blinding vision of light. No words were exchanged with the Savior, she said, but Fowler understood she had been chosen for a special purpose—to relay messages of hope and redemption from the Holy Mother to the outside world.

Starting three years later, in 1990, Jesus and Mary made monthly visits to her rural farmhouse to offer these messages of hope and redemption to all believers. Each session would last between half an hour and two hours; on at least one occasion, she said Satan came to her in a vision, but she turned him away.

Through much of the 1990s, the roads to Conyers were clogged with pilgrims yearning to hear Mary's message. They came from every direction, but most were from heavily Hispanic southern Florida and Mexico. They were directed toward a large field adjacent to Fowler's farm where they prayed on Mary's Holy Hill, filled bottles with water from the Blessed Well, or visited the small bookstore on the property.

"There are no words to describe the peace you feel here,"

Norma Lleras of Tampa, Fla., told *the New York Times* during a 1995 visit. "It's like a holy place."

Ammon S. Ripple, a building contractor who moved to Conyers from Maryland to be near the Fowler farm, said, "I believe in God, and God's presence is here."

On this day—Oct. 13, 1998—some 100,000 pilgrims pressed around the Fowler farm to hear the final message. Amid gasps and scattered applause, Nancy Fowler read her final public message from the Virgin Mary.

"If you are worried about the future, put not your attention to these matters," Mrs. Fowler read from handwritten notes. "The future holds no concern to those who truly seek God and love Him and remain in His favor."

As thousands searched the clouds for a sign, Fowler continues. "She, being the loving mother she is, reassured me that she would always remain with me," she said, without offering a reason why the messages were ending. "Just as she reassured me she would always remain with all of you."

People fell to their knees, gasped and clapped when Fowler said that a multitude of souls accompanied Mary in her vision. She said the souls were in purgatory but were being released into heaven in honor of Mary.

Some of the faithful said their cameras caught images of Mary along with strange colors and shapes emanating from the sun.

"I've seen different lights and different images," said Angie Moogalin of Chester, Va., clutching a Polaroid of Mrs. Fowler's house with another shape she claimed was a door above the house. "I come because of all the miracles I have experienced."

The Marian apparitions stopped Oct. 13, 1998, but Fowler continues to have visions of Jesus. She recently moved to Florida after transferring the title of the farm to a non-profit group called "Our Loving Mother's Children, Inc."

The Church has not authenticated the apparitions and indeed has distanced itself from the pilgrimages to Conyers. Yet the archdiocese of Atlanta continues to collect testimonies from those who claim to have experienced healings, conversions and other blessings.

"People are praying," said Atlanta Archbishop John Donoghue. "People are coming back to church who haven't been in a church for a long time. People's faith is restored. Conversions are taking place."

Miracle at Marpingen
Germany

DURING THE LATE NINETEENTH CENTURY, the new nation of Germany found itself locked in a long and bloody conflict between religious and secular authorities that threatened to tear Chancellor Otto von Bismarck's budding new liberal government apart.

At the heart of the turmoil was the government's unwillingness to share political power with the Roman Catholic Church. Despite the vigorous use of state power against disobedient clergy and uncooperative bishops, Germany's Cultural War—the so-called Kulturkampf—had plunged the nation into an almost fanatical feud between the two factions.

In the end, all Bismarck's strong arm tactics accomplished was to help mobilize Catholic opinion, intensify denominational differences between Catholics and Protestants and produced a flourishing Catholic political party.

It was amid this strife that a series of remarkable events occurred to unite people throughout the country and helped patch up many religious and secular differences. This was the repeated appearance of Mary, the Mother of Jesus, at Marpingen, an impoverished little village nestled in the gently rolling hills of the Saarland on Germany's western frontier with France.

The first apparition occurred July 3, 1876, when three 8-year-old girls, returning to their village from picking berries, saw a figure in white whom they identified as the Virgin Mary. After informing their parents and friends, the girls returned to the same site where Mary appeared to them several more times.

According to the young witnesses, the Virgin Mother had descended from Heaven to bring a special message to the troubled people of Germany. "She said we should all live in peace," they explained, adding, "she promised to come back in times of distress."

The controversy generated by the reported Marian apparitions resulted in large numbers of pilgrims flocking to the tiny village in hopes of seeing the Blessed Mother with their own eyes. Many villagers hoped Marpingen would become the equivalent of Lourdes, the French town where Mary had appeared two decades earlier in 1858.

Within days, the situation had clearly gotten out of hand—so much that on July 13, a company of heavily armed infantrymen was dispatched to the village to disperse the large numbers of pilgrims who had gathered to pray at the site where the Virgin Mary supposedly had appeared.

In the beginning, the government's liberal allies loudly condemned the apparitions as the result of female hysteria, peasant superstitions or conscious deception. There were even reports circulating that French agents might be involved.

According to David Blackbourn, a professor of history at Harvard University, the apparitions at Marpingen provided all the proof needed by the liberal government that southern Catholics were backward and stupid.

In his book, *Marpingen: Apparitions of the Virgin Mary in Nineteenth Century Germany*, Blackbourn writes, "The apparitions represented, in liberal eyes, everything they opposed: backwardness, superstition, disorder, the power of the priest and the rule of the ignorant mob."

Even without church encouragement, devotion to the Virgin of Marpingen continued well into the twentieth century. In the 1950s, another round of Marian apparitions occurred in Europe. Many still hoped that the village might become as famous as other shrines like Lourdes and Fatima, which are recognized by the church.

More than a century after the initial sighting, starting in May 1999, Mother Mary allegedly fulfilled her promise to return to Marpingen. Three local women picnicking in a forest were the first to spot the Holy Mother, but there would be at least 13 more visits to the same site where she had supposedly appeared back in 1876.

The new wave of visitations resulted in chaos as tens of thousands of pilgrims swarmed into Marpingen to take part in the Marian apparitions. Mary was last seen in October 1999, where 35,000 witnesses reportedly saw and heard her wish them a tearful farewell.

Some observers said they were aware of a "wonderful and intense smell, like roses," while others noticed a path of "glowing light" descending from heaven. Many said they heard angelic music floating over the forest, while a few claimed to have seen Mary herself, "full of grace," as she moved across the sky blessing the pilgrims, her veil motionless in the wind.

The Catholic Church spent more than six years investigating the second Marian miracle at Marpingen. While it concluded there was "justified doubt" about the supernatural character of the apparitions, the Church stopped short of accusing anyone of pious fraud.

"The vote now says that we're not sure," said Reinhard Marx, bishop of Trier, who led the investigation.

The bishop urged believers to continue venerating the Virgin Mary at Marpingen but stressed that miracles were not essential for those who believe.

Some believers, nonetheless, were hoping for a miracle. Father Jorg Muller, a therapist and author who also served as counselor to the Marpingen visionaries, analyzed the alleged apparitions and observed the three women in moments of religious ecstasy.

"Normally," Muller said, "the pupils contract when light is shone into them. Yet, in this case, the contractions are non-existent. Only after the apparition is over do the reflexes, such as blinking, return. One could not stage these by an act of will. That is out of the question."

After conducting a number of psychological tests with the three visionaries, Muller concluded the women did not suffer from neurosis and were not involved in any kind of manipulation.

In short, added Muller, no one can deny that what the women saw was real—a point tens of thousands of people already knew to be fact.

Tears of Blood
Italy

IN THE SPRING OF 1995, a 5-year-old girl named Jessica Gregori of Civitavecchia, Italy, was the first person to notice tears of blood running down the cheeks of a small white, statue of the Virgin Mary.

"The Holy Mother is crying," Jessica told her parents. They rushed into their front yard to see the crimson tears on the statue they had acquired from a priest who had purchased it on a pilgrimage to Medjugorje, Herzegovina, where many Catholics believe the Virgin Mary had been appearing.

Dumbstruck, Antonio Gregori called his priest. This was a miracle, something the Church had to investigate immediately.

Within days after learning of the "miracle" in the local newspaper, Italians were gripped by the mystery of the crying Madonna, made more compelling by reports of other crying statues that were popping up all over the province.

As the news spread, thousands flocked to Gregori's home to see the miracle with their own eyes. So serious was the case considered, a local judge ordered tests on the 17-inch statue to see if its tears matched the blood of Gregori family members.

Reports were inconclusive. Many investigators reported that the blood was "of unknown origin" and viewed it as a miracle.

The case was never closed—by either Church or local officials—and continues to produce reams of commentary in the press and among Church leaders. Church historians noted that the last wave of miraculous apparitions in Italy occurred in the 1940s during the turbulent postwar period. Sociologists talked about a "collective angst" caused by Italy's unstable political environment.

In spite of the hoopla, many Italians—always wary of fraudulent claims—feared a hoax. Once the wave of crying

Madonnas began to spread, the nation's largest consumer rights organization, Codacons, went to court in several communities, charging fraud and "abuse of public credulity."

"We live in a world full of connivers," Giuseppe Lo Mastros, president of Codacons, told the *New York Times*. "What we are seeing is the development of a miracle industry, or miracle mass production."

Lo Mastros said that out of 291 historical cases of crying Madonnas over the centuries, the Catholic Church has recognized only 14.

"I ask, why does no one know about these investigations?" he said.

Some have speculated that remote-control devices and special heat-sensitive contact lenses caused the statue to cry. But a CAT scan ordered by the local judge showed no hidden mechanisms inside the Civitavecchia Madonna.

One other test indicated the tears were male human blood.

Despite lingering questions, Civitavecchia, with a population of 60,000 and an unemployment rate of 21 percent, quickly set into motion plans to take advantage of its new popularity as a "miracle destination." A large sanctuary for its Madonna was built, complete with a spacious parking garage to accommodate throngs of visitors.

The local bishop, who greeted the first reports with skepticism, says he is now a believer. According to one newspaper reporter, the bishop personally witnessed the statue crying during weeks when it was kept sequestered in his residence.

The Madonna's biggest booster is the city's agnostic mayor, Pietro Tidel.

"Frankly, we are thinking of business," he said. "My position is that in a world in which people venerate hundreds of Madonnas, one more won't hurt."

It could take the Vatican decades to declare the crying statue a miracle, but Mr. Tidel sees no reason to wait.

"Let's pump it," he said. "People cannot follow the same pace as the Vatican. We will not wait 20 years to bring in hot dogs and religious souvenirs."

It has been more than a decade since the Civitavecchia Madonna was discovered weeping in the Gregori garden. The crowds—which peaked at several thousand the first few years—have dwindled somewhat, but the faithful continue to come in hopes of seeing a miracle.

"I believe she is crying," said Antonia Castaldi, a lacemaker who made the 48-mile trip from Rome. "With everything that is happening in the world, maybe God and the Virgin are getting tired, and this is their way of showing it."

Maria de Agreda: Sacred Woman in Blue
Spain, American Southwest

WHEN SPANISH MISSIONARIES reached the Texas wilderness in the early 1600s, they heard a lot of strange stories from local Indians about mysterious, white-skinned gods who had once walked among them.

According to some accounts, these divine visitors had spoken to them in a language different from theirs, but one they could understand. Most of these gods had come and gone in ages past, but all held forth a common promise—they would come again someday.

The story that got the most attention concerned a beautiful, young white "goddess," who, legend has it, appeared among several groups of Indians living in Texas and elsewhere in the Southwest. The Indians called her the "woman in blue" because each time she came she wore a blue cloak—similar, in fact, to those worn by the newly arrived Spanish priests.

Not only was this "woman in blue" a frequent visitor, she was said to have left behind material evidence of her earthly visits—including a portable stone altar adorned with religious emblems and the figures of several saints. There was even a figure of Christ himself!

Intrigued by such stories, missionary leaders wasted no time informing the church back in Spain about their findings. This seemed to be a mystery of profound spiritual significance: how was it that pagan savages living on the far edge of this strange, wild New World had come into possession of the very symbols of Christian faith?

Within a short while, droves of other missionaries, accompanied by soldiers and explorers, flocked to Texas. Their task: solve the mystery of the "woman in blue."

One of the missionaries who came was Father Damien Manzanet, who had recently read a new book, *The Mystical City of God*. In the book, Sister Maria de Agreda, a Castilian nun, told of her many visions in which she often traveled to faraway realms, including Heaven. God supposedly sent eight angels to guide her on her mystical journeys.

On one such spectral trip, she found herself mysteriously transported to a remote wilderness on the frontiers of New Spain—which we know today as western Texas and New Mexico—where she had introduced a heathen race to Christianity.

Sister Maria, a respected abbess who had entered the monastery at the age of 15, claimed to have made the mystical journey more than 500 times in the early seventeenth century. In glowing words, she related how she had been well received by dark-skinned savages who called themselves "Titlas" or "Tejas," and that they had miraculously understood her every word.

Maria's out-of-body travels apparently occurred only when she slept or lapsed into deep trances. Without being too specific, the sister said she would suddenly grow rigid in bed. A state of supreme ecstasy would seize her, and she would be whisked away at blinding speed to the wilderness where she worked and prayed among the savages.

By 1630 all of Spain was abuzz with talk of Sister Maria's "holy mystery." To make the story even more interesting, a group of 50 Jumano Indians had appeared at a convent in northeastern Mexico that same year, asking that missionaries be sent among them. When pressed to explain their sudden interest in European religion, the Indians said a graceful white woman— a "goddess"—had come to them long ago and instructed them in "the truths of the Christian faith."

Who could that white "goddess" have been? Except for the

wife or mistress of an occasional explorer or trader, there was no record of European women having visited that part of the New World. Even more perplexing were the religious artifacts apparently left behind by the "woman in blue."

The more Father Manzanet listened to the stories, the more convinced he became of a connection between Sister Maria's account of her out-of-body travels and the tales told by these brooding savages on the frontier. In her book, Sister Maria had called them Titlas.

Was that not what these Indians he encountered called themselves—*Titlas... Tejas... Techas*?

The similarities were all the proof the Franciscan priest needed to convince himself that it was Maria de Agreda who had visited the ancestors of these Indians long ago. Just why and when he wasn't sure. But the bottom line was that God had used Sister Maria and her miracles to lead him to the wilderness, too.

Like most seventeenth-century Spaniards, Father Manzanet believed strongly in supernatural forces and that divine intervention was an everyday fact of life. And like most of his countrymen, he readily embraced the possibility that Maria de Agreda had been telling the truth when she wrote about her otherworldly travels—that God had indeed sent her among the Indians in the New World to preach and spread the Gospel.

It was Maria's story, in fact, that had spurred legions of missionaries across the Rio Grande into the Texas hinterlands. While some established missions had sought to convert Indians, many searched for proof of the holy sister's travels. As they pressed deeper into Texas, the missionaries heard other stories about the "blue lady." One chief said she had healed his mother by touching her brow. Another legend told how delicate blue flowers always blossomed wherever she stepped.

Father Manzanet himself was once asked by a withered old chief for a piece of blue cloth in which to bury his wife. The Father, stunned by the request, asked why it should be blue.

"Because," said the chief, "that was the color of the cloak worn long ago by the beautiful young woman who had come to

Texas to tell us about God."

The story of the "woman in blue" would be like a magnet in later decades, drawing hundreds of other missionaries and explorers to the Texas territory. Today the Southwest abounds with legends about the mysterious "goddess," who some believe still roams the hills and deserts causing flowers to bloom.

Sightings continued into relatively recent times. In the 1840s, a phantom matching her description supposedly traveled the Sabine River valley aiding malaria victims. During World War II, the apparition was again reported in several locations throughout the American Southwest.

The "real" Maria died at Agreda, the village of her birth near the border of Aragon and Navarre, on May 24, 1665. Her remains, resting in a secluded crypt on the grounds of the convent where she long served, are said to be in an incorrupt state—that is, refusing to naturally decay, even after 335 years. The flush of her cheeks and her lifelike features still baffle the Catholic Church and modern science.

Miracle at Medjugorje
Bosnia

ONE SUMMER AFTERNOON IN 1981, six children playing in the woods near their remote mountain home of Medjugorje, in what was formerly Yugoslavia, looked up in the sky and saw the face of a "beautiful, shining" woman smiling down at them.

At first they were terrified and started to run away. Then a soft voice came to them and said, "Be not afraid....I have a message of great importance to you."

The children listened spellbound while the apparition, who identified herself as the Virgin Mary, told them that "atheists must convert and return to the ways of God" or be damned forever.

"Returning to God can be achieved through peace, conversion, fasting, penance and prayer," the voice went on, adding that "peace is the most important, for it makes everything else possible."

The apparition then "blessed" each child with 10 secrets.

The adolescents, who came to be called "seers" or "visionaries" by the locals, continued to experience daily apparitions. Some 2,000 apparitions were recorded by 1985, most of them occurring in the "chapel of apparitions," the rectory behind St. James Roman Catholic Church in Medjugorje.

The visions usually lasted three to four minutes, although the first apparition had lasted half an hour.

In addition to the apparitions, miraculous healings were soon reported in the area for a range of physical and psychological ailments, from eye diseases and vascular problems to substance addictions.

Other miracles occurred almost daily. In August 1981, the Croatian word for peace—*Mir*—was seen written in the sky at night above the cross on the hill where Mary first appeared. The area soon became known as the Hill of Apparitions.

The Virgin Mother's silhouette has also been seen on the hill. Like the "miracle of the sun" at Fatima, the sun has been reported to pulsate, spin hypnotically, change into a white disc, and shine in a rainbow of brilliant colors.

On Oct. 28, 1981, a bush spontaneously ignited on the hill. People rushed to extinguish it, but by the time they reached it, it had burned itself out, leaving no charring or burned evidence.

Mary reportedly told the young seers that Medjugorje was selected for visitation because the village of about 400 families included "many good believers who were capable of restoring their faith and serving as an example to other people in the world regarding the need to convert."

After their initial vision, the children spent at least six hours in prayer and fasted up to three times a week. They said they conversed with Mary in normal conversational tones and in their native Croatian. During the apparitions, experts examined the visionaries and found they did not react to light, hear any earthly sound or respond to being touched.

As a result of the apparitions, many villagers converted and began attending daily church services.

Pilgrims who visit the church and rectory say Mary appears to them during prayer. Others report unusual experiences, such as the changing of rosary chains to gold.

Photographs appear to show images of the figure of Jesus on the cross on the hill, Mary in prayer against the cross, Mary and child in the sky, and unnatural rays of light striking the cross.

After years of investigations, the Vatican has yet to validate the miraculous claims at Medjugorje. The official position seems to be one of "wait and see." One church spokesman confided, "We must...always beware of the Evil One presenting himself as an Angel of Light by offering something good to us that is still a lesser good than the one God is calling us toward."

In the early 1990s, efforts were made by the Congregation for the Doctrine of the Faith to ban church-sanctioned trips to Medjugorje. "It cannot be confirmed that supernatural apparitions or revelations are occurring here," one archbishop concluded.

That may be so, but while no evidence has been found to substantiate a miracle, the church unofficially admits nothing has been ruled out either.

The "miracle at Medjugorje" continues to make news, drawing thousands of pilgrims, journalists and curiosity-seekers each year. Some come in search of sensationalism, but most are sincere in their hopes of experiencing something miraculous.

Vision in the Clouds
Lubbock, Texas

ON THE AFTERNOON OF AUG. 15, 1988, some 12,000 people gathered at a small Catholic church in Lubbock, Texas, to witness a miracle. They came from all parts of the country. Some brought sleeping bags and tents, while others arrived in four-wheel drive vehicles and sleek motor homes.

The occasion was the Feast of the Assumption, one of the Roman Catholic Church's holiest festivals, which celebrates the day the Virgin Mary ascended into heaven. But this was to be no ordinary celebration of the feast.

With television cameras and reporters looking on and helicopters buzzing overhead, Monsignor Joseph James—the charismatic leader of St. John Neumann Catholic Church—wandered among the crowd, beseeching the multitude of worshipers to kneel and pray.

For weeks the monsignor had been promising his congregation that "something miraculous" was going to happen. He knew because Mother Mary had appeared to him in a vision on a recent trip to Medjugorje, in what was then Yugoslavia, promising to reveal herself to his congregation on that the Feast of the Assumption.

The news had spread far and wide, and soon hundreds of worshipers claimed to have experienced prayer-induced messages from the Blessed Mother.

"My dear little children," one of the messages said, "listen to me, your mother. I want to help you. I want you to be in heaven, where we can pray and serve our Father for all eternity. Yes, my dear ones, you must have signs and you will have these signs…but it will be up to you to believe."

Another message promised salvation to the pure of heart and to those who believed in the messages: "My children, do not be sad. Have joy in your hearts, have peace. Listen to the prayer that you ask for, the Lord will give it to you."

Most of the supernatural utterances were received by three regular churchgoers—Mike Slate, a retired Air Force officer; Mary Constancio, a former hospital therapist; and Teresa Werner, a housewife and mother. The three recipients reportedly went into trances following several minutes of prayer by the congregation, then automatically began "receiving" holy communication while fellow parishioners looked on in reverent silence.

When news of the messages broke, thousands of believers rushed to the church to see the miracle for themselves during regular and special services. The church wasted little time capitalizing on the series of reported miracles; more than 50,000 books containing the messages were rushed off the presses and into circulation.

Plans were being made for additional volumes as the number of visitors swelled. Promises were made that a major miracle would occur soon. Many churchgoers, including the monsignor, believed that all the signs pointed toward Aug. 15, the annual celebration of the Virgin Mother's miraculous ascension into the clouds.

Sometime during Mass on the appointed day, someone saw a strange cloud. Then another was seen—and another. At one point several unusual cloud formations seemed to come together to form a portrait of Jesus.

"The sun did appear to dance in the sky," one astonished reporter wrote.

But the celestial event was over in a flash. There was no rustling of wings or blaring of trumpets, as many in the crowd had anticipated. Not a single person claimed to have been "illuminated" or caught up in any special rapture.

"There were just the faces in the clouds that seemed to smile down for a few seconds, then dissolve into a spectacular display of lights," a visitor wrote.

Many people—especially those who had traveled long distances—were disappointed. Others, hoping to see a miracle, swore they had seen the face of Jesus in the clouds that day, along with that of the Virgin Mary.

A few claimed that their ailments had mysteriously cleared up.

Bob Golee, who journeyed to the service from Midlothian, Texas, said his chronic knee problems disappeared. Another woman said her back spasms were cured. Several claimed that illnesses ranging from cancer to warts had gone away.

Skeptics were quick to dismiss the phenomena as "collective visions" brought on by mass hysteria. Many who were there believe they were touched by a miracle.

"It was her, the holiest of mothers, who came down and smiled at us," a New Jersey housewife told a newspaper reporter.

Blessed Mother in the Hawthorn Bush
Belgium

THE DECADE OF THE 1930S was a troubled time for the little nation of Belgium. With fascism and Nazism on the rise throughout Germany and some of their bigger European neighbors, many Belgians feared it was only a matter of time before the world would again be plunged into war.

In the winter of 1932, one year before Adolf Hitler became dictator of the Third Reich, rumors began to circulate throughout Belgium about a remarkable Marian apparition. According to reports, the Holy Mother, floating in a cloud, had appeared before a group of startled schoolchildren attending mass in the tiny village of Beauraing.

The five children, aged between 9 and 15 years, claimed the Blessed Mother had appeared to them, clad in a blue gown and veil and hovering over a hawthorn bush. They said she opened her hands and smiled at them before promising to return with an important message.

Although chided for their story by local nuns, the children continued to be approached by the Blessed Mother—30 times in all, starting on the night of Nov. 30, 1932, and ending Jan. 3, 1933. Her message was clear and direct: sinners should convert and they would be saved from their sins.

"I am the Immaculate Virgin," she said. "I shall convert the sinners."

As news of the apparitions spread to nearby villages and towns, hundreds of believers braved the snowy cold to gather around the hawthorn bush for a glimpse of the Blessed Mother. Trains and buses were charted from faraway cities and towns.

While police struggled to maintain control of the crowd, many sang out, "Stretch Your Blessed Hand Out Over Belgium!"

At 6 p.m. on the evening of Dec. 8, one of the faithful shouted: "She is here!" In unison, the worshippers fell to their knees and beheld a vision of the Holy Mother floating in silence high over the bush.

Two weeks later, on the evening of Dec. 23, the apparition appeared again before the masses. This time she announced to the crowd: "I would like a church built here so that people can come here on pilgrimage."

Doctors who examined the five children around whom the apparitions centered were startled by their own conclusions: the youngsters to whom the Holy Mother communicated were in a state of total ecstasy. As proof, flaming matches pressed against their fingers failed to inflict pain or even burn the skin; the children also seemed completely insensitive to needles poked into their flesh.

"It is truly a miracle," one physician remarked.

That same month, 50 miles away in the village of Banneux, an 11-year-old girl named Mariette Beco happened to be in the kitchen with her mother when she looked out the window and saw a beautiful woman seemingly made of light suspended several feet above the ground.

"Mother!" the girl exclaimed. "A strange woman is in our yard."

Mariette's mother turned to look, but the radiant woman had disappeared. She closed the curtain.

"She was there," persisted the girl, who went on to describe the woman as clad in a dazzling white gown with a blue sash at the waist and a transparent white veil covering her head and shoulders. On her right foot was a golden rose; her right hand grasped a rosary of diamond-like brilliancy.

Pulling back the curtains for another peek, Mariette saw the lady again, still hovering over the ground and smiling at her as before. Mariette went to her room and, grasping her own rosary, prayed.

At school the next day, Mariette related her story to the young parish priest, Friar Louis Jamin. Thinking she must have heard accounts of the Beauraing apparitions, the priest dismissed the girl's story and urged her not to talk about it anymore.

Classmates eventually heard the story and teased Mariette cruelly. One called her Bernadette and another slapped her. But each day Mariette returned to the garden to pray and call on

Mary. On one occasion, the Blessed Mother asked that a chapel be built on the spot in her honor.

On, Jan. 18, Mariette was walking beside a stream near her home when she saw the luminous apparition again. Enraptured, she watched the vision slowly descend from the tree tops until it settled a few inches above the ground less than five feet in front of her.

"Put your hands in the water," the Blessed Virgin said. "This stream is reserved for me."

The apparition then disappeared, but it continued to return seven more times to Mariette—the last time during a rainstorm on, March 2.

"I am the Mother of the Savior, Mother of God. Pray much," Mary said to Mariette. She then blessed the girl as she had earlier and bid her farewell. "Adieu—until we meet in God," she said, then disappeared over the pine trees.

An Episcopal commission launched two official investigations of the Banneux sightings—once in 1935 and again in 1937. Evidence was collected and submitted to Rome. In 1942 the bishop of Liege approved the cult of the Virgin of the Poor, and five years later, in 1947, the apparitions themselves received preliminary approval by the Church.

Mariette eventually married and raised a family. She rarely spoke of her experiences in the garden again, and the apparitions never returned.

Our Lady of Guadalupe
Mexico

IN THE EARLY SIXTEENTH CENTURY, Mexico was awash in strange stories about bearded gods sailing in from the sea, bringing with them four-legged animals, shiny suits of armor and formidable weapons that roared like thunder.

Once ashore, the Spanish conquistadores marched quickly across the vanquished land, spreading the Christian Gospel to the natives—often at the point of a sword.

Conversion came easily in some parts, not so easily in others.

One impoverished Aztec who accepted the Gospel gladly was a peasant named Juan Diego. Diego's conversion was destined to play a miraculous role in a central Christian drama that would impact generations of Christians to come.

One Saturday morning in early December 1531, years after his conversion to Christianity, Juan Diego was hiking through the lonely Tepeyac hill country in central Mexico when he came to the site of a former pagan temple, some 15 miles outside of what then were the boundaries of Mexico City.

There, amid the silence of the wintry morning, he reportedly heard the strains of "celestial music" then looked up and saw a beautiful woman shrouded in a blazing ball of light as bright as the sun.

In Diego's native tongue, the apparition said, "I am the ever-virgin Mary, Mother of the true God who gives life and maintains its existence. He created all things. He is in all places. He is Lord of Heaven and Earth."

The vision went on to say, "I desire a church in this place where your people may experience my compassion. All those who sincerely ask my help in their work and in their sorrows will know my Mother's Heart in this place. Here I will see their tears; I will console them and they will be at peace."

She concluded by urging him to hurry to the bishop's house and let him know her wishes for a chapel to be built on the summit of Tepeyac.

The stunning vision was not unlike others being whispered about among the Indians of Mexico. Many associated these visions with the recent arrival of Spanish invaders, who had brought with them fortune seekers and religious preachers trying to convert the natives.

Diego, 57, did as he was told. However, upon arrival at the bishop's palace in Mexico City, he was turned away by servants who failed to understand the importance of his message. If he wished to see the bishop, they said, he would have to return with a sign.

Dejected, Diego returned to the hill where the vision first appeared. To his surprise, Mary came to him again in a billowing cloud of light and smoke and urged him to return to the bishop and deliver the message.

"My little son," she said, "the bishop shall have his sign...."

She instructed Juan to "go to the top of the hill and cut the flowers that are growing there. Bring them then to me...."

In a howling storm, Diego climbed to the top of the hill where he found a full bloom of Castilian roses. When he returned to Mary with the flowers, she rearranged the plants on his *tilma*—or cape—with her own hands. She said: "This is the sign I am sending to the bishop. Tell him that with this sign I request his greatest efforts to complete the church I desire in this place. Show these flowers to no one else but the bishop....This time the bishop will believe all you tell him."

When Diego returned to the palace and presented the flowers, the bishop and his advisers fell to their knees. Only it wasn't the beautiful roses that caused the change in their countenance; burned into Diego's cape was a picture of the Blessed Virgin, precisely as Diego had described her on his previous visit.

Thanks to Diego's action—and the miracle on his *tilma*—millions of Aztecs were converted to Catholicism.

In recent years modern scientists have tried—unsuccessfully—to understand or explain how the divine image was created in the fraying old cape. They are also puzzled as to how a 500-year-old cloth made of cactus thread, which normally lasts for no more than 30 years, could still be on display.

Nowadays, reproductions of the image said to have been left on Juan Diego's cloak appear in nearly every home and workplace in Mexico, including on the windshields of city buses and the bumpers of long-haul trucks.

Today, the original relic is housed in a large cathedral that is the by far the most popular religious pilgrimage site in the Western Hemisphere. More than 20 million pilgrims travel to Mexico City each year to see the tattered relic.

In documents now before the Vatican, the apparition is referred to as "without a doubt the most important factor" in the Catholic evangelization of the New World.

One final note: Guadalupe is said to be a corruption of an ancient Aztec word, *coatlaxopeuho*—she who crushes the serpent. Tradition has it that Our Lady of the Immaculate Conception identified herself as the woman in Genesis who tangled with the serpent in the Garden of Eden.

Other Important Marian Apparitions

THE PERIOD IMMEDIATELY FOLLOWING the death of Christ was a troubled time for the Roman world, as revolts spread from within and foreign invaders threatened the Empire's far-flung borders.

Starting about 40 A.D., rumors began circulating that the Blessed Virgin—Christ's own Holy Mother—occasionally returned from Heaven to bless the poor and oppressed and to reassure the faithful with messages of love and hope. Witnesses usually described her as clad in a long blue dress and head cover and shrouded in a globe of pure white light. The apparition was often heralded by thunder and lightning and accompanied by angelic beings.

Marian apparitions would become an irregular occurrence for the next 2,000 years. From Africa to South America, Europe to Asia, thousands of minor and major appearances have been documented. A comprehensive listing of all such visitations would fill a lengthy volume, but following is an overview, by country, of a number of important apparitions, starting with St. James' encounter in 40 A.D.

Saragossa, Spain

TRADITION HOLDS THAT JAMES was the first Apostle to be visited by the Holy Mother. The miraculous event supposedly occurred near Saragossa, Spain, where he had taken up refuge after fleeing persecution in Israel. While deep in prayer, Mary came to him in a "bright white light" and instructed him to build a church in her honor.

"This place is to be my house," the apparition told James,

before giving him a small wooden statue of herself and a column of jasper wood. "This image and column shall be the title and altar of the temple that you shall build."

About a year later, James arranged for a small chapel to be built in Mary's honor—the first church ever dedicated to the honor of the Virgin Mary.

James returned to Jerusalem four years later, was executed by Herod Agrippa, and became the first apostle to be martyred for his faith. Shortly after his death, several disciples stole his body and took it to Spain for burial. Impressed by a number of miracles performed by the disciples, the local queen converted to Christianity.

Eight centuries later a hermit digging in a field noticed an unusual star formation among a pile of rocks. Digging deeper, he uncovered the remains of the apostle and the small chapel built in his honor. Struck by the discovery, local church officials erected a cathedral in honor of St. James. Today, the cathedral is a major destination for thousands of Christian pilgrims.

Rome, Italy

BY THE FOURTH CENTURY A.D., Christianity had become fashionable among the Roman elite. Pious nobles seeking salvation donated their wealth and property to the Church, usually in honor of Mary and the Apostles.

John of Rome was one such nobleman.

One hot August night the Virgin Mary appeared to John and his wife in a dream and asked them to build a church on one of Rome's seven hills—the Esquiline. Thinking it was his duty to report the dream to the pope, John learned that Pope Liberius had experienced a similar dream the same night.

Prompted by the dream, John and Liberius traveled to Esquiline Hill on Aug. 5. There, in the snow, was the outline of a church—exactly as had been seen in their dream. Construction of a church began immediately.

Today, the Basilica of Santa Maria Maggiore is one of the busiest and largest churches on earth.

Walsingham, England

DURING THE MIDDLE AGES, Walsingham House was one of the most famous pilgrimage sites in the world. Dozens of English kings and queens visited Walsingham, including Henry VIII, who made at least three pilgrimages to the site before breaking with the Catholic Church in 1534 and forming the Church of England.

How did a simple English manor house become such a revered site throughout the whole of Christendom?

According to one version, the lady of the manor—Richeldis de Faverches—had a series of visions in which the Holy Mother showed her the Nazareth house where the angel Gabriel informed Mary she would give birth to Jesus. The Blessed Mother then instructed Lady de Faverches to build a replica of the Nazareth house and to dedicate it as a memorial to the annunciation to Mary and the Incarnation of Jesus Christ.

"Let all who are in any way distressed or in need seek me there in that small house that you maintain for me at Walsingham," Mary said. "To all that seek me there shall be given succor."

Lady de Faverches built the house as instructed. The shrine served thousands of pilgrims until Henry VIII destroyed the site four centuries later. The statue of Mary that resided in the house was burned several years later.

Alfred Patten, an Anglican priest, had Walsingham's Holy House rebuilt in the 1920s. The chapel became the Catholic Shrine of Our Lady in England and is now an active site for pilgrimages once again.

Aylesford, England

ENGLISH FRIAR SIMON STOCK was on a pilgrimage to the Holy Land when the Virgin Mary appeared to him in a cloud and presented him with a "scapular"—two pieces of brown woolen cloth tied together and embroidered with an outline of Mary.

"My beloved son, receive this scapular for your Order," the apparition told the friar. "It is the special sign of a privilege which

I have obtained for you and for all God's children who honor me as Our Lady of Mount Carmel. Those who die devotedly clothed with this scapular shall be preserved from eternal fire."

She described the brown scapular as a "badge of salvation.... The brown scapular is a shield in time of danger. The brown scapular is a pledge of peace and special protection, until the end of time."

The apparition instructed Friar Stock to return to Europe and to establish Carmelite communities near university towns in England, France and Italy. Several years later he was appointed Superior-General of this order.

Until the twentieth century, the brown scapular was regarded as one of the most important Marian relics in the world.

"Lady of LaVang"

WHEN AMERICAN SOLDIERS ARRIVED in Vietnam during the 1960s, they heard amazing stories about supernatural happenings in the vicinity of the Central Highlands. The stories stemmed from a series of visitations by the Holy Mother who reportedly performed miracles and brought peace and comfort to oppressed Christians during a time of civil and religious turmoil.

For much of the eighteenth and nineteenth centuries, various factions battled each other for power and domination. The northern regions of the kingdom fell under the authority of the lords of the Trinh family, while in the southern realm the Nguyen lords held power.

As the eighteenth century drew to a close, both of their rules were threatened by peasant uprisings and emerging rebel forces.

When French missionaries, aided by King Louis XVI, offered aid to a group of insurgents on Phy Quoc Island, the regional king issued an anti-Catholic edict that led to the destruction of all Catholic churches and persecution of Vietnamese Catholics and missionaries. Hundreds of Catholics were rounded up and executed. Survivors fled into the surrounding forest, which in those days was full of wild beasts, dangerous diseases and other terrors.

It was amidst this great suffering that the Lady of LaVang came to the people of Vietnam. The name LaVang was believed to have originated in the name of the deep forest in the central region of Vietnam now known as Quang Tri City where there was an abundance of a kind of trees named La' Vang. It was also said that its name came from the Vietnamese meaning of the word "Crying Out" to denote the cries for help of people being persecuted.

The first apparition of the Lady of LaVang was noted in 1798 by a group of Catholics fleeing persecution. One cold night as they gathered in the forest of La' Vang to say the rosary and to pray, a beautiful lady "shrouded in a bright white light" suddenly appeared. The lady, dressed in a long cape and clutching a child to her breast, was surrounded by angels.

In a soft, comforting voice, the apparition assured those in attendance she would protect them if they continued to pray to her. She also asked them to build a small church in the forest in her honor.

As news spread, thousands of oppressed Catholics made pilgrimages to the little church in the forest. The Virgin Mother made many appearances during the next 100 years and performed many miracles.

When Catholic persecution ended in 1886, construction on a much larger church began. This new church was inaugurated in a solemn ceremony that drew more than 12,000 people and lasted for almost four years.

The regional bishop proclaimed the Lady of LaVang as the Protectorate of the Catholics. In 1928, an even larger church was built to accommodate the increasing number of pilgrims. This church was destroyed in the summer of 1972 during the Vietnam War.

The history of the Lady of LaVang continues to gain greater significance as more claims from people whose prayers were answered were validated. In April 1961, the Council of Vietnamese Bishops selected the holy church of LaVang as the

National Sacred Marian Center. The next year, Pope John XXIII elevated the church of LaVang to The Basilica of LaVang.

On June 19, 1988, Pope John Paul II recognized the importance and significance of the Lady of LaVang and expressed a desire for the rebuilding of the LaVang Basilica to commemorate the 200th anniversary of the first apparition in August 1998.

Paris, France

ONE SUMMER NIGHT IN 1830, Sister Catherine Laboure, a Daughter of Charity in Rue de Bac, Paris, was awakened by a young child, about 5 years old, dressed in white.

"Come to the chapel," the child told Sister Laboure. "The Blessed Virgin is waiting for you."

At first Sister Laboure thought she was dreaming. Her biggest desire in life was to meet the Holy Mother.

When she realized she was fully awake, she rose from her bed and followed the child down to the chapel.

There, shrouded in the shadows of the little chapel, were hundreds of candles—lit and blazing as if it were Midnight Mass.

Suddenly she heard a noise that sounded like the rustle of a silk dress. Turning, she saw the Immaculate Virgin sitting in the Father Director's chair. The apparition was surrounded by a blaze of white light.

The child who had led her to the chapel pointed and said, "Here is the Virgin Mother."

Sister Laboure fell to her knees and began to weep.

"My child," the Blessed Mother said, "the good God wishes to charge you with a mission. You will have much to suffer, but you will rise above these sufferings by reflecting that what you do is for the glory of God."

Sister Laboure lifted her eyes and placed her hand in Mary's lap.

The Blessed Mother continued: "You will know what the good God wants. You will be tormented until you have told him who is in charge with directing you. You will be contradicted, but do not fear, you will have grace....Have confidence. Do not be afraid."

During this discourse with the Blessed Mother, Catherine was warned of dire future occurrences:

"The times are very evil," the Holy Mother said. "Sorrows will befall France; the throne will be overturned. The whole world will be plunged into every kind of misery."

Five months later, on the night of Nov. 27, Sister Laboure experienced another apparition. This time, Mary appeared dressed entirely in white holding a ball topped with a little golden cross. According to Sister Laboure's account, the Virgin Mother's feet "rested on a white globe...and I saw rings on her fingers, each ring set with gems."

The globe, she was told, represented the whole world. At the apparition's feet were writhing green serpents. Seconds later, an oval shape formed around the Blessed Virgin, and on it were written these words in gold: "O Mary conceived without sin, pray for us who have recourse to flee."

Upon seeing this vision, Sister Laboure heard a voice say: "Have a medal struck after this model. All those who wear it will receive great graces; abundant graces will be given to those who have confidence. Wear it around the neck."

At this point the oval seemed to turn, and Sister Laboure saw the reverse of the medal: the letter M surmounted by a bar and a cross, and below it two hearts, one crowned with a crown of thorns, and the other pierced by a sword.

After determining the veracity of Sister Laboure accounts, the local archbishop authorized that the medals be struck in accordance with the Blessed Mother's instructions. On the front of the medal was an image of Our Lady standing on the earth, her foot crushing the head of a serpent, hands outstretched and rays of light coming from her fingertips.

Around the medal was inscribed: "O Mary, conceived without sin, pray for us who have recourse to Thee."

Within months there was a flood of reported cures and spiritual conversions attributed to the medal—so much so, that it came to be called the Miraculous Medal.

Sister Laboure never revealed what she had seen to anyone but her confessor and superior. The rest of her life was spent as a simple nun. She died in obscurity in 1876. Her body lies in an incorrupt state of grace.

By the time of her death, there were millions of Miraculous Medals being worn by the devout all over the world.

Knock, Ireland

IN THE LATE NINETEENTH CENTURY, County Mayo situated in the heart of Ireland, was the center of great famine and economic turmoil. Families were being torn apart by epidemics, emigration and forced evictions.

Into this anguished environment there appeared a remarkable Marian apparition that brought hope and comfort to the long-suffering people of County Mayo.

The afternoon of Aug. 21, 1879, was wet, miserable and uncommonly cold. Margaret Beirne, a resident of the village of Cnock Mhuirre, was locking up the local church for the night when she noticed a "strange halo" hovering over the church. At about the same time, two other members of the church arrived and saw several statues floating over the church gables.

"Those are not statues," one commented. "They're moving. It's the Blessed Virgin!"

What they and 13 other church members saw in the fading light of day was a beautiful woman, clothed in radiant white garments and wearing a large, brilliant crown. On her right stood St. Joseph, his head inclined toward her. On her left stood St. John the Evangelist, dressed as a bishop. To the left of St. John was an altar on which stood a lamb and a cross surrounded by angels.

In the pouring rain, the witnesses, ages 6 to 75, watched the apparition for two hours, reciting the rosary. Although the rain soaked the observers to the skin, not a single drop fell in the direction of the gable. The ground beneath the apparitions was perfectly dry.

The Church response was mixed. After much debate, a commission was formed to collect the testimony of each witness. An investigation was also launched to study the series of purported cures and miracles that followed the sighting.

In 1879, the Commission of Inquiry concluded that what the witnesses had observed was a "real and truthful account." A subsequent investigation in 1936 came to the same conclusion.

Today the Lady of Knock Shrine is one of the most popular Marian sites in the world. Almost 2 million pilgrims visit the shrine each year. One famous visitor was Mother Teresa of Calcutta, who toured the shrine in 1993.

Fourteen years earlier, in 1979, a visit by Pope John Paul II commemorating the centenary of the apparition inspired an even greater devotion to the shrine and led to the Vatican's official endorsement.

Zeitun, Egypt

IN THE SPRING OF 1968, while the war in Vietnam was raging and millions of Americans were caught up in the counter-culture wave, a series of apparitions began to appear in the vicinity of the Great Pyramid of Egypt that changed the lives of thousands of people around the world.

Besides the pyramids, Zeitun, Egypt, was famous for a lot of things—but mainly for a Coptic church constructed to commemorate the area in Egypt where the Mother Mary had come with Joseph and Jesus when they fled from Herod.

Over a period of three years, more than a million people—including Christians, Jews, and Moslems—witnessed apparitions of the Blessed Mother appearing over the dome of St. Mary's Coptic Church on the outskirts of Zeitun.

Hundreds of miracles—many confirmed by medical authorities—were reported. Long lines of pilgrims, their faces streaked with tears, gathered each day to pray and seek healing. A number of miracles were broadcast live on Egyptian television and captured by professional photographers.

Egyptian President Abdul Nasser, an avowed Marxist, was

present for one of the Blessed Mother's visitations.

Authorities fearing a massive hoax searched a 15-mile radius surrounding the site but found no evidence. The local Coptic Patriarch, Kyrillos VI, pronounced the apparitions genuine, saying he had "no doubt" that the Mother of God was appearing above the roof of St. Mary's Coptic Church.

The apparitions ceased just as quickly as they had appeared. Then, starting in 1983, they started again—with widespread reports of a "beautiful woman clothed in light" appearing above the roof of the Church of St. Damian in Shoubra, Egypt, a suburb of Cairo. Throughout the 1980s, the apparition was seen by thousands of people walking above the church, always bathed in light and lasted up to five hours.

Shenouda III, head of the Coptic Church at the time, formed a commission to investigate the phenomenon. In 1987, the commission concluded as follows:

"Let us thank the Lord for this blessing on the people of Egypt and for the repetition of this phenomenon....We ask all the people to remain calm. Thus, they may worthily receive the blessing of the Virgin, of St. Damian and of all the saints....May this phenomenon be a pledge of well-being...for all nations."

Ezkioga, Spain

THE TINY BASQUE TOWN OF EZKIOGA was a quiet place until the summer of 1931. That's when two children playing with their dogs on a sunny hillside looked up into the clouds and saw the face of the Virgin Mary.

The sighting on June 29 set into motion a series of reported apparitions that continued for years. In the coming months hundreds more children and adults reported similar visions, and mini-Ezkiogas sprang up in surrounding areas.

Until the wave of apparitions ended, some 1 million pilgrims had descended on this remote region in the Basque country to see Mother Mary. The visions occurred at a time when the Roman Catholic Church in Spain, and in the Basque country especially, was reeling from attacks by civil authorities to suppress its teachings. The local bishop had already been expelled, visionaries had been locked up in mental hospitals and several churches had been torched.

This conflict between church and state during the early period Second Republic had been a common theme in western Europe for several decades. Across the Pyrenees was Lourdes, France, where a young shepherd girl had seen the Blessed Virgin in 1858. In Fatima, Portugal, other children made similar claims in 1917.

Unlike what happened at Lourdes, Fatima and some other places, clerical authorities rejected the claims made by the visionaries at Ezkioga. The Church worried that the visions were the product of all-too-human mischief or self-delusion, if not diabolically inspired. Church leaders were also afraid they were losing control of their congregations, as secondary cults sprang up around the manifestations and drew large numbers of the faithful away from the churches.

Condemnation by the Church, increased civil strife and growing war clouds combined to slowly diminish the number of Marian visions. Before long, the movement had ended, and Ezkioga remained only a cautionary memory as Spain, France and the other nations of Europe braced for the coming global war.

San Nicholas, Argentina

FOR MORE THAN TWO DECADES, historians, theologians and Roman Catholic Church authorities have been mystified by a strange series of occurrences involving a shy, middle-aged housewife that have transformed her small, sleepy Argentine hometown of San Nicholas de los Arroyos into a mecca for spiritual pilgrims from all over the world.

Gladys Quiroga de Motta, who quit school at age 11, has been transmitting messages said to be from Virgin Mary urging people to pray and accept God's way. The messages, often dealing in complex theological issues, have impressed scholars because of the deep level of sophistication and clarity of expression embodied in the ideas.

Many church officials wonder how a simple, uneducated woman with no special training in liturgical matters could comprehend, let alone communicate in writing, hundreds of conveyances said to come directly from Mary.

In 1985, shortly after Quiroga de Motta started receiving the messages, the bishop of San Nicolas, Monsignor Castagna, set up an Episcopal Commission to investigate the claims. After several months, the commission, made up of psychologists, graphologists and psychiatrists, declared Quiroga de Motta to be perfectly normal in every way, with no mental impairments or tendencies toward hallucination or psychosis.

That reaffirmed what millions of people who come each year to San Nicholas to meet with Gladys and hear her messages already knew.

"She's a saint," said one American schoolteacher who flew down from San Antonio to meet Quiroga de Motta and "just touch" the woman who many believe is a prime candidate for canonization.

On Sept. 25, 1983, Quiroga de Motta noted in her diary: "I saw the Virgin for the first time." Now, 26 years and more than 1,000 appearances by the Blessed Virgin Mary later, more than 300,000 people descend on San Nicholas on the anniversary of Quiroga de Motta's vision every year.

Quiroga de Motta said the vision came to her early one Sunday morning while she was alone praying. She said she saw the familiar image, dressed in blue and pink and holding the baby Jesus and a rosary. It wasn't until the image appeared to her a third time, on Oct. 7, that Quiroga de Motta dared ask Mary what she wanted.

"You have obeyed," came the reply. "Don't be afraid, come to see me. From my hand you will walk, and travel many paths."

This was to be the first of more than 2,000 messages, all of which Quiroga de Motta wrote down in a diary, that were communicated to her almost daily until Feb. 11, 1990. The Virgin repeatedly told her she was patron of the area and wanted a sanctuary built n her honor.

After sharing her story with the local church, a small sanctuary was finally built on the exact spot where the vision instructed Quiroga de Motta it should be. That sanctuary has now been replaced by a handsome new cathedral with a gigantic, million-dollar cupola that dominates the skyline.

Once an economically deprived town with high unemployment and slums, San Nicholas is now regarded as an economic miracle. Many attribute its good fortune the arrival of the Virgin Mother and construction of the new church.

The stream of pilgrims continue to flood into San Nicholas, all hoping for a chance to meet with Quiroga de Motta and perhaps get a glimpse of the Blessed Virgin. On most days, Quiroga de Motta's small front yard is littered with envelopes containing letters from the sick and desperate, beseeching her to pray and intervene.

Quiroga de Motta's visions have not been limited to the Virgin Mary. She often smells roses and incense, and once said Jesus himself has appeared to her more than 60 times. Dressed in a white robe, he has told her that "Evil has invaded the Earth, and darkness wishes to cover all."

She confesses also to frightening visions of demons and serpents belching smoke and fire. In one vision she saw "blind serpents drowning in green gel."

On Jan. 31, 1984, she wrote: "I see a big room, like a café.... young men and women, they seem drunk, something ugly. The Virgin says to me: 'These are calamities, human offal, no child of healthy parents should come to these places. God is not here, nor in sites like this.'"

Two months later, the upstairs floor of San Nicholas' only disco collapsed during a rock concert, killing five youngsters. Quiroga de Motta's grim premonition is now folklore.

Besides Marian visions, Quiroga de Motta also experiences stigmata—wounds suffered by Christ on the cross—every Thursday and Friday during Advent and Lent. The marks, which consist mainly of thumb-sized red sores on her wrists, have been examined by bishop-appointed doctors and been found to be authentic.

Dr. Carlos M. Pellicciotta, one of the examiners, described a typical outbreak: "It begins with a rash in the forehead...like lines of inflammation across the forehead. She had an intense headache....I gave her a corticosteroid pill, but it didn't help... then the first stigmatization starts. Some pigmentation in the wrists appear. By the Holy Friday she is crucified in bed. She suffers terrible pain."

Quiroga de Motta's miraculous gifts are said to include healing. A 7-year-old boy suffering from a terminal brain tumor was reportedly healed after Quiroga de Motta prayed for him. According to local priest Father Perez, "many others" who have come to Quiroga de Motta for help have been similarly cured or healed.

While the church approaches the miraculous claims with "great objectivity, an open heart but a cold mind," Father Perez treats every claim of a miracle with caution. He and other church leaders have frequently compared the events at San Nicholas involving Gladys Quiroga de Motta with Fatima and Lourdes.

Naju, Korea

JULIA KIM, A SOFT-SPOKEN KOREAN HOUSEWIFE, sits quietly on a draped sofa in the middle of her living room, hands folded piously in her lap, eyes closed, a serene smile on her bleeding lips.

Her lips are bleeding because, moments earlier, she had participated in Holy Communion, and now the wine and wafers were mysteriously changing into bits of flesh and blood— Christ's own flesh and blood the dozen or so witnesses gathered around her believe.

On a table next to Mrs. Kim, another startling phenomenon is occurring—a small, inexpensive statue of the Virgin Mary is shedding tears. One eye appears to weeping real tears, while droplets of blood seem to be trickling out of the other eye.

Everywhere there is the scent of fragrant oils.

"The Holy Mother is with us," Mrs. Kim says in a hushed,

reverent tone. "She is telling us to pray, to love one another, to end abortion and to get right with God."

A few minutes later, a hunched-over elderly man with a walker gently touches the weeping statue. His eyes light up, he smiles, he straightens up, backs away from the walker—and walks on his own.

"Another miracle," someone in the crowd of about 20 whispers.

For the past two-plus decades, miracles and phenomena such as these have been occurring with regularity in Mrs. Kim's modest home situated on a narrow street in a simple suburb of Naju, located on the southwestern tip of the Korean peninsula.

The miracles began in 1980 when Julia Kim, suffering from terminal cancer, had a vision in which Christ told her the suffering would soon pass. Soon after the vision, Mrs. Kim's cancer went into remission.

About the same time—June 30, 1985—the small statue of Mary in her living room started to cry. The weeping continued off and on until January 1992. That's when the statue began to ooze the scent of fragrant oils.

More visions and messages from Jesus and the Virgin Mary urged Mrs. Kim to continue to "pray constantly, to sacrifice for world peace and conversion of sinners, for the millions of babies being aborted, for families who are suffering, and for people who receive Holy Communion sacrilegiously."

Mrs. Kim's suffering continued as she continued to receive messages. She also experienced "terrible pain and afflictions" almost daily, including the pain of babies being aborted, the crucifixion of Jesus, and arrows piercing her heart. She also began to "take on" the pain of people for whom she was praying.

The visions and healings continued, eventually drawing tens of thousands of pilgrims to her small house in Naju. Many visitors actually witnessed the supernatural signs, such as the shedding of tears and tears of blood, the scent of fragrant oils, even Mrs. Kim's Stigmata—the re-enactment of the suffering endured by Christ on the cross.

As her reputation grew, Mrs. Kim traveled to other countries to preach and heal. She even met the Pope when she visited the Vatican in October 1995. During a private mass with the Holy Father, it was said she experienced the Eucharistic miracle again. For the 12th time, the "Sacred Host" turned to flesh and blood on Mrs. Kim's tongue.

The newsletter "Mary's Touch" reported, "Immediately after the Mass, the Holy Father came to Julia and witnessed this miracle. His Holiness blessed Julia and her companions."

On Sept. 17, 1996, another Eucharistic miracle took place before a group of leading church officials celebrating mass at Sacred Heart Cathedral in Sibu, Malaysia. More than 3,000 people witnessed the miracle, including Bishop Dominic Su.

"I was caught totally unprepared when this extraordinary Eucharistic phenomenon occurred in our Sacred Heart Cathedral," the bishop wrote in his official report about the incident. "Our Lord performed this miracle in order to confirm our faith in his Real Presence in the Eucharist."

Father Francis Su, who administered the Holy Communion to Mrs. Kim, wrote: "As I continued to distribute Holy Communion to the others present, those who were sitting close to her (Julia Kim) noticed blood in her mouth. The Sacred Host that she received from me transformed into visible flesh and blood."

He added, "I went to Julia and prayed over her. I could smell blood, and then I saw the Sacred Host on her tongue moving and forming the shape of a heart. Photographs were taken and some of them showed the 'Pieta' (Mother Mary holding the body of Jesus after he was taken down from the cross)."

Like most Catholics who experience Eucharistic miracles and visions, Mrs. Kim does not know why all this is happening to her.

"I was chosen" is how she explains it. "Through these messages and miracles, I have been able to bring many others to Christ and helped many people regain peace and love and humility in their hearts."

At home in Naju, Mrs. Kim continues to receive visitors. They come to spend a few minutes or a few hours, the sick and needy, the faithful, the curiosity-seekers. All come hoping to see a miracle.

Nowadays Mrs. Kim's living room has been converted into a small chapel. Religious relics fill the room, and on the walls and tables are photographs of people who have been healed.

Our Lady of the Rock: Mojave Desert

SOMETHING WONDERFUL ONCE CAME to the stark, scrubby desert lands outside California City, Calif.—something so wonderful and miraculous it changed the lives of tens of thousands of people.

It came in the form of a "beautiful young woman" floating high in the skies, a vision like no other, offering messages of hope and peace, along with the promise of eternal salvation to those who accepted Jesus Christ as their Lord and Savior.

Before the visions ended a few years ago, tens of thousands of people—mostly poor Catholic Latinos from the surrounding area—found God and say their lives will never be the same again because of what they saw and heard.

The visions began in the early 1990s when a middle-aged woman named Maria Paula Acuna came face-to-face with the Virgin Mary while traveling alone through the Mojave. The apparition appeared in the clouds and spoke to her, saying she should spread the word about God's desire for peace in the world.

The vision told her to return to the desert each Oct. 13 for more messages.

"Who was I to argue with the Blessed Mother?" Maria asked in Spanish.

Since that first encounter, Maria has been returning to the desert, rain or shine, the 13th of every month.

Nowadays she brings a crowd with her, though—sometimes 20 or 30, sometimes over a thousand. They bring lawn chairs, rosaries, binoculars, bottles of water and cameras, all hoping to see the Virgin Mother, to witness a miracle.

"The Blessed Mary always appears around 10," Maria told

the *Los Angeles Times*. "She looks like a big ray of light coming from the sky very slowly and then she appears in front of me."

She added: "She looks like a cloud. I see her very clearly. She's a very beautiful woman, very young, maybe 18 years old. About five feet, five inches."

Some of those who flock to the desert are part of the so-called "Marian Movement." These are devotees of Mary who travel to sites around the world renowned for visitations by Mary.

Many of those who come are regulars, having made dozens of trips with Maria to this site in the Mojave Desert—now christened Our Lady of the Rock—to take part in the excitement.

On one occasion, Maria said, "The light of the Blessed Mother looks like a crown and covers all the people here," before launching into a sermon in Spanish.

Her normal habit is to move through the crowd, listening to problems and laying her hands on heads as she prays, laughs and mingles. She stops long enough to kneel beside a small child on crutches and pray that he be healed.

Local Catholic authorities do not discourage pilgrims from making the monthly trek to the desert in search of wonders but so far have found no evidence to back up the sightings.

"The church's official position is that there are no apparitions," concluded Father Gregory Coiro of the Roman Catholic's archdiocese of Los Angeles, which spent more than a year investigating the desert phenomena.

The church's official line does not deter the faithful from following Maria to the desert. They know better. Some talk about the time rose petals fell from the sky as Maria prayed—and then mystically rose back into the sky. They remember when a rainbow appeared around the sun.

Maria isn't sure why she was told to return every Oct. 13 but suspects it might have something to do with reports of other Marian apparitions appearing on that day. She pointed to the famous sightings at Fatima, Portugal, when the Virgin Mary reportedly appeared to three children on May 13, 1917, and kept coming back on the 13th of each month.

Garabandal, Spain

ON JUNE 18, 1961, four girls playing on a meadow near their mountainous village of San Sebastian de Garabandal in northwest Spain heard "noise like thunder," then saw before them a dazzling white figure descending from the skies.

The figure—whom the girls recognized as St. Michael, the archangel—stared quietly down at the girls for several seconds then disappeared. The girls fled in terror.

Over the next two weeks, the angel confronted the girls repeatedly, only to disappear silently into the clouds after a few moments. Then, on July 1, he spoke for the first time. "The Blessed Virgin will appear to you tomorrow as Our Lady of Mount Carmel," he said before again vanishing.

This time the girls hurried back to the village—but not in terror—to spread the news. The next day, July 2, dozens of people, including many area priests, followed the girls to the site where they had seen the angel to await the promised event.

They were not disappointed with what they saw.

At about 6 p.m., the Holy Mother appeared, an angel on either side. The girls recognized one as St. Michael, the angel who had first appeared to them. Above the Virgin was a large eye that the children took to be the eye of God.

The Heavenly Mother smiled at the crowd, then whispered a few words to the four girls huddled at her feet, and went away, promising to return. Those who saw the apparition wept and prayed with joy, saying they couldn't wait for the Virgin's return to their village.

True to her word, the Virgin Mother returned—hundreds of times, in fact, over the next several months. She was occasionally accompanied by the Infant Jesus whom she carried in her arms.

In their diaries, the girls wrote about their private conversations with the apparition—about how the Holy Mother would kiss them and let them play with the Infant Jesus.

As the apparitions continued, new phenomena were

witnessed. On several occasions the four girls would race backwards arm-in-arm over the rugged, rock-strewn hillside, eyes dilated, heads thrown back in ecstasy, oblivious to danger. At times they would come to a dead stop—almost in defiance of the law of physics, and fall backwards to the ground in a straight, dead drop.

Doctors who examined the girls determined they were insensitive to pricks, burns, physical contact or bright spotlights shone directly into their eyes. More startling, their weight factor changed so much that two grown men had great difficulty in lifting one 12-year-old seer—yet, they could lift each other with the greatest of ease.

When these "ecstatic flights" ended, the visionaries were neither out of breath nor perspiring.

One of the many priests who witnessed the events at Garabandal was Friar Luis Andreu, a young Jesuit theology professor from Ona, Spain. On the night of Aug. 8, 1961, while observing the visionaries in ecstasy, Father Luis cried out, "Miracle! Miracle! Miracle! Miracle!"

On the drive home with friends later that night he exclaimed, "What a wonderful present the Virgin has given me! How lucky to have a mother like that in Heaven...."

Moments after making that pronouncement, he lowered his head and died. In a later vision, the Virgin Mother told the girls that Father Luis was in Heaven with her, adding that he had died "of great joy" for having seen her.

"The miracles of the church seem to me to rest not so much upon faces or voices or healing power coming suddenly near to us from afar off, but upon our perceptions being made finer, so that for a moment our eyes can see and our ears can hear what is there about us always."
—Willa Cather

WEEPING MADONNAS & BLEEDING STATUES

I s it possible for a porcelain statue to weep tears of blood? What are we to make of a 2,000-year-old wooden icon that opens and closes its eyes? Can the bones of a long-dead saint cure cancer?

In an age of space shuttles and quantum physics, questions like these seem oddly out of place. Yet, every year, thousands of people around the world step forth to claim they have experienced miraculous phenomena.

While many church leaders interpret miracles such as these as divine proof of supernatural intercession, others take a more cautious stance.

"Miracles are just paranormal events in religious clothing," says Luigi Garlaschelli, an Italian chemist who has spent years studying miraculous events in Europe. "I look for substance behind all things."

Another skeptic is the Rev. Peter Gumpel, an official at the Vatican's Congregation for the Causes of the Saints, an organization that investigates reports of miracles by candidates for sainthood. "Some of these things are medieval in origin," he said. "I stay away from them."

Gregory of Tours might have been the first scholar to record such a phenomenon. Writing in the sixth century, Gregory told of several statues of Christ and the Virgin Mary that had been observed weeping blood.

Such miracles have been reported since the beginning of Christianity. Early travelers to Jerusalem and elsewhere in the Near East mentioned seeing icons that appeared to shed tears of blood, some on a regular basis.

Some theologians have speculated that the phenomenon could be related to Christ's ordeal in the garden of Gethsemane where Luke said he "sweats great tears of blood falling down to the ground."

Most images and statues weeping blood are of Jesus' mother, the Virgin Mary. Believers say the tears are caused by Mary's great sadness; she is sad, they say, because the world is full of sin and suffering.

The Roman Catholic Church has always avoided associating itself with claims of miracles—at least until Church authorities have had time to conduct a rigorous and thorough investigation of the events.

This process can sometimes take years, decades and even centuries to complete. Meanwhile, hundreds of miraculous events continue to be reported each year around the world, some of which make headline news. Most of these miracles can be attributed to natural causes—hallucinations, mistaken observations and outright fraud—but many appear to be supernatural in nature.

Many officials, however, quietly admit they are at a loss to explain the many statues and icons that "weep" genuine tears reported in historic times as well as the present day. Some of these statues—and even icons—are known to have open and closed their eyes at certain times and exuded fragrant oils and the scent of roses.

Such phenomena are not confined to followers of the Christian faith, having been experienced by Muslims, Jews and a number of people of other faiths who claim to have witnessed similar miracles.

How is it possible for statues made of marble, metal and wood to bend and occasionally groan? How can freshly painted wooden icons shed tears of blood? This question has long been debated within the Christian community, more so by the

Roman Catholic Church and less so, perhaps, by evangelical worshippers who tend to be more prone to miracles of all kinds— faith healing, snake handling, iodine consumption, "laying on hands," "speaking in tongues," and collective visions of Jesus Christ and angels.

Some specialists see such phenomena as the products of psychological stress, mental illness and mass hysteria, while believers defend them as spiritual events, forms of revelation or apparition.

The Catholic Church has always been very careful about approach—particularly in the case of weeping statues. Whenever a case is reported, the local bishop is charged with forming a committee to look into the phenomenon. Rarely is the outcome favorable for a miracle. This can be frustrating for believers who sometimes accuse the Church of being too reluctant to get involved and too secretive in its findings.

But reports about bleeding or weeping statues continue to occur monthly, from California to Lebanon, Romania to Tobago. While authorities investigate, evidence seems to be mounting that supernatural causes are behind the miracles, as demonstrated by the following cases.

Lake Ridge, Va.

IT BEGAN WITH A STATUE—a small, delicate plaster reproduction of Our Lady of Grace, ordered from a Pennsylvania mail-order catalog. Nothing flashy. Just an ordinary 12-inch image of the Virgin Mary robed in blue with eyes gazing down in earthly contemplation, arms outstretched, tilted head shrouded in a glowing halo.

It wasn't until droplets of water welled in the eyes of the statue and slid down its smooth cheeks onto a wooden desk in the living room of James and Ann Bruse that people in the small northern Virginia town of Lake Ridge began to whisper about a possible miracle.

By the time the statue "wept" in front of 500 people and miraculous healings were rumored to be taking place around this upscale town just an hour's drive from the nation's capital, the Roman Catholic Church knew it had a full-fledged public relations campaign on its hands.

A recent Gallup Poll found that at least 83 percent of Americans believe in miracles—that statues of the Holy Mother can shed tears, that statues of Jesus Christ on the cross can open and shut its eyes at will, that "crosses of light" can appear in bathroom windows and on the sides of pool halls, barns and trailers.

At the same time, there is a conflicting urge among many believers to dismiss miracles such as these as fakes. The religiously inspired maintain that events like those in Lake Ridge are proof that God is using his powers to call sinners back to him. Skeptics, including much of the press and the scientific community, liken "weeping statues" and other miracles to the UFO and Bigfoot phenomena—products of ignorant, delusional, or hysterical mindsets of people who enjoy weird happenings that tend to distract them from otherwise dull, monotonous lives.

Even the Roman Catholic Church—which has recognized just 14 Virgin sightings and weeping statue episodes in the past two centuries—allows that, at some point, it's up to the believer to decide.

On Thanksgiving Day 1992, the son of James and Ann Bruce—"Jimmy" Bruse, a recently ordained priest serving at St. Elizabeth Ann Seton Catholic Church—walked into the family living room and stopped. There, on his father's desk, was the statue of the Holy Mother he had given his parents as an early Christmas present. To his astonishment, a drop of water fell from the statue's cheek.

"It's crying," Bruse's mother said from behind him.

"There must be some explanation," James Bruse said, entering the room. The former tea salesman picked up the statue, turned it upside down and gave it a good shake. He examined it with his flashlight, rubbed his fingers over the smooth plaster.

The tears kept coming.

In the days that followed, the statue dripped intermittently, sometimes when the Bruses were at home, sometimes when the house was empty. But it always seemed to happen when Jimmy—Father Jim—was around.

Before long, four other statues in the house started to weep—so much that Mrs. Bruse placed them in bowls to protect the furniture. The family speculated that "the Holy Spirit" is in the room," or "it's a sign from God."

It seemed like everywhere Father Jim went—churches, homes, offices—statues wept. Even his boss, the Rev. Daniel Hamilton, revealed that a statue in his office of St. Elizabeth Ann Seton that had been given to him by Father Jim was shedding miracle tears.

Hamilton contacted his superior, Bishop John R. Keating of the diocese of Arlington, for help—and was told in no uncertain terms to keep the matter quiet. Hamilton and Father Jim knew this was something they couldn't just sit on, so they hopped in a car and drove to the bishop's house. The moment they walked into the house, a statue of Mary on the bishop's polished wood mantel began to cry.

Keating was astonished.

"We must not talk about this until a thorough investigation can be completed," he told the priests.

But on March 1, the big fiberglass Madonna at St. Elizabeth's began to weep before 500 parishoners as Father Jim said mass. Some 3,000 people mobbed the church the following Sunday. People fell to their knees before the Madonna, weeping, praying aloud and straining for a glimpse of the tears.

Other miracles—spinning suns, rays of vibrant colors, statues and rosaries changing colors and amazing healings— were said to be taking place all over Northern Virginia. Reports of healings, weeping statues and other phenomena continued after August 1992 when Father Jim was ordered by Church authorities to stop talking to the press.

When news first broke about the weeping statue, critics charged the Bruse family with staging the whole thing. Some accused Father Jim of using "black magic" to make the statue cry, while others say he arranged a variety of elaborate gimmicks to fake the tears.

That didn't stop thousands of believers from descending on the church to see the controversial statue with their own eyes. Although most did not see tears, they asserted how the event had changed their lives and brought them back to church.

The tears and blood, many felt, were "God's way of getting our attention."

As for Father Jim himself, he believes that Christ is using the events to show us He is real.

Barberton, Ohio

SOMETIMES MIRACLES HAPPEN in unexpected places.

St. Jude Orthodox Church is no cathedral sporting flying buttresses and stained glass. It's a simple, vinyl-sided little building tucked between a tool factory and a railroad track in a bleak and aging industrial section of Barberton, Ohio.

But it's here that hundreds of people have been coming for years to see a miracle—a colorful painting of the Virgin Mary that some say weeps real tears.

Akron resident Melinda Sullivan, 31, saw the miracle with her own eyes. She saw it while she and her husband sat on a wooden pew inside the church's garage-sized sanctuary praying to the 12-year-old icon, titled The Holy Protection of the Virgin Mary.

"I believe I saw it weeping," she said in an interview with a Knight-Ridder newspaper. "I wanted to see it with my own eyes. To me, it's a miracle."

Word spread quickly about the weeping, drawing dozens, then hundreds of curiosity seekers to the little church on a weekly basis.

Was it truly a miracle? Did the Virgin Mary really weep—or did the witnesses see only what they wanted to see?

"People are hungering for inspiration, for signs of inspiration," explained the Rev. Michael Dimengo, communications director for the Cleveland Diocese of the Roman Catholic Church. "To them (the witnesses), this was one of those signs."

Colfax, Calif.

PEOPLE COME TO THIS SMALL California town nestled in the foothills of the Sierra Nevada range by the thousands to wait in line outside St. Dominic's Church for an opportunity to see an image that many believe looks like the Virgin Mary appearing on a wall over a statue of Jesus.

"I think it's a miracle," said Marie Cammarota, 60, who drove all the way from Sacramento to see the image after she heard about it on the news.

The apparition appears each day for just one hour, from about 9:30 to 10:30 a.m. The church seats only 100 at a time, and those fortunate enough to cram inside for a peek at the miracle are rarely disappointed.

"It was weird, man," said Tyler Placio. "I think it's what you want it to be. If you're into religion, then you see the Virgin Mary."

Everyone agrees they see something. The image usually starts as faint, curved lines of red, blue, green, purple and pink light. The lines darken and extend into a shape that many say looks like the top half of a figure. Then it fades away.

Some say the image is only the reflection from sun light streaming through a stained-glass window. But most of those who see the image disagree, pointing out that the image always appears, even on cloudy days.

Bishop Francis Quinn of the Sacramento diocese says if the image persists, he will establish a commission to investigate.

"It could be the image of the Blessed Mother in a silhouette pose," Quinn theorized. "She (appears to be) holding the infant Jesus in her arms to the left side."

Bethlehem

WHAT MORE APPROPRIATE PLACE to witness a miracle than the birthplace of Jesus Christ?

In recent years, hundreds of witnesses—Jews, Muslims and Christians alike—have come forth to say they've seen a painting of Jesus hanging inside the Bethlehem Church of the Nativity that sheds red tears resembling blood.

The weeping was first noticed by a 60-year-old Muslim woman who cleans part of the church every morning. Sadika Hamdan told reporters she was working alone in the shrine when suddenly, "a light came from the column and the picture of the Messiah Jesus, peace be upon him, began to cry."

She described the scene as "beautiful, beautiful. He opened and closed his eye, and later tears fell, red tears."

At first she was "very frightened" and wondered why Jesus would be speaking to her, a Muslim. When she fetched the priests, however, they saw it and knew it was a miracle.

"I have been coming to this church for 22 years," Hamdan said, "and it is the first time in history that I have seen such a sight."

Besides tears, some of the hundreds of people who visit the church daily say they have seen the painting of Jesus wink at them.

Ambridge, Pa.

A LUMINOUS, LIFE-SIZE STATUE of Jesus Christ hanging from a ceiling at Holy Trinity Church in Ambridge, Pa., has been attracting thousands of visitors ever since the statue's eyes supposedly opened during a Good Friday service in 1989.

The church parking lot has been jammed with visitors ever since reports about the miracle appeared in the local and state media. Church Pastor Vincent Cvitkovic says there's a constant stream of traffic passing by the small white church 15 miles northwest of Pittsburgh, and, at times, the crowd threatens to overwhelm the calm of this community.

One visitor, Evelyn Borrelli, 44, of Glassport, said she packed her car with her children and friends and drove 40 miles to this Ohio River town to see the weeping statue.

"I wanted to be as close as I could be, and I wanted my children to experience it too," she said. "I truly believe it was a miracle."

A spokesman for Bishop Donald Wuerl, head of the Roman Catholic diocese of Pittsburgh, said church officials are withholding judgment on the event until they can conduct an official investigation.

But many of the worshipers say they don't need an official investigation; they're already convinced that what they saw is a miracle.

"I don't know how to explain it," said Don Otto of Coraopolis, who attended a Good Friday prayer service. "It was like electricity running through you. It was an overwhelming experience. Tears came to me."

The Rev. Cvitkovic said he often pointed out the crucifix to his congregation of 300 families, saying it was unusual in that it depicted a still-living Christ, with eyes open.

Dominic Leo of Beaver, an artist who helped restore the 60-year-old statue and had touched up the eyes with acrylic paint, confirmed the eyes were open when the crucifix was hung.

Cvitkovic said it would be nearly impossible for someone to have tampered with the crucifix because the church is locked when services are not held.

Those who come now to Holy Trinity sit quietly, hands folded, eyes transfixed on the crucifix. Some are clearly moved, breaking into tears, while others come only out of curiosity.

Hampstead, N.Y.

LATE NIGHT PHONE CALLS were nothing new to the Rev. George Papadeas.

As the busy pastor of St. Paul's Greek Orthodox Church in Hampstead, N.Y., he was used to having his sleep interrupted in the wee hours by distraught parishioners in need of guidance.

On the night of March 16, 1960, however, he received a call that changed his life.

"I had just turned off the light and gone to bed," he said, when the phone rang, "precisely at 1:30 a.m."

The young woman on the other end of the line was clearly distraught. "Father," she pleaded, "I beg you to come over to our house at once. You've got to see the miracle."

Papadeas recognized the woman's voice immediately. It was Pagona Catsounis, wife of Pagionitis Catsounis; they were born devout members of his church.

"Miracle?" the clergyman grumbled. "What kind of miracle can it be at such a late hour?"

"It's the Blessed Virgin," Mrs. Catsounis stammered. "She is weeping!"

The young woman explained how she had gone into the living room earlier to pray and found tears streaming down the cheeks of a small icon of the Holy Mother hanging over the sofa. Her husband had seen it, too.

"It's really happening, Father," Mrs. Catsounis persisted. "Even as I speak, her tears cover the picture."

Papadeas had been well trained in the study of miracles. That didn't necessarily mean he believed in them, and on the way over to the Catsounis house that night he wondered what unsettling event had caused the young couple to think they had experienced a miracle.

When he arrived, he was astonished to find several other members of the congregation waiting for him.

"See," they told him, pointing excitedly toward the icon.

He blinked in astonishment. Sure enough, there were tears—unmistakable tears—welling up in the Blessed Virgin's left eye!

"When I arrived," he later wrote to the bishop, "a tear was drying beneath the left eye. Then, just before the devotion ended, I saw another tear well in her eye."

He said the tear "started as a small, round globule of moisture in the corner of her left eye, and it slowly trickled down her face."

As far as Papadeas was concerned, he had witnessed a miracle.

When news spread the next day, hundreds of visitors descended on the Catsounis household to witness the miracle, which was well publicized by newspapers and radio stations throughout the city.

To the delight of the crowds, the Virgin continued to shed copious tears, often in view of witnesses. On March 23, seven days after Mrs. Catsounis had first noticed the tears, the icon was taken to St. Paul's for safekeeping—and to give the Catsounis family some much-needed relief from the curiosity seekers.

By then the weeping had all but ceased, yet thousands of visitors flocked to the church weekly for a glimpse of the Blessed Virgin, whose picture had been enshrined on the altar.

Miracle or not, many of those who came to St. Paul's sincerely believed they had witnessed some kind of divine apparition. Their conviction was bolstered by media accounts.

While downplaying such events, the Catholic Church estimates that 200 similar apparitions have been recorded in the past six decades or so. Most were dismissed as hallucinations, illusions or outright fraud, but 14 are considered "worthy of pious belief," including the Catsounis sighting.

While the Church is yet to rule on the Catsounis sighting, family members and other observers do not see any point in waiting on official approval of what they believe was a genuine miracle—a miracle that helped redefine their faith and change their lives forever.

Limpia, Spain

THE SAD PORCELAIN EYES OF CHRIST on the larger-than-life crucifix in the little parish church of Limpia in northern Spain seemed so real that they appeared to gaze deep into the very heart of churchgoers.

Then, on the morning of March 30, 1919, a 12-year-old girl kneeling in prayer below the crucifix looked up and saw Christ's eyelids flutter open.

"The eyelids opened, and they looked down on me," the girl told two missionary Capuchins visiting the church.

Both priests examined the statue and found nothing extraordinary. They assumed the girl had imagined things or simply made up the story. Then several adults stepped forward to say they, too, had seen the eyes move—not once, but on several occasions. Two men said they had seen tears flowing down the statue's cheek.

The next month, the parish priest, Don Eduardo Miqueli, wrote his bishop, describing what his parishioners claimed to have seen and the religious fervor that gripped his church.

Soon, thousands of pilgrims flocked to Limpia. Bells rang, firecrackers popped, and triumphal arches were built outside the church to shelter the masses.

One visitor from Germany, the Rev. Baron von Kleist, wrote: "Many said that the Savior looked down at them—at some in a kindly manner, at others gravely, and at yet others with a penetrating and stern glance. Many of them saw tears in his eyes; others noticed that drops of blood ran down from the temples pierced by the crown of thorns."

Kleist added: "One saw froth on his lips and sweat on his body; others again saw how he turned his head from side to side and let his gaze pass over the whole assembly of people; or how at the Benediction he made a movement of the eyes as if giving the blessing; how at the same time he moved the thorn-crowned head from one side to the other."

According to Kleist, some observers swore they heard a "deep, submissive sigh" escape the statue's lips.

Thousands of people gave sworn testimony to having witnessed manifestations of the kind described by Kleist. Some observers were so affected they fainted. Others fled the church and could not be persuaded to return.

Many devout men and women saw nothing, though they spent hours watching. In fact, most of those who visited the church—4,000 a day for more than two years—saw nothing.

One witness who claimed to have seen the miracle was a noted physician, Gutierrez de Cossio of Santander. In a newspaper article, Dr. Cossio said, "In the whole of my medical practice, nothing has ever made such a deep impression on me, not even the sight of the first corpse which I saw as a young student."

Another doctor, Maximilian Orts, examined the face of the statue through binoculars from a distance of seven yards and saw a "drop of bright red blood" trickle from the right eye down into the carved lock of hair below the ear.

Dr. Orts told himself that it was all an optical illusion. He moved from the nave to a side chapel. But there he saw the process repeated. Finally, convinced despite himself, he cried out, loudly enough for those around him to hear, "There can't be a doubt; it is blood!"

Czestochowa, Poland

FOR CENTURIES, Christian pilgrims have been trekking to this small Polish town to pay homage to an ancient portrait of the Holy Mother and Christ Child that believers say heals the sick and wounded.

Known as the "Black Madonna" because soot has caused discoloration, the painting is generally regarded as one of the most revered likenesses of Mary in the world. Since the fall of communism, the enigmatic painting has attracted millions of visitors who come in search of miracles and answers to their prayers.

According to legend, the Black Madonna was painted by St. Luke the Evangelist. It was while working on the painting that Mary revealed much about the life of Jesus that Luke would go on to reveal in his gospel.

The painting went through a series of ownerships before winding up in the possession of Constantine. When the Saracens attacked Constantinople, the portrait was displayed from the walls of the city, causing the invaders to flee in terror. The portrait was credited with saving the city.

The painting eventually wound up in the hands of Charlemagne, who subsequently presented it to Prince Leo of Ruthenia in northwest Hungary. There it remained until the 11th century when the city was under attack. During the siege, the king prayed to the painting; in the confusion that followed, the invaders began attacking each other, and Ruthenia was saved.

By 1382 the Black Madonna was owned by a Polish prince named Ladislaus. During a Tartar invasion, a series of arrows hit the painting and lodged in the throat of the Madonna. Fearing the worst, the prince fled, taking the famous painting to the town of Czestochowa, where the portrait was hidden in a small church.

Sixty years later, an attack on the city by Hussites left the painting badly damaged. One invader reportedly struck the painting with his sword. But before he could strike another blow, he fell to the floor, writhing in agony until he died. Both sword cuts and the arrow wound are still visible in the painting.

More serious damage was avoided in 1655 when a group of monks successfully defended the portrait against forces of Sweden's King Charles X for 40 days. Many saw this as a miracle; the Lady of Czestochowa became the symbol of Polish national unity, and the king of Poland placed the country under the protection of the Blessed Mother.

Another Marian miracle associated with the painting supposedly occurred in 1920 as the Russian army was massing along the banks of the Vistula River threatening Warsaw. According to witnesses, when an image of the Virgin was seen in the clouds over the city, the Russian troops withdrew.

"The miracles on earth
are the laws of heaven."
—Jean Paul Richter

SACRED FIRES, FRAUDS & ODDITIES

From flying monks to ancient saints whose bodies resist decay and corruption, religious history is a smorgasbord of curious happenings that pose tough challenges to all but the strongest of believers. Miraculous fasting, healing shrines, bilocation, prophecy, drinking poison, firewalking, handling of serpents, odor of sanctity, glossolalia and the rapture are just a few of the traditional miracles found in many faiths.

While mainstream scientists seek alternative explanations to these and other sacred mysteries, religious people insist they are "gifts" from God and require no further proof as to their legitimacy.

Bilocation

IS IT POSSIBLE FOR A PERSON to be in two places at precisely the same time?

Throughout recorded history, stories have been told about men and women being mysteriously transported from one place to another, sometimes across oceans to opposite continents. This phenomenon, known as teleportation—or bilocation—has fascinated and intrigued scientists, historians and theologians for centuries.

The term "teleportation" first came into use in the early 1900s, having been coined by writer Charles Fort to describe strange disappearances. But the phenomenon itself, usually referred to as bilocation, has been known about for at least 2,000 years and is seriously regarded in most of the world's major religions as a miraculous gift.

Many famous people, starting with St. Peter and St. Anthony, were said to be gifted with the miracle of bilocation. In the New Testament there is a reference to Philip the Evangelist who baptized an Ethiopian on the road from Jerusalem to Gaza. As found in Acts 8:26-40, the Ethiopian disappears from view immediately after the baptism and reappears in a city about 40 miles away.

While the Catholic Church publicly remains ambivalent about teleportation, it considers the phenomenon one of the key miracles necessary for sainthood and "reserves" it for those of great sanctity.

Other religions speak of bilocation. Icelandic sagas, for example, share tales about warriors who were able to fall into a trance and transport themselves thousands of miles away in battle. A number of Indian gurus reportedly possessed the same trick—going to sleep in one place and waking up in another location.

Some scholars have referred to the Ascension of Jesus Christ into Heaven as the first known case of bilocation. According to the Gospel of Mark (16:14-19), Jesus and the remaining eleven disciples were seated around a table when he told them to spread the Gospel, whereupon he was "received into Heaven to sit at the right hand of God."

The Gospel of Luke says that while Jesus was in the act of blessing the disciples near Bethany, he was "carried up" into Heaven. In a third account of the Ascension, in Acts of the Apostles (1:9-12), Jesus continued to preach the Gospel for 40 days after the Resurrection before he was "taken up and received by a cloud." Two men clothed in white appeared prior to the event and told the disciples that Jesus would return in the same manner in which he was taken.

St. Anthony of Padua, the "patron of lost things," is credited for having experienced bilocation on at least one occasion. This happened in 1226 while he was preaching in a church in Limoges. In the middle of the sermon, he suddenly realized he had a "previous engagement" in another church, then stopped, pulled his hood over his head and knelt silently for several minutes.

In that exact moment, the congregation in the other church saw the saint suddenly appear in their midst, read a passage from the Bible and then, equally suddenly, disappear. The kneeling figure in Limoges then stood up—and continued his sermon!

In the 17th century, European explorers in the New World heard bizarre accounts about a Spanish nun named Sister Maria who mysteriously appeared among the Indians and taught them the ways of the Roman Catholic Church. The Jumano Indians of New Mexico called her the "woman in blue" because she was said to be clad in the customary blue dress worn by Catholic nuns.

Sister Maria reportedly traveled to the American Southwest at least 500 times between 1620 and 1631 and converted hundreds of Native Americans to Christianity.

On Oct. 24, 1593, a Spanish soldier on guard duty in Manila in the Philippines suddenly found himself standing in the main square of Mexico City, still wearing the uniform of his Philippine regiment. Unable to explain how he had mysteriously traveled 9,000 miles in the blink of an eye, the soldier was charged with witchcraft until an investigation proved he was telling the truth.

The ability to teleport oneself without any visible means is mentioned frequently in the Bible. In the Acts of the Apostles, St. Peter was supposedly transported from Herod's prison. Old Testament prophets were also occasionally teleported. Elisha witnessed Elijah's being whisked away by a whirlwind. Habakkuk was carried from Judea to Babylon to give food to Daniel in the lion's den, and Ezekiel told how "The spirit lifted me, and brought me unto the East gate of the Lord's house."

Perhaps the most remarkable story of them all involving bilocation concerned a Capuchin monk, Padre Pio, who developed a habit of "dropping in" out of nowhere. Before his death in 1968, Pio reportedly teleported himself on many occasions. During World War II, he was observed by several Allied pilots "hovering" in the air over his hometown of San

Giovanni Rotondo, arms outstretched as if to protect it from falling bombs.

One American pilot met Pio after the war and recognized him as the brown-robed monk he had seen floating in the air outside his airplane over southern Italy.

Between 1907 and 1909, witnesses in San Jose, Costa Rica, reportedly saw three children—ages 12, 10 and 7—teleported through the air during a spiritualist séance. The children had been sitting in a room one moment, observed by several adults, then the next, they were gone. The children were found outside in the garden brought inside the house, and then the incident happened a second time.

The children said a "mysterious pressure" had taken them by the arms and gently lifted them up from the room and put them down outside in the garden.

St. Joseph of Cupertino (1603-1668)

ON THE AFTERNOON OF OCT. 4, 1630, as a procession of chanting clerics worked its way solemnly through the crowded streets of Cupertino, Italy, someone suddenly shouted—and the long column of brown-robed monks and veiled nuns came to a halt.

"He's flying," a spectator screamed, pointing toward the sky.

Hundreds of heads looked up and saw an incredible sight— one of the monks, a newly-ordained Capuchian monk named Joseph Desa, was actually soaring through the air. At one point he hovered, some 50 feet overhead, arms outstretched, seemingly asleep or in a deep trance as startled onlookers gazed up.

When he came down and realized what had happened, the embarrassed young monk lifted his robes and hurried away. How could he have done such a thing on the feast day of St. Francis of Assisi, the most important day in his hometown of Cupertino?

For several years, Desa had been aware of his strange ability to levitate—to lift himself off the ground and fly or soar through the air. Until today, he had been able to keep his secret hidden from the brothers at the monastery. Now everyone knew about his bizarre gift, and there was bound to be trouble.

Trouble had stalked Desa all his young life, going back to his childhood years when he couldn't seem to do anything right. He lacked every natural gift possible, was incapable of performing the simplest household task, and couldn't carry on a conversation, pass a test or hold down a job.

Even his parents seemed cursed by bad luck. The day he was born, his widowed mother was living in a tumble-down shack because his debt-ridden father, an impoverished carpenter, had been evicted from their house shortly before his death.

Desa grew up a sickly child, always the butt of jokes from his companions who teased him unmercifully and called him a fool. Later, when he tried to enter religious life, the Friars at Minor Convent refused on account of his ignorance. The Capuchins at Martino near Tarento accepted his application, but his ineptitude, carelessness and abstractness soon led to his expulsion.

His fortune finally turned when the Monastery of Grottela not far from Cupertino allowed his admission as a servant. His duties were to keep the donkeys fed and groomed and take care of the gardening and cleaning.

Desa was elated. And it couldn't have come at a better moment—his own mother had grown impatient with his bumbling inabilities and had recently booted him out of their home.

At the monastery, Desa's ambition was to become a monk. Unfortunately, that required an academic examination, something he would surely fail. Fortunately, the superior graded only a handful of the exams and, thinking they were all about equal, issued passing marks to the whole class, including Joseph. Despite his many limitations, Joseph Desa, at the age of 25, was now a full-fledged monk.

It was at the monastery where Desa's life changed dramatically—and immediately. The turnabout began one day when a stranger visited his cell and gave him a new monk's habit.

"When I put it on, all my despair disappeared immediately," Desa later wrote. "No one ever knew who that religious was."

From that day on, Desa seemed to develop great virtues, humility, obedience, love of penance, and a new sense of purpose. He plowed into religious studies, fasting and praying long hours every day. Although he lacked the ability to read and reason well, he seemed to be "infused by knowledge and supernatural light" that surpassed that of most of his fellow monks.

It was about this time that he started developing a reputation for ecstasies, miracles and that strangest gift of all, levitation. He experienced levitation so often he became known as the Flying Friar. His flights became so frequent, in fact, his superiors eventually refused to allow him to take part in community services out of fear his "flights" would cause too great a distraction.

But Desa could not contain himself. On hearing the names of Jesus and Mary, he would simply "go into ecstasy" and remain in that state until a superior commanded him to return to his senses. He would also levitate, sometimes to great heights, when he heard hymns and other "sweet music."

His most famous flight occurred during a papal audience before Pope Urban VIII. When Joseph bent down to kiss the Pope's feet, he was suddenly "filled with the reverence for Christ's Vicar on earth" and lifted into the air. It took a direct command from the Minister General of the Order to bring him back down to the floor next to a rather startled Pope.

On another occasion he is said to have picked up a 36-foot cross by himself and flown it through the air to the top of a steeple. At a Christmas service, witnesses watched him soar to the high altar where he knelt in the air, raptured in prayer, while a choir sang carols below.

When he wasn't flying around, praying, fasting, and levitating, Desa found time to perform miraculous healings. He was extremely popular with children and the local peasants. That he rarely accepted money for his help, caused a lot of strife with his cash-strapped superiors. He was chastised often and warned not to levitate. Many times he was ordered to remain in his cell for long periods as punishment for flying.

Word of the monk's miraculous feats reached far beyond the rustic confines of Cupertino. Thousands of pilgrims from all over Italy and other parts of Europe called on Desa each month, including kings, queens, knights, emperors, bishops, cardinals and popes.

All the hoopla was too much for his jealous brothers and stressed-out superiors. He was subsequently transferred to another monastery, then another, finally arriving in Osimo in 1657 where he continued to experience supernatural manifestations daily until his death on Sept. 18, 1663, at age 60.

One month earlier he had become ill with a fever, but he was comforted in knowing he would soon be united with God. He wanted desperately to experience "one last flight," but his last weeks on earth were spent in a sweat-soaked bed.

After receiving the last sacraments and a papal blessing, Joseph Desa of Cupertino died on the evening of Sept. 18, 1663. He was buried two days later in the chapel of the Immaculate Conception before great crowds of people who were touched by his Franciscan life and witness.

St. Joseph was beatified by Benedict XIV in 1753 and canonized July 16, 1767, by Clement XIII. In 1781 a large marble altar in the Church of St. Francis in Osimo was erected so that St. Joseph's body might be placed beneath it.

Because of his many "flights," St. Joseph is the patron saint of air travelers and pilots.

The Blood of St. Januarius

IT IS A WARM DAY IN MID-SEPTEMBER, and the richly ornate chapel inside the great Cathedral of Naples is packed with thousands of worshippers who've come from all over the world to see a miracle.

The occasion is the Feast of Gennaro—Januarius—the fourth century patron saint of Naples, and all eyes are focused on the gilded altar where a young priest unveils a remarkable relic—a human skull, said to be that of St. Januarius himself, enshrined in a silver case.

Next to the skull lies an ancient glass reliquary containing a thick, dullish-brown mass.

As the officiant approaches the high altar, arms raised, the sunlight glittering off his golden vestments, a rattle of prayers is heard from a dozen or so black-garbed old women huddled near the back of the chapel—the so-called Aunts of St. Januarius— who suddenly begin to convulse and wail hysterically.

It is at that precise moment that the archbishop carefully picks up the reliquary, gives it a good shake, then raises it high for all to see. In the twinkling of an eye, the dark mass turns liquid—a bright, bubbly fluid that sparkles radiantly in the dim light.

"It is liquefied," he solemnly intones.

Seconds after the announcement, the church is shaken by a loud, 21-gun salute from cannons stationed at the nearby 13th century Castle Nuovo.

"The blood of Saint Januarius," someone in the congregation tearfully proclaims.

Weeping and chanting, long lines of worshippers then start wending their way to the altar to touch—and sometimes kiss— the ancient vial of blood. The word "miracle" is whispered over and over as the archbishop recites in Latin, "*Il miracolo e fatto*"—Glory to God's miracle.

The "miracle of Saint Januarius," as this celebration of the blood has come to be called, happens four times each year—the feast of St. Januarius on Sept. 19; on the feast of the transfer of the saint's relics, which occurs the Saturday before the first Sunday of May; during its octave; and on Dec. 16, the anniversary of Naples' escape from the eruption of Mount Vesuvius in 1631.

The event, which began more than six centuries ago, has blossomed into one of Italy's most famously odd religious festivities, drawing busloads of Catholics and non-Catholics eager to witness the transformation. Church officials credit the phenomenon with the conversion of countless thousands of pilgrims.

While skeptics scoff at the ceremony, believers insist it's divine proof that God still cares about his children.

"God's ways are inscrutable," explained one church leader. "All that can be said is that it certainly helps to maintain one's faith in the supernatural, in the power of God and the intercession of the Saints."

Very little is known about St. Januarius. His life seems as mysterious as the congealed blood inside the transparent glass reliquary at Naples Cathedral. In the catacombs below the city, there is a centuries-old portrait which, legend says, depicts the venerated saint wearing a halo and clutching a staff. Beyond that, historians don't know much about the man so honored and revered by Catholics.

Tradition holds that Januarius was a bishop of nearby Beneventum before he suffered the wrath of Roman Emperor Diocletian sometime in the year 305 AD. According to one account, he and several other Christian clergymen were thrown into a fiery furnace, but the flames failed to harm them. At that point, Timotheus, president of Campania, had them cast into a lion's pit in an amphitheater. When the animals refused to attack, the enraged Roman blamed black magic and had them all beheaded.

Before the axeman's blade swung, Timotheus allegedly was smitten with blindness, whereupon Januarius cured him. Five thousand people were supposedly converted to Christ before the martyr was decapitated.

After the execution, Timotheus allowed Januarius's followers to gather his body parts and take them to various locations. They eventually wound back up in Naples. Many miracles have been attributed to the relics—including halting the eruption of Mount Vesuvius in 1631.

The most popular miracle associated with Januarius, however, concerns the "liquefaction of blood" ceremony. Archbishop Orsini of Naples was the first to mention the blood cult phenomenon in 1389. Throughout the Middle Ages and into modern times, rumors continued to swirl about the vial of blood, which has been linked to countless miraculous cures.

Prior to the ceremony and throughout most of the year, the blood of Januarius is kept safe in a hermetically sealed glass vial, completely dry and resembling a blob of red currant jelly. It is only when the thick glob of blood is placed in close proximity to the saint's skull that the amazing transformation takes place.

The liquefaction sometimes takes place after a few minutes of prayer, sometimes after several hours. On some occasions the process lasts late into the night. But it always happens, say church officials.

"Sometimes the blood boils up and bubbles, filling almost the entire vial," one Naples bishop wrote on May 14, 1881. "At other times it liquefies...at other times the whole mass liquefies more fully, and sometimes a very small portion of it changes."

Especially noteworthy is the fact that the blood, when liquefied, increases in volume and weight—contrary to the laws of physics. This phenomenon has been observed and studied by numerous scientists and doctors as well as theologians.

In recent years, other towns in the region and elsewhere in Italy claim to possess the blood of other saints with similar miraculous curative powers. As with Januarius, the blood of these saints is said to remain in a congealed state until a certain feast day when it turns into liquid.

Scientists who have examined the vials of blood have failed to explain the phenomenon. As recently as 1988 a team of researchers called in by Cardinal Michael Giordana, the archbishop of Naples, was unable to make a determination.

One of the investigators was Professor Pierluigi Bollone, president of the International Center for the study of the Shroud of Turin. He declared that spectrographic photos of the process demonstrated to his satisfaction that the liquid was arterial human blood.

"It's a miracle," he was quoted as saying.

Many theories beyond the supernatural have been advanced over the years. One suggests that unknown "magnetic forces" from nearby Vesuvius are responsible for the weird properties of the liquid, while others attribute some kind of psychokinetic power.

What does the Catholic Church itself think?

According to Cardinal Giordano: "The official church allows the veneration of relics, but it has never issued a judgment—and never will—on the miraculous character of the liquefaction. The only miracles on which our faith is based are those of the Gospel."

Today, St. Januarius—known also as San Gennaro—is regarded as a saint and martyr in both the Roman Catholic and Eastern Orthodox traditions. Neapolitans revere him especially as a protector against eruptions of Mount Vesuvius, but he is more widely known for his relics at the Cathedral of Naples and the liquefaction.

Firewalking

THE BEARDED YOUNG MAN pulled off his shoes, rolled up his pants legs, then stepped barefooted onto the bed of hot coals. Head raised high, he proceeded to stroll across the fiery path, oblivious to the searing heat.

He was firewalking, re-enacting an ancient mystical tradition that tests not only a walker's stamina and courage but a walker's faith as well. Even before the young man had completed his walk, other brave walkers edged onto the coals and began to hop, skip and stroll briskly across the blistering path.

Some see firewalking as a miracle. Others say it's a complete joke, no more dangerous than sticking a hand in the oven or face over an open flame. Skeptics utterly dismiss the involvement of the supernatural, while many of the faithful argue that a "higher power" protects them while out on the coals.

People have been firewalking for thousands of years, mostly shamans and mystics, to honor the gods and to pay tribute to the natural element of fire. The act is seen as a way to purify their lives and bring healing and peace to the world.

Today, thousands of normal people "firewalk" every year. Some do it for religious reasons, others for the sport. The tradition is most visible in India and Africa and among some North American Indian tribes, but practitioners also flourish in

China, Japan, Europe, Australia, South America and elsewhere.

From early Christian sects to Buddhism, nearly every religion has dabbled in firewalking at one time or another, some more passionately than others. The geographical dispersion of the tradition suggests it must have been one of humanity's earliest rituals in the distant past.

While not officially recognized by the Roman Catholic Church or any mainstream Christian denomination, firewalking has roots deep in the Christian tradition. St. Peter Igneus supposedly was one of the earliest holy men to firewalk in ancient times.

The oldest recorded firewalk occurred more than 4,000 years ago in India when two Brahmin priests competed to see who could walk farther over hot coals. Across the ocean in North America, firewalking was a popular ordeal among various tribal populations. French explorers and missionaries traveling through Canada in the 17th century told of numerous firewalking ceremonies.

Father Le Jeune, a Jesuit priest, wrote to his superior, saying that a sick woman walked through two or three hundred fires with bare legs and feet, not only without burning, but all the while commenting on that she could feel no uncomfortable heat.

Some 30 years later, Father Marquette reported similar firewalks among the Ottawa Indians, and Jonathan Carver writes in his 1802 book, *Travels in North America*, that one of the most astounding sights he saw was the parade of warriors who would "walk naked through a fire…with apparent immunity."

Until recent years, firewalking was found mostly among fakirs of India and elsewhere in the Far East. Eastern Orthodox Christians in Greece and Bulgaria participate in the ordeal during some popular feasts, while firewalking is used regularly in religious ceremonies among African-born Hindus and the Kung Bushmen of the Kalahari.

Miracle or not, firewalking has become a popular sport among New Agers, corporate executives and jet-set travelers to the Pacific Islands. Organizers of firewalking ceremonies claim the practice is good for the spirit because it forces practitioners to meditate, to "think cosmic."

Some experts say firewalking is similar to other "trial by fire" ceremonies used in previous centuries to test one's faith or to determine guilt or innocence. During the Inquisition, judges used several fire-related techniques to identify heretics or witches—searing suspects with hot irons or burning them at the stake.

In some voodoo rituals, individuals possessed by gods and demons are said to be impervious to any pain, including fire. These performers have been known to dance naked over crackling bonfires and to "eat fire"—stick burning sticks and hot coals down their throats to demonstrate their mastery over dark forces.

Joan of Arc's heart and entrails were said to have been miraculous spared from the flames that otherwise cooked her 19-year-old body at the stake.

The Holy Fire of Jerusalem

FOR CENTURIES, WORSHIPERS HAVE BEEN coming to the Church of the Holy Sepulcher in the ancient walled city of Jerusalem to witness one of the oldest and holiest of all Christian miracles —the so-called Holy Fire from Heaven.

According to tradition, the fire comes down the first Saturday after the spring equinox and Jewish Passover to light the holy flame inside the tomb where Jesus Christ was taken after being crucified on the cross at Calvary.

The Miracle of the Holy Fire, as the ritual has been called since at least the eighth century, is regarded by Orthodox Christians as "the greatest of all Christian miracles." Some scholars suspect the event might be even older, perhaps going back to at least the first century.

The ritual begins this way:

Early on the morning of Holy Saturday—Orthodox Easter Sunday—Israeli police enter the tomb to inspect for hidden matches or other fire-starting devices. Then, precisely at 1:45

p.m., the Patriarch of Jerusalem arrives, escorted by a large procession of archpriests, priests and deacons waving liturgical banners. The procession circles the tomb three times and then stops in front of its entrance.

That's when the Patriarch, stripped of all his glittering liturgical vestments except for a white robe which is searched thoroughly, enters the tomb with two large unlit candles. All illumination is extinguished at that point. The ancient tomb is plunged into total darkness.

If all goes well—and it always does—he will emerge seconds later from the darkened tomb with both candles lit. The crowd, usually numbering in the thousands, literally goes wild, erupting in songs, chants, handclapping, dancing and shouts of praise. Some rock back and forth, weeping and muttering silent prayers.

Amid all this drama, a second miracle then occurs when candles and oil lanterns held high by the worshipers ignite spontaneously by a mysterious blue flame. The blue flame then flickers about the church, lighting other candles until gradually fading out.

"I believe it to be no coincidence that the Holy Fire comes in exactly this spot," said one eyewitness, Patriarch Diodorus I who witnessed the miracle 19 times until his death in 2000. "The Gospel says that when Christ rose from the dead, an angel came, dressed all in a fearful light. I believe that the intense light that enveloped the angel at the Lord's resurrection is the same light that appears miraculously every Easter Saturday."

The Patriarch said the light can not be described in human terms. "It usually has a blue tint, but the color may change and take on many different hues," he explained. "The light rises out of the stone as mist may rise out of a lake. It almost looks as if the stone is covered by a moist cloud, but it is light."

The first written account of the Holy Fire—also known as the Holy Light—dates from about 385 when Etheria, a noble woman from Spain, visited the Holy Sepulcher of Christ and wrote that the entire church filled with an "infinite light."

Five centuries later, in about 870, an itinerant monk named

Bernhard describes an angel who came down after the singing of the "Kyrie Eleison" and ignited the lamps hanging over the burial slab of Christ, "whereupon the Patriarch passed the flame to the bishops and to everyone else in the church."

Some scholars point to an even earlier reference to the phenomenon that reportedly occurred in the first century. St. John Damascene and Gregory of Nissa told about how the Apostle Peter saw the Holy Light in the Holy Sepulcher shortly after Christ's resurrection.

Symbolically, the descent of the Holy Fire is said to commemorate the moment of Christ's resurrection, when the power of God descended into the tomb of Christ, transforming death into life. The Easter hope is renewed as the flame spreads among the crowd, lighting candles and lanterns.

Numerous miracles have been attributed to the tomb in recent centuries. In 1579, the holy fire reportedly ripped apart a column outside the church after Turkish authorities refused to admit the Orthodox Patriarch. The split column can still be seen today. Two 11th century Roman Catholic priests were severely punished when they tried to steal the Holy Fire for themselves.

The Church of the Holy Sepulcher, also called the Church of the Resurrection, was built by Constantine I in 335 on the ruins of a temple to Aphrodite erected by the Roman emperor Hadrian. Twice destroyed, the church was finally rebuilt as a single, large structure during the Crusades and rededicated on July 15, 1149.

Levitation

WHEN A PERSON IS LIFTED off the ground without any visible means of support, that person is said to be levitating. As bizarre as this phenomenon sounds, history is full of stories about people, mostly saints, nuns and other religious figures, rising mysteriously into the air in full view of witnesses, sometimes to great heights for hours at a time.

Known also as ascensional ecstasy, ecstatic flight, or ecstatic walking—when the body appears to run rapidly without touching the ground—levitation is one of the least understood phenomena acknowledged by the Roman Catholic Church as a recognized gift from God.

During the Middle Ages, levitation was thought to be a manifestation of evil. Witches, fairies, ghosts and demons were said to possess the powers to levitate and to cause normal humans to as well. In the Bible, levitation is usually seen as a diabolical ploy of Satan.

The earliest documented case of full levitation involved the first century heretic Simon Magus, who was judged evil, while the most celebrated person known to have levitated was an Italian saint named Joseph of Cupertino who once levitated several feet above the ground in full view of Pope Urban VIII. He also levitated before cardinals and other members of the church, but his most amazing feat came when he levitated to the topmost spires of St. Peter's Cathedral.

In all, St. Joseph was said to have levitated at least 100 times, earning him the nickname the Flying Friar. He died in 1663 and was canonized in 1767 by Pope Clement XIII because of his unique ability, viewed by the church as a "work of God."

St. Teresa of Avila was another well-known saint who reported levitating. This happened usually while in a trance, but she was always conscious and even saw herself being lifted up. Another saint who experienced this phenomenon and wrote about it was the Venerable Maria Villani, who mentioned on five different occasions that she was suddenly swept off her feet and remained in the air for extended periods of time.

Father Paul of Moll, known as "The Wonder-Worker of the Nineteenth Century," was a priest who is said to have also enjoyed the gift of levitation. On one occasion, penitents watched the priest rise several feet off the floor during Holy Eucharist.

On multiple occasions, St. Francis of Assisi was recorded to have been seen in levitation several feet above ground. He was also observed to "fly among the trees" on more than one outing. A nun named Passitea Crogi, who died in 1615, was reportedly observed by several nuns as she lifted off the ground several feet and remained in that position for two or three hours.

St. John of St. Facond, according to the Acta Sanctorum, liked to levitate at night. He was seen suspended in the air many feet above the ground where he often remained all night long.

Other well-known saints and holy figures who are said to have levitated on a regular basis were Gemma Galgani (d. 1903), St. Frances Xavier (d. 1552), St. Dominic (d. 1663), St. Philip Neri (d. 1595), St. Margaret of Metola and Castello (d. 1320), and Passitea Crogi (d.1615). Some of these people, especially the nun Passitea Crogi, were witnessed floating above the ground for two and three hours at a time.

Altogether, about 200 Catholic saints supposedly levitated, including St. Edmund, then archbishop of Canterbury, Sister Mary of Bethlehem; St. John of the Cross; St. Adolphus Liguori in Foggia; and Father Suarez of Santa Cruz in southern Argentina. St. Teresa of Avila and St. John of the Cross supposedly levitated together up to the ceiling of St. Peter's Cathedral.

Documented cases of levitation have also been reported in the religious traditions of Hinduism and Buddhism. Milarepa, the great 13th century yogi of Tibet, is said to have possessed many occult powers, including the ability to walk, rest and sleep while levitating.

The Ninja of Japan also mastered the art of levitation, as did the Brahmins and fakirs of India.

In 1906, a 16-year-old schoolgirl from South Africa supposedly rose five feet in the air while demonically possessed. When sprinkled with holy water, she reportedly came out of her states of possession.

During the 19th century, a number of physical mediums claimed to have experienced levitation. The most famous was Daniel D. Home, a Scotsman regarded as the greatest occultist in the history of modern spiritualism. Home had his first vision at the age of 13, his first levitation in Manchester, England, in 1855. He was excommunicated by the Roman Catholic Church as a sorcerer.

To authenticate cases of levitation, Pope Benedict XIV proposed a rigorous series of liturgical and scientific testing procedures.

"First of all," he wrote, "the fact must be well-proved in order to avoid all trickery." He added: "That because of the law of gravity, well-proved levitation cannot be naturally explained; that it does not, however, exceed the powers of angels and the devil, who can lift bodies up; that consequently the physical, moral and religious circumstances of the fact must be carefully examined to see whether there is not diabolical intervention; and that, when the circumstances are favorable, one can and must see in it a divine or angelic intervention, which grants to the bodies of the saints an anticipation of the gift of ability which is proper to glorified bodies."

Today scientists tend to be very skeptical of this type of phenomenon, attributing it largely to mass hypnosis of the audience, clever illusions, drug-induced hallucinations or outright fraud.

Rationalists say levitation might be achieved through a pattern of deep breathing, but so far no satisfactory explanation has been advanced to account for this mystical phenomenon.

Incorruptibles

IN THE LATE 1930S, at the height of the Soviet terror against the church, a squad of communist soldiers forced the archbishop of Chernihiv, a priest named Pachomius, to don a pair of gloves and crack open a tomb containing the ancient relics of a fourth -century martyred archbishop named St. Theodosius.

Expecting to find nothing but old bones, the Soviet scientists and soldiers were astonished to find the remains of the saint looking almost as fresh and new as the day he had been entombed some 1,800 years prior.

Ukranian newspapers carried some mention of the event, but it wasn't until the fall of the Soviet Union five decades later that full details of the miraculous discovery were made known to the outside world. In their journals, the scientists had expressed utter shock at the discovery and admitted more study would be required of this phenomenon.

Some called it a miracle. How else could they account for a corpse lasting so long?

Miracles or not, perfectly preserved bodies of long-dead people have been found all over the world. These bodies— especially those of saints and other holy people—are said to be "incorrupt." That is, they have been able to resist the natural ravages of decay and decomposition without benefit of mummification or other embalming processes.

In Anglican, Catholic and Orthodox Christian cultures, if an un-embalmed body or body part remains incorruptible after death, it is generally viewed as a sign that the individual is eligible for sainthood. Mummified corpses and others that have been treated with preservation properties do not qualify.

Many incorruptibles have been found in close proximity to other bodies that decomposed normally. Some, buried in bare earth and in such damp conditions that their clothing had long rotted off, remained intact, apparently unaffected by the ravages of their natural surroundings.

From the beginning, many people in the church viewed the phenomenon as tangible proof of the sacredness and purity of a saint. Instead of being buried in the ground, the incorruptibles were placed into sumptuous reliquaries and exposed above or behind the altar for everyone to see. From the Middle Ages through today, churches containing these relics have become popular destinations for pilgrims.

Legendary tales of supernatural powers have often been associated with these incorrupted bodies, many of which remain on full display at churches and shrines throughout Europe. Some people who come in contact with these remains claim to experience feelings described as "ecstatic." Others have detected the scent of fragrant oils emanating from the cadavers and, upon closer examination, have noticed bleeding, perspiration and body warmth.

Other supernatural characteristics sometimes associated with incorruptibles include the absence of rigor mortis; actual bleeding; and, in rare cases, some kind of "ritualized" movement of the limbs—for example, during a blessing or prayer.

While it isn't really known why some saints are preserved from corruption and not others, the church strives to review the life and deeds of each incorruptible subject to determine his or her level of holiness. Faith and virtue are two determinants generally considered in the process.

History indicates that the martyred St. Cecelia, the first century patroness of musicians, was the first saint whose body experienced the phenomenon of incorruption. Her body, discovered in 1599 in a church in Rome erected in her honor, was found in the same position—and condition—in which she had died 1,500 years earlier.

Preserved bodies generally fall into one of three categories— those accidentally preserved, those deliberately preserved, and those said to be incorruptible. Accidentally preserved bodies are those entrapped in lava, sand, bog or some other environment that protects them from decay, while deliberately preserved corpses are those usually mummified or otherwise artificially kept from decomposition.

Incorruptible bodies, the third category, are said to be that way because of supernatural or divine intervention. While scientists have remained baffled by this phenomenon ever since the first were discovered in secluded chambers and tombs of old churches in the early centuries after Christ, some theologians insist God made certain bodies incorrupt for a reason—perhaps as a mystical sign of his promise of the Resurrection.

While incorruptibles are seen primarily as a Christian phenomenon, other cultures have examples of revered, incorrupt dead. The followers of Paramahansa Yogananda maintain that his body was incorruptible months after his death. In the Aug. 4, 1952, issue of *Time* magazine, medical authorities who examined Yogananda reported: "The absence of any visual signs of decay in the dead body...offers the most extraordinary case in our experience...."

The article continued: "This state of perfect preservation of a body is, so far as we know from mortuary annuals, an unparalleled one....Yogananda's body was apparently in a phenomenal state of immutability....No odour of decay emanated from his body at any time...."

Incorruptible bodies are said to be lifelike, moist and flexible. Many contain a sweet, rose-like scent even years after death. "Partial incorruptibles" have been found throughout the centuries; in these, certain parts of the body decay normally, while other parts such as the heart or tongue remain perfectly free of decomposition.

These "relics," as they are commonly referred to by the church, are usually kept in one of two kinds of exquisitely crafted containers of gold and silversmithing—a sepulcher inside the altar, or in a reliquary. Reliquaries can be anywhere— up front by the altar, tucked away in a corner or concealed in a dark crypt. Depending on what sacred relic is inside them—a limb, head or full body—they come in a variety of shapes and sizes, ranging from glass and stone boxes shaped like caskets to massive cavities in the configuration of Noah's Ark.

Whether displayed upfront by the high altar or below in shadowy crypts, the incorrupted remains of these holy ones have become big tourist attractions at churches, cathedrals and shrines throughout Europe. Pilgrims willingly open up their hearts—and pocketbooks—for the opportunity to kneel beside the remains of revered saints and other holy leaders and pray, to touch and take photos.

In Europe, practically all of the incorruptibles have been positively identified and determined to be worthy of canonization because of their publicly devout lives.

Following are just some of the incorrupt bodies recovered in the past 2,000 years. Most are still on display.

--St. Bernadette Soubirous. Her body is on display in the Chapel of St. Bernadette in Nevers, France.

--Blessed Paula Frassinetti. Her body is on display in the Chapel of the Convent of Santa Dorotea in Rome, Italy.

--St. Catherine Laboure. Her body is on display under the side altar in the Chapel of Our Lady of the Sun in Paris.

--St. Jean-Marie-Baptiste Vianney. His body is on display above the main altar in the Basilica at Ars in France.

--St. Fincent Pallotti. His body is on display under the main altar in the Church of St. Salvatore in Onda, Italy.

--St. Teresa Margaret. Her body is on display in a glass case at the Monastery of St. Teresa in Florence, Italy.

--St. Andrew Bobola. His body is on display under the main altar in the Church of St. Andrew Bobola in Warsaw, Poland.

--Blessed Osanna of Manua. Her body is on display under the altar in Our Lady of the Rosary in the Cathedral of Manua, Italy.

--St. Catherine of Bologna. Died in 1463. Her body has been incorrupt and on display in an upright position for more than 500 years.

--St. Rita of Cascia. Died in 1457. Her body is on display in a glass case in the Basilica of St. Rita in Cascia, Italy.

--Blessed Margaret of Metola. Her body is on display under the high altar of the Church of St. Domenico at Citta-di-Castello, Italy.

--St. Zita. Her body is on display in a glass reliquary in the Basilica of St. Frediano in Lucca, Italy.

--St. Sperandia. Her body is on display in the Benedictine convent church of Cingoli, Italy.

--St. Alphege. He was archbishop of Canterbury and was captured, put in prison, and eventually murdered by his captors in 1012. Ten yeas later his perfectly incorrupt body was discovered.

--St. Withburga. Her remains were on display for more than 300 years until destroyed during the Reformation.

--St. Agatha. Parts of her incorrupt body are still in existence today.

--St. Cecilia. Her body was discovered incorrupt in 1599. She is known to be the first saint to be incorrupt.

Laying on of Hands

IT WAS SUMMERTIME in rural Tennessee, and an old-fashioned tent revival was in full sway.

Some 200 people, most of them wearing cutoff jeans, tank tops and bibbed overalls, crowded inside the hot tent to sing, clap, cheer and stomp their feet while they listened enraptured to the preacher's thunderous pronouncements about the coming "end times."

With his audience hanging on to every impassioned word, the preacher—a fiery man in his mid-40s sporting bare sleeves and khakis—strutted about the impromptu stage, waving his arms and dramatically thumping his tattered black Bible each time he made a point.

Finally he came to the part everyone had been waiting for—the "laying on of hands."

"And then Jesus stretched forth his hands in love and touched the leper," the preacher intoned. "Then the leper called out to Jesus and said, 'Lord, if you will, make me clean.' And Jesus said, 'I will, be clean,' and the leper was healed immediately...."

Amid a chorus of hallelujahs and "praise the Lord," those not in wheelchairs or on crutches jumped to their feet and began to sway back and forth. While the congregation danced and sang, many shuffled toward the front.

One by one, they knelt before the preacher, heads bowed, arms reaching and waving. Laying his hands on top of each head, the minister commanded they be healed "in the name of Jesus Christ, the Almighty Father and Savior, amen!"

Some fought back tears as the power of God took control, cleansing their souls and healing their bodies of ailments and afflictions ranging from arthritis to cancer. One old man, upon being touched, rose from his wheelchair and exclaimed, "I can walk!"

Tent revivals such as this, common in America from the 1930s to the 1950s, faded with the coming of radio and television. Thanks to the electronic medium, salvation and healing was now only a click away, plus the new form of service allowed the faithful to worship in the privacy of their own homes.

Central to the old-fashioned tent revival service was the laying on of hands, a religious practice found throughout the world in varying forms. In recent years, this form of "miracle healing" has made a dramatic comeback as more and more

Americans turn to nontraditional evangelical services such as those found in the Pentecostal and Charismatic movements.

In Christian churches, the laying on of hands is used as both a symbolic and formal method of invoking the Holy Spirit during a variety of services, including baptism, ordination of church officers and especially healing.

In its "healing" form, the laying on of hands is based on biblical precedent set by Jesus. In the New Testament, Christ employed this rite to restore life to the daughter of a woman named Jairus (Matthew 9:18) and to give health to the sick (Luke 6:19). Today, the act is more often seen as a way to cleanse one's spirit and create union with the Holy Spirit.

There are many examples of miraculous healing throughout the Bible. For example, in Matthew 8:14-15, we read: "And when Jesus entered Peter's house, He saw Peter's mother-in-law lying sick with a fever. He touched her hand and the fever left her, and she rose and served him."

Another is found in Luke 22:50-51: "And one of them struck the slave of the high priest and cut off his right ear. But Jesus said, 'No more of this!' And He touched his ear and healed him."

But healings are still said to occur, and it is this mystical process that seems to attract so many followers to the Pentecostal and other fundamentalist movements today.

In ancient times, the laying on of hands was an action aimed at conferring a blessing of authority. Jacob blessed his son Joseph in this fashion, and Jesus laid his hands on children to bless them and on the sick to heal them. In the Old Testament, priests were ordained by the laying on of hands.

In the New Testament the "Holy Spirit" was conferred through the act of laying on of hands. Apostles laid hands to heal, cast out demons and perform other miracles. The practice was used in the early Christian church for ordination ceremonies and is still used in a wide variety of other services, including blessing, anointing leaders, consecration, deliverance, prophecy and confirmation, where a bishop, priest or minister lays hands on the confirmed and prays for the Holy Spirit to enter him.

Laying on of hands is also used in the ceremony of baptism. After signing the forehead with the sign of the cross, the priest lays hands on the head then prayerfully beseeches God to accept the recipient into his Holy Family.

Church scholars warn of a "dark side" to the act, however.

"Untrained people should refrain from trying to lay on hands because we know from the Gospels that demons can leave a person and enter into another," commented one authority. "Those who lay hands on others in pride can take on sins instead of them being transferred to Jesus...and inadvertently impart curses instead of blessings."

People who have experienced having hands laid upon them often talk about the feeling of "peace and power" that comes over them, "tingling sensations" and a "relaxing surrender" and a compulsion to "lift up our hands and drink of the spirit."

Before he ascended to Heaven, Jesus told his followers that all who believed in the Gospel and were baptized would be able to lay on hands to heal the sick in his name and they would recover. The Apostle Paul went about laying on hands and healed many, as did Barnabas.

Known also as "the Divine Touch," this process was performed by kings in England and France and was believed to cure a number of diseases. The rite of the king's touch began in France with Robert the Pious, but legend later attributed the practice to Clovis as the founder of the kingdom, and Edward the Confessor in England.

The belief continued to be common throughout the Middle Ages but began to die out with the Enlightenment. Queen Anne was the last British monarch to claim to possess this divine ability, though the Jacobite pretenders also claimed to do so. The French monarchy continued to believe and perform the act up until the French Revolution.

Milk Drinking Statues of India

EARLY ON THE MORNING of Sept. 21, 1995, tens of thousands of people crowded New Delhi temples as rumors spread that idols of Hindu gods were drinking milk offered by devotees.

The miracle was first reported around dawn in a small temple on the outskirts of Delhi, when a statue of Ganesh, the Hindu god of wisdom and learning, appeared to gulp down several spoonfuls of milk offered by a worshipper.

Soon more reports surfaced alleging that statues of other gods were drinking milk. Said to be lapping up the white liquid from pots, pans, jugs and bottles were Shiva, God the Destroyer in the Hindu trinity; his consort Parvati; and Nandi, Shiva's bull.

At one Delhi temple a priest said more than 5,000 people had crammed into his temple.

"We are having a hard time managing the crowds," complained a Delhi housewife who waited two hours to feed the white marble statue of Ganesh. "The evil world is coming to an end and maybe the Gods are here to help us."

Within hours, news swept across the country about the extraordinary miracles taking place in Delhi. Not to be left out, thousands of other people in other towns and villages hurried to temples to make similar milk offerings.

By late afternoon, the number of faithful converging on temples had grown into the millions. Traffic in many cities was halted as police struggled to establish order among the surging crowds bearing containers full of milk offerings. Things got so out of hand the Indian stock market shut down, as did much of the government.

Soon after journalists broke the story and broadcast reports to other parts of the world, the same thing started happening in other countries with Indian populations—Hong Kong, Nepal, Singapore, Thailand, Dubai, the United Kingdom, Australia, Japan, Canada and the United States.

In England, Hindus reported similar miracles taking place in temples and private homes. At one temple in London, 10,000 people over a 24-hour period witnessed the 15-inch statue of the bull Nandi and a bronze statue of the cobra Naag drinking milk from cups and spoons.

Sushmith Jaswal, 20, said she was skeptical at first, but concluded: "It is a miracle. God is trying to show people he is here."

At the Geeta Bhavan Temple in Manchester, England, a 3-inch silver Ganesh sipped milk from a bowl. Rakesh Behi, 35, fed the silver elephant several times and said, "Did you see how quickly Ganesh drank? How can anyone not believe this miracle?"

In Southall, Asha Ruparelia, 42, said she fed a clay statue of Ganesh 20 pints of milk overnight. "Nearly 600 of my friends and relatives have come here to see the miracle."

After observing one such feeding, Rebecca Mae, a reporter with the *Daily Express*, wrote that "the statue appeared to suck in half a spoonful while it was held level by the worshipper. The rest was sipped reverently by the devotee."

Srikant Ravi, who is in charge of a popular temple dedicated to the monkey god Hanuman in central Delhi, said, "It is sheer magic....The gods have come down to solve our problems."

Other reactions ranged from disbelief to incredulity. Scientists from the federal Department of Science and Technology theorized that the offered milk was probably "absorbed" in the granite or marble idols, not sucked, and that it most likely spilled away in trickles not clearly visible.

But the faithful dismissed any suggestions of a hoax, saying that what they had seen was a "true sign" from God. Besides, they say, not all the statues were marble or granite; some that drank milk were made of metal.

"We believe this is a miracle," said one Indian priest in London. "All I know is that our Holy Book says that wherever evil prevails on earth then some great soul will descend to remove the bondage of evil so that right shall reign."

He added, "These happenings...may be a sign that a great soul has descended, like Lord Krishna or Jesus Christ."

The phenomenon ended almost as swiftly as it had begun. Within days, the idols worldwide somehow all stopped drinking milk. More than a decade later, the faithful are waiting for them to get thirsty again.

Odor of Sanctity

SOME CALL IT the "smell of death." Others, especially in the Catholic Church, describe it as the "smell of eternal life."

It's the so-called "odor of sanctity," a commonly reported phenomenon normally associated with the incorrupted remains of saints and other holy people, but also among those nuns and priests who have experienced stigmata—the wounds Christ suffered on the cross.

Said to resemble the fragrance of roses and other flowers, the odor of sanctity—or osmogenesia—continues to baffle church authorities as much as it does the skeptics. Even before their deaths, some saints were said to be surrounded by this "heavenly" aroma as they went about their daily business praying, healing and carrying out the affairs of the church.

Not all odors were said to smell like flowers. When Padre Pio, the famed 20th century Italian priest, experienced episodes of bilocation or stigmata, he was reportedly surrounded by the rich aroma of tobacco.

St. Valery, who died in 619, and St. Joseph of Cupertino, who died in 1663, were among the many others said to be blessed with the perfumed odor. Celestial fragrances were said to fill rooms when they entered. St. Hermann (d. 1230), Blessed John Baptist Da Fabriano (d. 1539), St. Catherie De' Ricci (d. 1589) and Blessed Mary of Oignies (d. 1213) can be counted among those who gave off "beautiful" fragrances when in prayer.

The most compelling of miracles relating to the odor of sanctity are those of the Incorruptibles. Church records indicate that when the tombs or caskets of these long-dead people were opened, they emitted a mystical and pleasant fragrance.

Some saints whose bodies were known to emit a heavenly fragrance after being exhumed years after death were St. Theresa of Avila (d. 1582), St. Paul of the Cross (d. 1775), St. Rose of Lima (d. 1617), St. Camillus De Lellis (d. 1614), and St. Mary Magdalen De Pazzi (d. 1607).

Shroud of Turin

IN A CHAPEL OF THE CATHEDRAL at Turin in northern Italy lies a shroud that millions of Christians revere as the burial cloth in which the crucified body of Christ was wrapped. While some dismiss it as a fraud, others say it's a miracle—proof of Jesus Christ's resurrection.

On the cloth, which is about 14 feet long and 3 feet, 6 inches wide, the dim, brown image of a dead and disfigured man can be seen—almost like a photographic imprint. At the top can be seen the compelling features of a bearded man so like the commonly accepted face of Christ that those who cherish the shroud are convinced that the resemblance must be more than mere coincidence.

If genuine, the cloth is the most impressive and moving relic to have come down to us from the time of Christ.

But is it real?

For centuries, skeptics have repeatedly proclaimed doubts of its authenticity. Controversy still rages—but 20th century science has, surprisingly, made the voices of the skeptics less strident than they used to be.

Tests by impartial scientists are producing increasingly firm evidence that what is revered by so many is, in fact, the shroud of someone who was crucified in Palestine around the time that Jesus died. Whether the body was that of Christ can probably never be ascertained.

The burial cloth under investigation bears marks on its left-hand portion of the front and on its right-hand portion of the back of a man around 35 to 40 years old and about 5 feet 6 inches tall. There is evidence of a wound in the ribs and of bleeding from the forearms.

Even more striking are bloodstains in the head area—proof, say some, that a crown of thorns had been placed around the victim's head.

One of the most controversial issues, of course, is how the shroud came to bear such clear imprints of the body it covered. Another equally vexing problem arises from the fact that there is no record of its existence before 1357, when it was publicly exhibited at the small French town of Lirey.

At that time the cloth belonged to a noble French family, the de Charnys, who never explained how it had come into their possession. Among the many people both inside and outside the Church who nevertheless had faith in its authenticity were the powerful dukes of Savoy, to whom the controversial relic was bequeathed in 1453.

At first they kept it in their capital city of Chambery, where it was slightly damaged by fire in 1532. Then, in 1578, they moved their capital to Turin, where the shroud was enshrined in a cathedral chapel built expressly for it. There it has lain since, venerated by many—although the Catholic Church itself has never declared it valid.

Skeptics suggest the figure imprinted on the shroud was simply painted sometime in the 14th century. One American expert, Walter McCrone, insists that the bloodstains are unnaturally red for 2,000-year-old blood and were likely made by some artificial substance—probably rose madder, a paint pigment favored by medieval artists.

On the other hand, scientific tests have revealed that blood found in the shroud contains the right mixture of calcium, protein and iron.

Textile experts have also concluded that the weave of the linen is of a type common in Palestine 2,000 years ago and that its fibers contain traces of cotton, which does not grow in Europe.

Using a new technique that helps decipher the faded contours of shapes imprinted on the fabric, a team of researchers recently found startling new evidence of the shroud's authenticity— including images from a Tiberian amulet, Roman nail, spear, sponge and crown of thorns.

"Images like these abound all over the shroud," Dr. Alan Whanger, professor emeritus at Duke University Medical Center, told the *Washington Times*. Whanger, a research member with the Association of Scientists and Scholars International for the Shroud, says the new process offers "clear confirmation" that the images are those of the Nazarene.

Because the objects were stained with the victim's blood, Whanger said they would have been wrapped in a burial shroud according to Jewish custom. Whanger and other members of his team dismissed a 1988 carbon-14 study that concluded the shroud was a 14th-century forgery.

"Those labs still won't open their data for scrutiny," Whanger said.

In 1990 the Vatican said the carbon testing methods had been "strange" and that more tests should be conducted. Before his death, Pope John Paul II, on the advice of the Pontifical Academy of Sciences, called the shroud a "relic," another word for authentic.

Simon Magus

SIMON MAGUS HAS BEEN CALLED a lot of names—none very flattering.

Back in the early days of the Christian Church, the man regarded as the "father of all heresy" was branded a warlock, a sorcerer, a prophet, a miracle worker, a witch, a false messiah and a magician.

It was the last name "Magus," from the Latin word for magician, that has stayed with him down through the ages.

In the beginning, long before he tried to buy his way into the church and fly to heaven, Simon Magus was a pretty popular guy, hanging out with the likes of St. John and St. Peter, both heavyweights in the early Christian movement.

Magus, an educated and deeply religious man, greatly admired the apostles and their teachings. His admiration for the power of Christian evangelization was so strong, in fact, he even sought baptism by Philip the Evangelist—the same man who had baptized Peter and John.

But Magus wanted more—lots more. Once he saw the power of St. Peter and other Christian miracle-makers in action, he resolved to possess their secrets at all costs.

So began the tragic downfall of a man whose reputation

as a notorious schemer and practitioner of the black arts would doom him to eternal damnation. His name, in fact, is said to have given rise to the term *simony*, which describes the sin of trying to buy or sell sacred objects or to connive one's way into ecclesiastical office.

According to second-century historian Justin Martyr, Magus' misfortunes started during a visit to Rome at the time of Emperor Claudius (41-54 AD). While the emperor and crowds of spectators looked on, Magus is said to have regaled them with showy demonstrations of his own great skills as a miracle-worker and magician.

Some sources say Magus learned the black arts in the land of Samaria, his home country. There, among the remote hills and desolate river valleys, magic and sorcery were commonplace, as were harlotry, shamanism and demonism. In this dark and sinister domain, Magus was greatly revered for possessing vast preternatural powers. Contemporaries said he "amazed the nation of Samaria" with his "uncanny magical arts."

He even founded a strange new sect—Gnosticism—and placed himself at the godhead. Under the title of "The God that is Great," Magus traveled widely into Phoenicia, Palestine—even to Egypt—preaching the heretical gospel in which he claimed to be the true messiah himself.

"I am God," he proclaimed, "And I have come to you. Already the world is being destroyed. And you, O men, are to perish because of your inequities."

He told his followers: "But I wish to save you, as you see me returning again with heavenly power. Blessed is he who has worshipped me now!" In apocalyptic style, he added: "But I will cast everlasting fire upon all the rest, both on cities and on country places. And men who fail to realize the penalties in store for them will in vain repent and groan. But I will preserve forever those who have been convinced by me."

Simonianism, as this branch of Gnosticism came to be called, considered Simon Magus as "the first God," or "Father," and he was sometimes worshiped as the incarnation of the Greek god Zeus. All this time he zealously followed the practices of Christianity, even attending a religious school founded by Dositheos after the death of John the Baptist. He also studied Arabic-Jewish magical medicine in Alexandria and is thought to have been a student of Hellenistic culture.

His powers are said to have grown so strong he could make himself invisible. At will he could levitate, elongate and even change himself into an animal. It's no wonder he was known far and wide as the "master sorcerer" and the "king of mysteries."

As he roamed the ancient Near East spouting his bizarre brand of mysticism, casting out demons, and performing miracles, he won a lot of converts. One was a beautiful young woman named Helena, whom Magus believed was the reincarnated Helen of Troy. Magus had found Helena in a brothel in Tyre, but through her "fallen state" he saw an opportunity to "resurrect her spirit" for his own religious purposes.

According to his enemies, Magus' religion allowed all manner of sinful practices. One observer noted, "Their secret priests...served the lust of the senses and practiced magic with all their might, employ conjurations and spells, concoct love potions and methods of seduction, and engage in dream-interpretation and dark prestidigitator's arts."

Followers reportedly worshiped statues of Magus and Helena, which were described as similar to Zeus and Minerva.

On a visit to Rome, Magus encountered the apostles Peter and John who, according to Acts 8:9-24, had come there to preach the Gospel. Wandering mystics and religious outcasts often sought out the streets of Rome as a forum to sound off their beliefs, attract converts and demonstrate their spiritual masteries. So it was with Peter and John, the two most famous followers of the crucified Jew named Jesus.

Magus was utterly fascinated with the two bearded strangers—especially the way they could "lay on hands" and heal the sick and lame. Legend has it that is he confronted Peter and demanded he sell him the key to his mysterious power.

"Give me this power, that any on whom I lay my hands shall receive the Holy Spirit," he said.

Magus' haughty request greatly offended the Christians.

They could not imagine anyone having the gall to try to buy the holy power.

Peter rebuked the arrogant Samarian, saying, "May your silver perish with you because you thought you could obtain the gift of God with money." Furthermore, "You have neither part nor lot in this matter, for your heart is not right before God. Repent, therefore, of this wickedness of you, and pray to the Lord that, if possible, the intent of your heart will be forgiven."

Magus was speechless. Humbly, he replied, "Pray for me to the Lord that nothing of what you have said may come upon me!"

According to the Acts of Peter, Magus refused to repent and, instead, continued his deceitful ways.

But the deed had already been done anyway. Magus' arrogance quickly earned him the wrath of the mightiest of the Christian apostles. It was a deed so dark and blasphemous that his name would go down in church history as Simon the Great Heretic.

On a subsequent visit to Rome, Magus again encountered his old nemesis, Peter, and challenged him to a magical showdown before the new emperor Nero (54-68 AD). Still furious at Peter for his earlier dressing-down, Magus announced he would prove his power was greater than that of the apostles by flying off the top of the Roman Forum and straight to heaven.

With the raucous crowd cheering him on, Simon the Magician scaled the lofty heights, lifted his arms in dramatic fashion—and plunged to his death. Some accounts say Magus fell because, mid way into the flight, Peter beseeched God to end the blasphemy, and God answered.

Following Magus' flashy death, numerous myths sprang up about his life and legacy. One held that he was a demon in human form, citing his unusual powers of levitation, elongation and metamorphosis.

"Everything is a miracle. It is a miracle that one does not dissolve in one's bath like a lump of sugar."
—Pablo Picasso

HEALING WATERS & HEAVENLY CURES

For as long as anyone can remember, stories have been told about miraculous healing waters that sometimes cure or offer relief to people suffering from ailments and afflictions ranging from schizophrenia to cancer.

One sip, say the faithful, can cause cancer to go into remission, restore eyesight to the blind and allow those who are crippled to throw away their crutches.

Spanish conquistador Ponce de Leon sailed to Florida in the 16th century in search of a magical, bubbling spring that supposedly offered eternal youth to those who partook of its waters. He never found the fabled fountain, but stories persist throughout the world, from Asia to South America, about similar mystical, flowing waters.

Even today, pilgrims travel to faraway places—Calcutta, Dusseldorf and Rio de Janeiro—to drink and bathe in waters said to be blessed with divine healing properties. A favorite destination among celebrities is Tlacote, Mexico, where famed basketball star Magic Johnson recently went to drink water from a spring that medical advisers said might help cure his AIDS condition.

In the United States, victims of arthritis, tuberculosis, the gout and other diseases often pay generous sums of money to find relief at "miracle springs." Similar springs have been discovered in China, Australia, Japan, Germany, Russia, England and elsewhere.

Probably the most famous story about healing waters originates in Lourdes, France. In 1858, 14-year-old Bernadette

Soubirous claimed that a manifestation of Mary, the mother of Jesus, instructed her to tell the world about a nearby grotto where she would find a flowing spring that contained special healing properties.

Bernadette did as she was told. Nowadays, millions of pilgrims wait in line each year with jugs, cups and pitchers to drink the spring's cool, pure waters. Many claim to receive partial or total cures of physical and emotional ills.

Healing waters are nothing new to followers of the Christian faith. Since the time of the Apostles, Christians have considered healing waters a "gift of the spirit." Even non believers who drink from "blessed" waters sometimes report relief from chronic illnesses, depression, anxiety and other physical and emotional ailments.

Do "healing springs" really work? Can they cure as advertised?

While mainstream science generally frowns on the subject, some specialists suggest that the secret behind the properties of healing waters has to do with the way active hydrogen (atomic hydrogen) and hydrogen (molecular hydrogen) interact in water.

Lourdes, France

HUNDREDS OF MARIAN APPARITIONS are reported every year, but the mother of all sightings, the one that launched them all—at least in the modern era—occurred in the rugged foothills of the Pyrenees in southern France in the winter of 1858.

That's when an impoverished young shepherd girl out gathering firewood near the Grotto of Massabielle with her sister and a friend encountered the vision of a beautiful woman who identified herself as the "Immaculate Conception," the Virgin Mary, mother of Jesus Christ.

The girl was Bernadette Soubirous, 14-year-old daughter of a poor mill worker named Francois Soubirous and his wife, Louise, a laundress. Hard times had fallen on rural France, forcing the Soubirous family and most others to rely on their religious devotion to get by. Besides tending sheep, Bernadette—described as a frail, somewhat simple-minded girl—also waited tables in her aunt's tavern.

She had returned to Lourdes in January 1858 to attend the free school run by the Sisters of Charity and Christian Instruction so she could complete preparations for Catechism and Holy Communion.

It was early on the morning on Feb. 11 that Bernadette had her vision—a vision that has inspired generations of believers ever since and turned Lourdes into a holy shrine for Catholics all over the world.

Ironically, only Bernadette was able to see the "beautiful woman," who appeared to her a total of 18 times over the course of several weeks. During the ninth vision, the lady told Bernadette to drink from the spring that flowed under the rock. Confused, the girl replied there was no spring; in fact, the ground was rocky and completely dry.

But Bernadette did as she was told. Digging with her hands, she was soon rewarded for her effort when a small puddle bubbled up from below ground. Over the next several days, a steady stream began to flow.

So began one of the most remarkable stories in modern church history. In the century and a half since Bernadette dug the stream, countless millions of people from all parts of the world have made pilgrimages to Lourdes to drink water from the spring.

Thousands say they've been healed from afflictions and ailments of all kinds—cancer, tuberculosis, brain tumors, arthritis, and mental impairment. The Catholic Church has recognized 67 miracles at the site, the latest being an elderly Italian woman who was lowered into the chilly waters at Lourdes during a pilgrimage in 1952.

Now age 94, Anna Santaniello had a variety of ailments, including Bouillaud's disease, a rheumatic condition that causes trouble with speaking and walking, as well as acute asthma attacks, cyanosis of the face and lips, and swelling of the legs.

In an interview with Vatican Radio, Santaniello said, "I told them all I wanted to go—even if I must die seeing Our Lady."

She said, "I prayed with a loud voice so she would hear me. 'Blessed Virgin, you must help me,'" she said. "Everyone was praying for me....They had me kiss the statue of Our Lady that they had there on a small altar."

After a few minutes in the icy baths, "I felt a great warmth, precisely around my heart," she said. "I felt calm. I got up and told the volunteers (who wanted to help her back on the stretcher) to "go help the others because I can do it on my own."

Santaniello's story was forwarded to her home diocese, the Archdiocese of Salerno-Campagna-Acerno, where a special commission sat on the study until 40 years later when a new archbishop at Salerno agreed to reopen the investigation. In 2005, the Roman Catholic Church officially recognized Santaniello's case as "Miraculous," the 67th "miracle cure" officially attributed to the sanctuary in southwestern France.

Santaniello's miracle was not unlike so many others that have been reported over the years, most of which fail to earn recognition from either the church or the media. Scientists, historians, theologians and other experts still come to Lourdes every year—not to seek healing, but to interview the faithful who claim to have been touched by the "holy spirit" at the shrine and try to understand the true miracle of Lourdes.

"There is a lot of interest among doctors right now in the power of faith and religion to produce cures," said Dr. Raj Persaud, a London psychiatrist who visits Lourdes often to investigate whether patients have been cured by divine intervention or something else. "Several scientific studies have found that praying for the seriously medically ill does seem to produce medical benefit."

It is ironic that, while so many other people have found miracles in the waters she discovered, Bernadette Soubirous passed on the opportunity to drink from the spring and possibly save herself in her long battle against the tuberculosis and asthma that would eventually claim her life.

On March 25, Bernadette announced that another vision—

the 13th—instructed her to erect a chapel on the site. Authorities refused to listen and even tried to shut down the popular spring which was producing 27,000 gallons of water each week. When Empress Eugenie, wife of Napoleon II, intervened on Bernadette's behalf, construction went forward.

Never one for drawing attention to herself, Bernadette joined the Sisters of Charity convent, moving into their motherhouse at Nevers at the age of 22. She spent the rest of her life there, working as an assistant in the infirmary and later as a sacristan, creating beautiful embroidery for altar cloths and vestments.

During a severe asthma attack, she asked for water from the Lourdes spring, and her symptoms subsided, never to return. However, she did not seek healing in this way when the tuberculosis she had contracted while working at the Lourdes shrine flared up and claimed her life at the age of 35 on April 16, 1879.

Her body was first exhumed on Sept. 2, 1909, only to find it "incorrupt"—preserved from decomposition. The corpse was exhumed a second time on April 3, 1919, and found to still be in a perfect state of preservation.

In 1925, relics were taken from her body and her face was sprayed with a film of wax. The remains were then placed in a gold and glass reliquary in the Chapel of St. Bernadette at the motherhouse in Nevers.

Bernadette received Beatification in 1925 and Canonization in 1933 under Pope Pius XI—not so much for the content of her visions, but rather for her "simplicity and holiness of life."

Today, St. Bernadette is remembered by the Roman Catholic Church as the patron saint of sick persons and of Lourdes.

Minster, England

TWO ANCIENT WELLS GUSHING through an abandoned abbey garden in a tiny village on the Isle of Sheppey in Kent, England, has been drawing thousands of miracle seekers since the discovery of a submerged prehistoric bronze statue of a fertility goddess in the early 1990s.

Archaeologists say the wells, which date back 3,500 years and are about 40 feet deep, contains some of the purest water found in Europe. People who have sipped from the wells claim it has cured a variety of illnesses, ranging from cancer to blindness.

Each day, visitors clutching water jugs and canteens trek down to the wells to collect supplies of water to take back home. Some come from as far away as Germany and France, confident that water from the wells contains miraculous healing powers.

Government-sanctioned tests have found the water to be pure, with no traces of sewage or chlorine. A number of valuable trace elements, such as potassium and magnesium, were also found in the wells, which are now listed as a Grade One historical site by English Heritage.

Equally remarkable is a prehistoric statue of a three-headed fertility goddess found in the water recently by local amateur archaeologists. Ian White, who dredged up the bronze statue from beneath centuries of silt at the bottom of the deep well, credits the statue with helping his wife give birth to a healthy baby girl.

For years, he and his wife had tried to have a baby. Nothing worked—doctors, drugs and other treatments—until he found the statue. The Whites firmly believe that the "triple-headed goddess," the name they gave to the prehistoric artifact, was responsible for the birth of their baby.

"There is little doubt of a life force here," archaeologist Brian Slade told writer Brian James. "It is ancient, pre-Christian, but I believe it is a force for good."

According to legend, the wells were famous in ancient Europe as a "healing center," a place where fertility rites were regularly practiced. The "Three-Headed Goddess" is also said to date to that time. Minster Abbey was founded by nuns in 640 by the Saxon St. Sexburga, the widowed queen of Kent.

Tlacote, Mexico

EACH DAY, more than 10,000 people come to Jesus Chahin's remote chicken ranch near the dusty village of Tlacote, Mexico, in search of a miracle.

They've been coming for years, millions of them, some from as far away as Europe and Asia, lumbering along the rocky path in creaking wheelchairs, others hobbling on crutches and walkers or carried on the shoulders of friends, family members or total strangers.

They bring with them plastic jugs, canteens and metal cans—anything to collect a few liters of the precious, life-giving waters said to flow in a muddy well on Jesus' remote farm some 150 miles north of Mexico City. Most believe a few sips of these special healing waters can cure whatever ails them, from AIDS, glaucoma and cancer to obesity, baldness and high cholesterol.

Like other "healing springs" in Germany, India and elsewhere around the world, the miraculous waters on Jesus' farm—dubbed by the press as the "Lourdes of Mexico"—are said to have cured countless thousands of pilgrims who came and drank. According to Jesus' own estimate, more than 20 million have been to Tlacote since May 1991 when he first discovered the water's unusual healing and curative properties.

That happened when one of his sick dogs quickly recovered after drinking from a muddy puddle. When word spread about the water's miraculous healing power, others came and drank—and they, too, were healed. Then more came, and more.

At first local medical authorities refused to acknowledge anything special about the water—until several gallons shipped to a nearby army hospital were credited with healing 600 Mexican soldiers.

Nowadays, visitors suffering from diabetes, heart disease, cancer, arthritis and other ailments brave sizzling temperatures, dangerous terrain and long lines stretching for miles to drink waters from Jesus' well.

Jesus Chahin, who refuses payment for the water, attributes its curative powers to the fact it weighs less than normal water—by at least 44 grams, according to a 1993 CBS report. State health officials disagree, saying tests show the water is completely normal for the region, but completely safe to drink.

Many of those who come could not care less about scientific explanations or natural causes. To them, God put the miracle waters on Jesus' farm for a purpose—to heal whatever ails them.

"This is miracle stuff," commented a Texan who lost 50 percent of his vision in an industrial accident. After his wife sprinkled a few drops of the water on his eyes, his eyesight is "halfway back to being normal."

Another visitor said his mother's cancer went into remission after drinking some of the water. A real-estate agent from Chapala, Mexico, had been unable to walk for years. He also suffered from kidney problems. On the advice of a friend, he drank a jug of water from Tlacote and, within days, regained use of his legs and kidneys.

Tlacote has become so popular that special buses are now chartered daily from San Antonio. That idea began when a San Antonio newspaper editor, Tino Duran, traveled to Tlacote to do a story—and to seek medical help himself.

Duran's experience was so positive that he decided to get the bus service started so that other people in San Antonio could journey to Tlacote safely and inexpensively.

While doctors are at a loss to understand what is going on at Tlacote, millions of people who have been healed or touched by the miracle water simply say it's God's work.

"Every day I wake up and I know that God has given me this pain," said Antonia Gonzales, who suffered from arthritis for 30 years. "I know, too, that it is too great for me to bear, so I pray and I offer it back to him. He gives it to me and I give it right back to Him. That is how I am able to bear it."

Nadana, India

SINCE 1992, THE PEOPLE OF NADANA, a village nestled in a remote jungle area about 120 miles north of Delhi, have been praising the qualities of a bubbling well that many claim can heal the sick and afflicted.

Many locals who have bathed in or drunk from the formerly

deserted well say it cured a wide range of ailments, including arthritis, cancer and gastro-intestinal problems. A 5-year-old polio victim was reportedly cured after taking a bath there.

Today, a constant stream of pilgrims, many from faraway countries, flock to the well to partake of its miraculous healing powers. As many as 20,000 are said to arrive daily, mostly aboard buses chartered from nearby towns and villages.

The well has developed a special reputation of being able to heal skin diseases, according to Share International. Pilgrims are said to derive benefits from bathing or floating in the waters, then taking home large jugs to drink.

The owner of the well, a village leader named Mamraj, reportedly turn down a large sum of money for the well because he said God gave the water to the people, not for making money.

Nordenau, Germany

ONE HUNDRED MILES from the bustling German city of Dusseldorf lies the small, picturesque village of Nordenau, a popular ski resort in the populous district of Schmalenberg.

For more than a century, people from all over the world have been coming here to ski, hike, canoe and picnic among the dark, evergreen forests and scenic mountain trails. Nowadays, they also come to drink water from an underground spring said to possess special healing powers.

The spring bubbles from a cave on property owned by Theo Tommes, whose Hotel Tommes lies nearby. Back in 1992, while investigating an abandoned slate mine to use as a wine cellar, Tommes entered the cave and noticed a "bright white light" that seemed to fill the whole cavern.

Later, Tommes' mother entered the cave and saw a series of small crosses of light within the glowing white light. Experts brought in to investigate the mysterious cave concluded that the grotto was highly charged with energy.

Only then did they discover the spring—a "wonderfully clear" spring flowing from an underground source near the back of the cave. Analysts at the German Fresenius Laboratires tested the water and found it especially pure and clean. They also found that it was 8 percent lighter than ordinary water.

Another German laboratory, Hygene Institut des Ruhrgebiets Gelsenkirchen, also certified the water to be extremely light, perhaps 8 percent lighter than ordinary water. Stranger still, water the spring spirals to the left, but five metes further on it spirals to the right.

It wasn't long until stories began circulating about the spring's miraculous healing properties. As these stories spread in the media, hundreds of people in hope of a miracle cure for various ailments started journeying to Nordenau—some from as far away as Paris and Prague.

Few were disappointed.

According to the German newspaper *Bild*, an old woman complaining of blindness sprinkled some of the water on her eyes and was healed. An ex-miner said the water cured his back injury, allowing him to throw away his crutches.

Stories like these continued to gain widespread dissemination in European newspapers. Before long, pilgrims started arriving from places like Brazil, Mexico, Japan, Australia and the United States.

Today, the Nordenau spring is one of the most popular "healing springs" in the world, along with Tlacota, Mexico, and Nandana, India. Nobody understands the secret behind the spring's curative powers, but one German geo-physician, Dr. Johannes Koch, suspects it has something to do with radiation inside the cave plus the fact the spring is a meeting place for at least three watercourses.

"It's very strong at this point," he said of one part of the cave that remains dry year-round. "It's giving power, filling people up with energy."

A German reporter, Guido Brandenburg, drank some of the water and said, "After five minutes my fingertips vibrated....I felt as if an electric current flowed through me."

Barnwell, S.C.

LUTE BOYLSTON LOVED the land.

As a farmer, born and bred in the South, he saw the fields and woods surrounding his South Carolina homeland as God's gift to the people—a reward, he felt, for honest, decent folk who worked hard and led righteous lives.

It annoyed him when friends and neighbors abused God's gift. For years, the Barnwell County planter watched his beloved land slowly deteriorate—first from careless agricultural use, and later from the encroachment of civilization.

When houses, shopping centers and parking lots began gobbling up great chunks of virgin territory, Boylston began to worry. Where would it all end? How much land would be left to his grandchildren? His great-grandchildren?

For years he stood helplessly by while developers, outdoor recreationists, and even other farmers pillaged the countryside. Then, one warm, summer day in July of 1944, he did something a bit unusual to protect his farm. He climbed into his pickup truck and drove into town, stopping to collect his attorney and then heading to the courthouse to file a new property deed.

In that deed—still on file in the Barnwell County Courthouse—the 76-year-old farmer gave explicit instructions that upon his death part of his property would be deeded over to God. After all, reasoned Boylston, it had been God's land in the first place.

In the unusual bequest he stated that he didn't believe "the white people who dispossessed the Indians ever appreciated the value of God's will sufficiently to help in any way preserve for posterity this gift of God Almighty to mankind."

The piece of land deeded over to God happened to be the site of Barnwell County's famous "Healing Springs." For decades, men, women and children from across the country had been flocking to the springs to drink, bathe, and play in the cool, clear waters bubbling from the ground. Many of those who did so claimed the waters possessed miraculous healing powers.

Boylston himself recognized the divine power of the

springs as well. In his deed of land to God, he made it clear that "the Almighty had intended the cool waters of the wells to be a source of comfort to the afflicted....I return to Him the most treasured piece of earth that I have ever owned or possessed."

The farmer's princely act earned him a big blue and white sign posted beneath several huge trees and a granite marker beneath a clump of oak trees surrounding the springs. Waves of people continued to enjoy the springs, which now, officially, belonged to God—the only piece of land on earth legally deeded so.

American Indians had been the first to know about the mystical little patch of ground. Local legends suggest some of these tribes worshipped the waters—or at least spirits in the waters. Early settlers drank from the springs as well, and the mystical tradition continued.

During the Revolutionary War, soldiers often camped around the springs to rest, bathe, and—according to some accounts—help heal wounds suffered in combat.

By the middle of this century, the Healing Springs had become a favorite destination for thousands of travelers from all parts of the country—even Canada and Europe. Eventually, the springs were named an official state attraction. On any given Sunday, gangs of visitors descended on the one-acre plot of land to sip from the springs and splash their faces and arms. They came armed with plastic jugs and glass jars, metal buckets and wooden barrels—anything that would hold the life-giving waters from the Healing Springs.

Inevitably, the garbage began piling up. Plastic candy and cigarette wrappers. Beer cans. Discarded human debris which occasionally reached unmanageable proportions.

Boylston's quiet little spring in the woods, the spring he had returned legally to God, was rapidly becoming a dumping ground for human refuse. Ironically, many of the people who came to the springs for comfort and healing were the same ones causing most of the mess. In stepped the state of South Carolina. If Barnwell County didn't take action soon to clean up the springs, the popular tourist attraction would lose its official status.

Disgusted by heaps of debris left over by man and nature, groups of concerned citizens joined forces to restore "God's little acre" to its former pristine condition. Spearheaded by the local chamber of commerce, the cleanup campaign was a roaring success. Healing Springs regained favor with the state and is still a state tourist attraction. Thousands of people still go there each year to partake of the waters' mysterious properties.

One such visitor is Sammy Lee Dunn, who claims to have been making the 150-mile round-trip to Healing Springs for the past 50-plus years. The elderly Saluda County retiree believes the spring water is filled with "the Lord's mysterious powers. It's in there. And I ain't about to quit coming as long as the Lord will let me."

"A miracle is an event which creates faith. That is the Purpose and nature of miracles. Frauds deceive. An event which Creates faith does not deceive: therefore it is not a fraud, but a miracle."
—George Bernard Shaw

SPEAKING IN TONGUES:
The Language of the Angels

Mystics and religious leaders have long written and preached about the various states of ecstasy said to come over the faithful during praise and worship services, of seeing angels and saints and visions of God and His heavenly kingdom.

One of the most common but misunderstood phenomena in the church today—especially among the Pentecostal and Charismatic practitioners—is the ecstatic ability to "speak in tongues," a gift that harks back to the time of the Apostles and one that continues to baffle, amuse and disturb Christians of all denominations.

Even seasoned theologians with a thorough understanding of the Bible debate the value and meaning of speaking in tongues. Adding to its mystification is the fact that many Christian cults, the occult, Eastern mystics and New Agers claim to have mastered the gift of communicating in languages completely alien to them or those around them.

Speaking in tongues, or glossolalia—from the Greek *glossa*, tongue, and *lalo*, to speak—signifies the ability to speak in a language of unknown origin to either the speaker or his audience. This language, which has been described as gibberish and bizarre babble, is considered by some to be the "language of Heaven" or "language of angels."

Skeptics dismiss these cases as nonsense, saying that people claiming to speak in tongues are simply caught up in a state of trance, self-hypnotism or a heightened state of emotionalism brought on by religious ecstasy. Some compare the phenomenon to snake-handling practices where ecstatic believers, "caught up in the fire of the Holy Spirit," literally embrace Mark's admonition to "take up serpents" as a dangerous demonstration of their faith.

Medical studies in the early 20th century linked glossolalia to schizophrenia and other mental disorders, but modern research now disputes those claims. In 1972, John Kildahl, argued in *The Psychology of Speaking in Tongues* that glossolalia was "not necessarily a symptom of mental illness," and that "glossolalists suffer less from stress."

According to the New Testament, the first case of speaking in tongues occurred during the Pentecost—50 days after Christ's crucifixion—when the Holy Spirit was revealed to a group of believers. "Tongues of fire" are said to have shrouded the heads of the Apostles, who miraculously began to speak in languages unknown to them or anyone present.

Luke records the account in the Book of Acts, which occurred while the believers were gathered in a house near a Jerusalem temple.

"Suddenly there came a sound from Heaven as of a rushing mighty wind, and it filled all the house where they were sitting. And there appeared unto them cloven tongues like as of fire, and it sat upon each of them. And they were all filled with the Holy Ghost, and began to speak with other tongues, as the Spirit gave them utterance" (Acts 2:2-4).

Speaking in tongues occurred again in Caesarea 38 years after Pentecost, this time in the home of the Roman centurion Cornelius (Acts 10:44-48). Unlike during the Pentecost, when Jewish believers spoke in tongues, here the tongues were spoken by Gentile believers. As noted by Peter, this served as a sign to verify to many Jewish Christians that the gospel applied to Gentiles as well.

The last incident of tongues recorded in Acts takes place 13 years after Caesarea in Ephesus. Paul laid his hands on 12 disciples, baptizing them in the name of Jesus, when suddenly they began to speak in tongues (Acts 19:1-7).

Altogether, speaking in tongues is mentioned in the Bible at least 35 times.

Even today, Christians continue to claim they have witnessed or personally engaged in speaking in tongues. Although guardedly accepted by Catholics and Protestants, this belief forms a fundamental point of Pentecostal and Charismatic doctrine, which many consider the fastest growing sect within Christianity.

Some Charismatic Evangelists identify three different activities that comprise "tongues"—the "sign of tongues," in which listeners hear their native language by means of divine power; the "gift of tongues," which refers to a belief that the Holy Spirit sometimes conveys a message understood by listeners as well as the speaker; and "praying in the spirit," which suggests that a believer engaged in glossolalia is speaking directly and only to God.

Aside from Christians, other religious groups also observed various forms of glossolalia, including the ancient Oracle of Delphi where priestesses of the god Apollo spoke in strange utterances and certain Gnostic magical texts from the Roman period where nonsensical syllables were used.

Closer to the present, Spiritism—or Spiritualism—during the 19th century was developed into a religion of its own, thanks to the work of Allan Kardeck, and the phenomenon was seen as one of the self-evident manifestations of spirits.

Glossolalia has also been observed in shamanism and the Voodoo religion of Haiti; it can often be brought on by the ingestion of hallucinogenic drugs or certain psychedelic mushrooms and other plants.

According to evangelist Tom Brown of Tom Brown Ministries, speaking in tongues is the most talked-about phenomenon in the Christian world.

"Pentecostalism and the Charismatic movement have brought speaking in tongues to the forefront, and these branches of Christianity are without doubt the fastest growing segments of Christianity," says Brown. "These movements are impacting the world even more than the Reformation did."

Brown said many people inaccurately define speaking in tongues as "speaking gibberish" or "talking nonsense." The truth, he points out, is that "speaking in tongues is the most intelligent, perfect language in the universe. It is God's language."

Evangelists such as Brown believe that glossalalia is the "language of heaven" because, as Brown puts it, "It is what is spoken in Heaven....The only difference is that the people in Heaven understand what they are saying."

Some Charismatic leaders such as Brown argue that speaking in tongues is essential to salvation. When believers are baptized in the Holy Spirit, they maintain, they learn to speak in tongues.

"Speaking in tongues is the physical, biblical evidence that one is baptized in the Holy Spirit," says Brown. "Jesus says that those who believe in Him will speak in new tongues" (Mark 16:17).

A decade ago, speaking in tongues was encountered only in Pentecostal churches, revival meetings, Quaker gatherings and some Methodist groups. Today, says Friar George Nicozisin of the Greek Orthodox Archdiocese of America, glossolalia is also found in some Roman Catholic and Protestant churches.

And while the Orthodox Church does not necessarily condone speaking in tongues or believe the gift is essential for salvation as do some Charismatics, it does not rule it out either, according to Nicozisin.

"The Greek Orthodox Church does not preclude the use of Glossolalia," says Nicozisin, "but regards it as one of the minor gifts of the Holy Spirit."

Nicozisin said the Church's view on speaking in tongues is based on St. Paul's words in Chapter 14: "I thank God that I speak in strange tongues more than any of you....But in church worship I would rather speak five words that can be understood, in order to teach others, than speak thousands of words in strange tongues."

Some church leaders hold to the view that this spiritual gift ceased after the Apostolic age. Others maintain that the gifts of

God are varied, and that speaking in tongues is not "proof" that one has been baptized in the Holy Spirit or has reached spiritual maturity or immaturity.

All agree that what matters most is "absolute commitment" to the lordship of Jesus Christ.

"If I speak with the tongues of men and of angels, but do not have love, I have become a noisy gong or a clanging cymbal," writes Paul. "And if I have the gift of prophecy, and know all mysteries and all knowledge; and if I have all faith, so as to remove mountains, but do not have love, I am nothing..." (1 Corinthians 13:1-2, 13).

"The miracles of nature do not seem miracles because they are so common. If no one had ever seen a flower, even a dandelion would be the most startling event in the world."
—Unknown Source

CROSSES OF LIGHT

Shortly past midnight on Dec. 8, 1992, Joann Noriega walked into the bathroom in her modest house in Montclair, Calif., and saw in the moonlight a "big, beautiful cross" framed in her window.

Then she saw something else —the silhouette of a woman's face that seemed to be "aglow" against the bright cross.

In the 17 years she had lived in her house, Noriega had never seen anything quite like this. Thinking it was some kind of hallucination created by the moonlight, she opened and closed the window several times.

But the cross and figure of the woman would not go away.

Noriega dropped to her knees and prayed.

"It was the Virgin Mary," she was quoted as saying. "I had no doubt. I didn't even try to guess at it."

When she looked up again, she saw a "host of angels" shrouded over the image of Mary and the cross.

"It was like the Immaculate Conception," she said.

The vision in the window lasted for a week. Nowadays, she says, the Virgin on the cross returns every full moon.

Understandably, Noriega's cross of light attracted a lot of attention, especially in the media. Newspaper and television stories ran, and soon, large crowds of curiosity-seekers flocked to her modest home to see the apparition with their own eyes.

Other phenomena have occurred in the home—additional crosses in the window, rainbows on the ground, oil seeping from a candle in her bedroom, and the sound of bells. The fragrant smell of roses often permeates the house while visions of the Virgin Mother occasionally appear.

Each week, Noriega holds a Friday night prayer meeting in her living room. It is here that the Virgin often appears.

"Inviting people here to pray and see the crosses makes them feel good," Noriega said. "They can feel the Holy Spirit. They can feel all these warm feelings."

Many miracles have occurred in the house, Noriega explained. Sick people have been healed. Depressed pilgrims have gone away singing and laughing, she said. One former drug addict said, "I believe I've been in the worst places in my living hell....But now I know, whatever happens, God is there for me. He's already proved it."

Mysterious crosses of light similar to those that appeared in Noriega's bathroom window have been showing up in different parts of the world for the past 20 years or so. These apparitions, ranging from a few inches in height to more than 40 feet, seem to conform to a particular pattern—a brilliant, even-armed cross within a diamond shape. They appear in frosted glass and give the impression of floating, suspended in midair, between the glass and the light source.

Many people say the glowing manifestations are God's way of sending a signal that Christ will soon return. Some lights, rumored to possess miraculous powers of healings, attract large crowds of believers.

A number of researchers and theologians have compared them to Marian appearances, weeping Madonnas, stigmata and other church-related phenomena that have been seen and studied for centuries.

And while skeptics dismiss the lights as nothing more than hallucinations or fraud, many religious people firmly believe they are "divine signs" that Christ is coming again.

"People see what they want to see," said Dr. Stjepan Mestrovic, a professor of sociology at Texas A&M University. "Whether it's real or not, trying to explain it scientifically, I think, is irrelevant. You have a group of people who are bound together by a belief and faith."

The first documented case was in 1988, according to the *Pasadena (Calif.) Star News*. That's when residents reported seeing a cross shining through a bathroom window of an apartment in El Monte.

Eyewitness Mona LaVine told the paper she saw "a cross of a pale golden light—and simply beautiful."

The owner of the apartment replaced the glass a few days later, but the cross kept reappearing in the new glass. Over the following two weeks, 12 more crosses appeared around the Los Angeles area.

What's behind the rash of sightings? Buddy Piper, a researcher for *Share International*—a New Age publication—has spent the past couple of decades researching and writing about the phenomenon. He says most crosses of light appear in the windows of private homes, that only a few cases occur in churches.

"They are appearing around the world," Piper was quoted as saying. "I have seen scores and scores of cross manifestations in the United States. They generally come in depressed areas of cities and they generally come in bathroom windows."

Tabernacle Church of Christ in Norfolk, Va., is one such place. Members of the small Pentecostal church, housed in a tiny brick building crammed between two modest houses on Tidewater Drive, have seen dozens of crosses of light flickering in the church windows in recent months.

"The crosses are real," says Pastor Mattie Jenkins. "They're there. It's the glory of the Lord."

Member Chris Smith described the crosses of light as "so beautiful….Once you see it, you're not going to believe it. The different colors and how they change. Oh, it's so beautiful!"

The first person to see Tabernacle crosses was Brenda Riddick.

"They just appeared there," she said. "I looked out the window and I saw them. It was so bright and beautiful."

In Altadena, Calif., near Los Angeles, the Reverend P.G. Pierce and his family regularly see the brilliant image of a cross shining through the bathroom window. A newspaper photo and accompanying article said the image appears to be shining through the window from the outside, but when people go into the back yard to find the source of the phenomenon, they find nothing.

"Whether or not a miracle exists," commented the *Los Angeles Herald Examiner*, "it is clear that many people in Los Angeles want desperately to see and touch a fingerprint of the Creator...."

The newspaper added: "All but the most committed of atheists would like to have a sign, any sign. Everyone wants to know that we are here for a reason, and that a higher entity stopped by to tell us so."

One evening in early November 1995, gigantic crosses of light started appearing in the windows of a small Knoxville, Tenn., church pastored by the Rev. Joe Bullard. Bullard and his wife, Mildred, were the first to notice a "radiant white light" that seemed to surround the entire building.

Two days later, right in the middle of a sermon, Bullard and the congregation were startled when they saw a "gigantic, bright white light—at least 40 feet tall"—in the shape of a cross centered on a wall inside the Copper Ridge Baptist Church. Suddenly, crosses of light began appearing in all five sanctuary windows, which had been installed in the church 26 years earlier.

The odd thing, said Bullard, was that the crosses were not inside the windows themselves, but suspended in mid-air similar to a holographic image.

"It was spooky, but we knew it was the Lord's work," the pastor said.

Before long, thousands of people were flocking to the 135-year-old church to see the apparition with their own eyes.They came during the night as well to breathlessly behold the fiery apparition which manifests itself as a reddish-gold glow.

In the days that followed, word got out that the crosses had miraculous healing powers. While there were scores of undocumented claims that the manifestation could cure cancer and restore sight, one woman, Joan Anderson, told the *Kokomo Perspective* that a trip to the Knoxville church resulted in an inoperable brain tumor being completely healed.

Bob Hurley, a skeptical columnist with the *Greenville Sun*, visited the church and came away a believer.

"I can't get the hair on the back of my neck to do anything but sick straight out these days," he wrote. "The crosses are indeed in the windows at the Copper Ridge Baptist Church. That is a fact. It doesn't matter if you believe or not....Now that I've seen the crosses with these two eyes, I'm a believer."

From sophisticated Manhattan to the swamps of Louisiana, the Philippines to the Yorkshire Dales, stories about mysterious manifestations of light in the shape of a cross continue to make headlines.

In 1999, parishioners at the Greater Macedonia Baptist Church in the small town of Port Sulphur, La., had just finished celebrating mass on Christmas morning when they noticed two crucifix-shaped lights blazing in the church windows.

When news got out, the tiny community was inundated with thousands of pilgrims anxious to see the crosses of light, described as gold or bronze-colored. A local television station caught the crosses on film and convinced many the manifestations are real.

Parishioner Lois Gibson said the crosses had "brought the whole community here closer together, irrespective of creed or nationality. It is a sign...that it is possible for us all to live in harmony together."

What one Florida announcer called "the miracle of 37th Street" was a cross of light that appeared in the bathroom window of Riviera Beach resident Ida Rollins shortly before Christmas in 1994.

So popular was the sighting that the *Miami Herald* reported that police had to throw up barricades around Rollins' house to keep back thousands of curiosity seekers.

In spite of the crush of people around her home, Rollins believes the cross is a "sign from God, a message of hope" for one of the poorest areas in town.

Rollins' message reflects the prayers and beliefs of the vast majority of people who claim to see the mysterious crosses. From all corners of the world—New Zealand, Croatia, Zambia, Egypt,

Canada and Brazil—witnesses of all religious backgrounds are convinced the glorious manifestations are divine messages from God.

"It's a "wake-up call," said one preacher from the Philippines. "Our Maker is trying to tell us to change our lives, to do right, because the end of time is not far away."

*"To me every hour of the light
and dark is a miracle. Every
cubic inch of space is a miracle."*
—Walt Whitman

STIGMATA:
Wounds of Passion

*STIGMATA—Spontaneous appearance of the wound marks of
Jesus Christ, on a person's body. These marks include the nail
wounds at the feet and the hands, the lance wound at the side,
the head wounds from the crown of thorns, and the scourge
marks over the entire body.*

On the morning of March 29, 1998, a Roman Catholic
priest working in the Caribbean island nation of Antigua
began to speak strangely and bleed profusely from his
wrists and ankles.

Parishioners who rushed to the priest's aid were reportedly
"thrown to the floor by an invisible force." Each time they
approached the suffering priest, they were struck by that same
mysterious force and pushed back.

Church officials from the local diocese were clearly baffled
by the inexplicable behavior of the priest, a 40-year-old Canadian
native named Gerard Critch who continued to experience the
strange symptoms for more than a week. They were especially
concerned because he complained of "excruciating pain" from
the flowing wounds in his hands, feet and side.

After a preliminary examination, they declared he might
be suffering from an extremely rare and controversial condition
known as stigmata. Though stigmata is not technically a disease,
people afflicted with it usually experience intense pain and
suffer wounds that mimic those endured by Jesus Christ as he
lay dying on the cross at Calvary.

Hundreds of cases of stigmata have been recorded throughout history, most of them exhibiting signs similar to Rev. Critch's—bleeding hands, feet, forehead and side, speaking in a strange tongue, visions of Jesus Christ and angels.

Although the Church stopped short of saying Rev. Critch was a "true stigmatic," they couldn't deny that something strange took hold of the popular middle-aged Canadian priest that warm morning in 1998.

"That something unusual took place is undeniable," a spokesman for the diocese said in a statement. "Several persons have seen these occurrences and have been affected."

One of those witnesses was R. Allen Standard, a banker from the United States who flew Critch to New York City on his private jet for treatment at an American hospital.

"The wounds were real," Stanford told the Associated Press in an interview. Among other phenomena, Stanford said he saw oil oozing from the marks on the priest's feet "as it did with Jesus."

Could all those witnesses have been wrong? Did Rev. Critch "fake" his wounds as alleged by some critics?

The Rev. Kevin Molloy, a priest at Corpus Christ Church in St. John's, Newfoundland, said Rev. Critch "would never do anything like that." He described the priest as a "good man" who was doing "good work" with his parishioners.

"For this to happen is just overwhelming," Molloy said. "It's amazing news, really, because this is something very rare."

The Roman Catholic world has known about stigmata for the better part of 800 years. Historically, this phenomenon stems from certain monastic practices of the Middle Ages, especially among Dominican and Franciscan orders of monks and nuns, who were known for their vows of poverty, strict rules and harsh treatment of their bodies.

Said to be extremely rare, this mystical experience occurs mostly among women, usually around the age of 33—the purported age of Christ when he died on the cross.

Even today, stigmatics clad in loin cloths and crowned with thorns gather on hilltop locations around the world to recreate

Christ's Passion in brutal and bloody drama by having their hands and feet nailed to wooden crosses each Easter Sunday.

Why do they do this? Skeptics might say such painful action is a product of lunacy or ecstasy, take your pick. During long spells of prayer and dedication, believers sometime enter a kind of deep hypnotic state in which their senses are deluded to the point they actually believe they are receiving "holy wounds" from Christ in some supernatural way.

Father Herbert Thurston, who made a lifelong study of this phenomenon, was quoted as saying:

"The impression left upon me has been that the subjects who were so favored or afflicted were all suffering from pronounced and often hysterical neuroses. Many of them were intensely devout...but in others piety was combined with eccentricities and with apparent dissociations of personality which were very strange and not exactly edifying."

He concluded: "I find it difficult to believe that God could have worked miracles to accredit such people as his chosen friends and representatives."

But Catholics and other believers say that stigmata is just one of the many mysterious gifts God shares with selected individuals. Others include speaking in tongues, bilocation—the teleportation of one's body to another location—healing and prophecy.

While it isn't always easy to understand these gifts, those who receive the marks of Christ or any of these other divine gifts are said to be truly special people.

Writing in a newspaper column, Father William Saunders, pastor of Queen of Apostles Church in Alexandria, Va., says: "The stigmata is a sign of union with our crucified Lord. The genuine stigmatic must have lived a life of heroic virtue, have endured physical and moral suffering, and have almost always achieved the level of ecstatic union with Him in prayer."

According to the Catholic Encyclopedia, "many ecstatics bear on hands, feet, side, or brow the marks of the Passion of Christ with corresponding and intense sufferings. These are called visible stigmata. Others only have the sufferings, without any outward marks, and these phenomena are called invisible stigmata."

Many stigmatics believe their suffering can release souls suffering in Purgatory. This belief is closely associated with other well-known monastic practices, including the wearing of hair shirts, flailing oneself—or others—with leather whips and sticks, pricking one's flesh with sharp objects and submitting flesh to fire for cleansing.

Although the Catholic Church accepts the notion that stigmata is a genuine gift of God, medical and psychiatric examinations have shown most cases to be the result of hysteria, fraud or some mental imbalance.

St. Francis of Assisi, one of the most famous saints in history, is generally accepted as the first person to receive these strange wounds. His stigmatization occurred—along with visions of Jesus Christ and angels—while he prayed outside a cave high on a remote mountaintop during the Feast of Exultation of the Holy Cross in 1224.

Other sources say that an Englishman named Stephen Langdon experienced the phenomenon two years earlier, in 1222, while in the presence of the archbishop of London. At least one report indicates that an obscure Flemish nun named Mary of Oignies showed similar signs 12 years earlier in 1212. This last report has been all but discarded by the Church because Mary apparently had a reputation as a self-mutilator.

Even if St. Francis wasn't the first true stigmatic, his case was without doubt the first well-documented one and may thus be considered the first undisputed case of stigmata.

At least 20 more cases of stigmata were reported during the 100 years following St. Francis' death. Symptoms were basically the same—visions of Christ, Mother Mary or angels, followed by excruciating pain and bleeding from various parts of the body. Some stigmatics claimed to "wrestle" or "battle" with demons, as did St. Francis.

The trend continued in successive centuries, as hundreds more people, mostly Christians of all denominations and from all regions of the world, exhibited on their bodies physical marks similar to those suffered by Christ—wounds in hands and feet as if nails had been hammered through; marks on the forehead corresponding to a crown of thorns; wounds in the side as though speared; and stripes across the back similar to scourging.

In all, there are around 321 generally accepted cases of stigmata, mostly from Roman Catholic countries, of all ages and sexes. Of these, 62 have been beatified or sainted. No verified cases of stigmata have been found before the 13th century.

Stigmata often correspond with the Passion and Death of Christ, including the Last Supper and Easter. Stigmatics reportedly speak to visions of Christ and angels during this period and smell strange, perfumed scents.

Exactly what is stigmata—and how do seemingly healthy, normal human beings of all faiths suddenly start oozing blood and oil for no apparent reason? Theologians and physicians have been trying to answer those questions for centuries.

The Encyclopedia Britannica defines stigmata as "a phenomenon observed in a number of Christian saints and mystics for which no satisfactory explanation has been offered yet. It consists of the appearance, on the body of a living person, of wounds or scars corresponding to those of the crucified Christ."

The Apostle Paul, writing in the first century after Jesus' death, described strange marks on his body: "I bear in my body the marks of the Lord Jesus" (Galatians 6:17).

In the original Greek, "marks" was written as "stigmata" (to prick, puncture), a word commonly used by both Greeks and Romans to describe a mark pricked or branded upon the body of slaves and soldiers with the name of their master.

Christian martyrs were sometimes branded with the name of Christ on their foreheads. Some Christians marked themselves on the hands or arms with a cross in the name of Christ.

Paul's statement has been interpreted by some to mean the marks on his hands, feet and side had been given to him by God to reflect visual evidence of what Christ endured on the cross.

The phenomenon occurs in two basic forms—visible stigmata in which wounds and blood are clearly visible, and invisible stigmata through which the recipients suffer silently and display no physical signs of their pain.

Explanations range from self-mutilation and hysteria, often brought on by long periods of solitude, meditation and prayer, to supernatural causes. Experts contend that the vast majority of stigmatics are so emotionally and physically tied to their belief that they experience a blissful, ecstatic state of mind similar to rapture.

A few stigmatics—most notably Magdalene de la Cruz (1487-1560)—went on to confess having faked their marks. Some people who fake the phenomenon are said to suffer from Munchausen syndrome, a psychological disorder characterized by an intense desire for attention.

In a number of closely examined cases, the wounds of stigmatics have been shaped as letters and symbolic markings. For example, a bloody cross appeared on the forehead of a French prioress, Sister Jeanne des Anges (1602-1665), and the names Joseph, Mary and Jesus were written in blood on her left hand.

Most startling of all, some post-mortems have revealed marks or signs on the inner organs of a number of stigmatics. St. Clare of Montefalco (1268-1308) was said to be gifted with the spirit of prophecy as well as the grace of working miracles. Once she said to her sisters: "If you seek the cross of Christ, take my heart; there you will find the suffering Lord."

After her death the heart was removed from her body and doctors found, clearly seen on the cardiac tissue, imprints of the instruments of Christ's passion, including a tiny crucifix in the middle about the size of a thumb. A blood sample was taken from her incorrupt heart and put in a vial, which remains on display at the Church of the Holy Cross in Montefalco, Italy.

The heart of St. Teresa of Avila (1515-1582), which is still kept as a holy relic, is said to bear a mark as if it had been penetrated by a lance. St. Veronica Giuliani (1660-1727) reportedly bore the initials "J" and "M" for Jesus and Mary on her heart. Shortly after her death, surgeons removed the heart and found the initials, along with images of a cross, a crown of thorns, and a chalice, exactly as Veronica had said they would find.

Stigmatics often go for long periods of time without food or water, sometimes taking only wine and wafers at Communion. Angela of Foligno (1250-1309) reportedly went without nourishment for 12 years. St. Catherine of Siena (1347-1381) gave up bread, surviving on communion wafers, cold water and bitter herbs.

Illness is another frequent characteristic. Most stigmatics experience long and painful ailments during which they are bedridden and subjected to convulsions, blindness, deafness, mutism and paralysis. Most were born into poor families and suffered sicknesses throughout their entire lives. A genuine concern for the needy was another frequent characteristic, as was a burning desire to pray, worship and otherwise please God.

In their zeal to please God and "suffer for Christ," self-punishment became part of the daily routine for these tortured individuals during the late Middle Ages. Angela of Foligno, for example, drank water that supposedly came from washing the sores of lepers. Catherine of Genoa (1447-1510) ate scabs and burned herself. Eustochia Calafato (1424-1468) wore a pigskin undergarment to prick her flesh, whipped herself, melted candle wax over her head, burned her face and used ropes to "stretch her arms in the form of a cross."

Others rubbed lice into self-inflicted wounds, thrust nettles into their breasts, rolled in broken glass, jumped into ovens, and lacerated their bodies until the blood flowed.

Believers say stigmatics endure such agonies of the body and spirit because they wholeheartedly believe that these personal and painful sacrifices can actually reduce the level of suffering in the world. In other words, they are "imitating Christ" and his suffering, said one theologian.

According to the Catholic Encyclopedia, "The sufferings may be considered the essential part of ...stigmata; the substance of this grace consists of pity for Christ, participation in His sufferings, sorrows, and for the same end—the expiation of the sins unceasingly committed in the world...."

Many skeptics argue that stigmatic wounds are just plain psychosomatic—the result of overpowering religious obsession, hysteria, or, in some cases, sexual frustration. Others charge they are outright hoaxes, designed to bring fame and perhaps monetary compensation to the individual or shame to the Church.

Believers, however, point out that true stigmatists never accept money for their wonders. Instead, they devote their entire lives to a strict regime of prayer, poverty, suffering and meditation.

The gift of stigmata, they insist, is the real deal—one of many unexplained "holy gifts" from God. Others include speaking in tongues, prophecy, healing, levitation and bi-location—the ability to transport one's body from place to place via supernatural or mystical means.

Following are a few examples of notable people—saints and ordinary people alike—whose stigmatic claims either have been embraced by the Church or continue to be the subject of rigorous investigation.

St. Francis of Assisi (1182-1226)

PRIOR TO BECOMING one of the greatest saints of the Roman Catholic Church, St. Francis of Assisi—born Francesco Bernardone, son of a wealthy cloth merchant—achieved a certain level of fame as a poet, troubadour, crusader and knight.

Before his death at the age of 44, Francis achieved everlasting fame as the "Patron Saint of Animals" and as a man who forfeited a life of luxury and comfort to answer the call of God as an obscure hermit monk in the wilds of Umbria.

He is also credited with being the first documented person in Church history to experience the bizarre phenomenon known as stigmata.

This supposedly happened in September 1224, two weeks before his death, during a month-long holy retreat with three companions to Mount Alverna (La Verna) 3,000 feet high in the remote Apennines.

The group had gone into seclusion to worship and be near God. Two weeks after their arrival, Francis went off on his on to pray. He asked not to be disturbed because he knew from an earlier vision that his time on earth was running out.

"Brothers, I am not going to live much longer," he confided in his friends. "My song is ended. So I would like to be alone in order to immerse myself in God and weep over my sins."

Once by himself, according to biographer St. Bonaventure, a demon appeared to Francis and ridiculed him for having abandoned a life of luxury for that of a visionary monk.

"Comfortable monasteries! Magnificent churches!" the demon hissed, "That is what you have achieved with that phantom of yours, Lady Poverty! Just between ourselves, admit that you were born crazy....Your name will become a curse... God has abandoned your order...."

The confrontation with the demon left Francis weak. His muscles cracked with pain; his eyes burned as if on fire.

Later, after two straight weeks of nonstop fasting and prayerful meditation in the cold mountain air that had left him extremely weak, an angel suddenly appeared to Francis.

This was no ordinary angel; it was a seraph—an angel with six mighty wings, said to hold the highest rank in the angelic order. What's more, the angel was attached to a cross with the image of Jesus Christ emblazed upon it.

"All of a sudden there was a dazzling light," writes St. Bonaventure. "It was as though the heavens were exploding and splashing forth all their glory in millions of waterfalls of colors and stars."

In the center of that bright whirlpool was a "core of blinding light that flashed down from the depths of the sky with terrifying speed until suddenly it stopped, motionless and stood, above a pointed rock in front of Francis."

Before Francis loomed a figure with wings nailed to a cross of fire.

"Two flaming wings rose straight upward, two others opened out horizontally, and two more covered the figure," Bonaventure recounted. "And the wounds in the hands and feet and heart were blazing rays of blood. The sparkling features of the Being wore an expression of supernatural beauty and grief.

It was the face of Jesus.

Then: "Streams of fire and blood shot from His wounds and pierced the hands and feet of Francis with nails and his heart with the stab of a lance. As Francis uttered a mighty shout of joy and pain, the fiery image impressed itself into his body, as into a mirrored reflection of itself, with all its love, its beauty, and its grief."

When his companions found him later, cold and unconscious, they were horrified. They described the wounds on the hands and feet as "fleshy" and "nail-like, round and black, standing clear of his flesh." Furthermore, the right side of his chest bled as if it had been pierced by a lance, and his skin looked as if it had been slashed.

During the days that followed, Francis' clothes were often soaked in blood. The marks remained until his death and reportedly caused him much pain.

Francis died on Oct. 3, 1226, possibly from cancer or malaria that had been contracted years earlier on his missionary travels throughout Europe and North Africa. He was canonized two years later in 1228. In 1979 he was declared a patron of ecologists by Pope John Paul II.

Even before he died, questions were raised about why Francis had walked away from his father's riches in order to journey through life as a poor beggar and monk. Growing up in the small town of Assisi, he had been blessed with everything a boy could want—fine clothes, money, talent and intelligence. Handsome and showy, he enjoyed mixing with other young aristocrats who enjoyed spending their nights in wild parties.

When he was about 20, he was captured during a military campaign and held prisoner for a year. Some say it was this brutal experience that caused him to turn to religion. After returning home, he gave away his material possessions—including the clothes on his back—and began to preach purity and peace to anyone who would listen.

His father was furious with Francis and eventually stripped

him of his inheritance. That was fine with Francis, who by then had taken to wearing rough clothes and vowed to follow God. He told his father goodbye and walked out of town naked—to the astonishment of his former friends.

His first ministry was gathering rocks to rebuild chapels and churches in the area. He also began serving lepers and other outcasts of society. By 1209 he began to attract a large following, and with papal blessing, founded the Franciscan brotherhood. The friars traveled throughout central Italy and beyond, preaching for people to turn from the world to Christ.

Throughout his life, Francis emphasized simplicity and poverty, relying on God's providence, rather than money and possessions. The brothers, who were often mocked, were spat upon and had stones thrown at them, worked or begged for what they needed to live, and any surplus was given to the poor.

Francis also had a special love and relationship with animals. It was said that wild animals acted tame in his presence and seemed to understand when he talked to them. At times, according to Bonaventure, birds and squirrels would sit on his shoulders and sing and chatter while he prayed outdoors.

He fasted regularly and spent many hours in prayer daily. The brothers reported he would often go into ecstasy during prayer, completely unaware of his surroundings.

In 1220, exhausted and ill, he formed a group called the First Friars, and four years later underwent his mystical experience on Monte La Verna. Until the end, he and the brothers continued to travel, preaching poverty and asking people to take up the cross and follow Christ.

St. Catherine of Siena (1347-1381)

DURING HER VERY SHORT LIFE, St. Catherine of Siena was known to possess many special gifts from God—the ability to cast out demons and heal the sick, levitating during prayer and frequently having visions of Christ and the Virgin Mary.

Before her death at the age of 33, this feisty, fearless Dominican nun instructed queens and kings on how to behave and corresponded with popes and peasants alike. She survived the Black Death, famine and numerous civil wars to emerge as one of the most respected and revered saints of all time.

Born March 25, 1347, into a prosperous merchant-class family—her father was Giacomo Benicasa, and her mother was Monna Lapa, daughter of a famous Italian poet—Catherine was the 23rd of 25 siblings. During her lifetime the papal residence moved from Rome to Avignon and back again, and the great western Schism pitted Pope against anti-pope.

At a very young age Catherine sensed the world was in serious trouble and resolved to do what she could to help the poor and needy. Always attracted to prayer and solitude, she saw her future in the church—preferably as a Dominican friar, but she knew that was out of the question because she was female.

Early on, she took a vow of virginity and committed herself to Christ and her church. Her parents were opposed, but at the age of 17, she entered the Third Order as a nun. After three years of seclusion, she devoted herself to caring for the poor and the sick, especially those afflicted with the most repulsive diseases.

In Siena, Catherine's reputation as a healer and mystic blossomed. Men and women of all ages and from all levels of society flocked to her, including assortments of ne'er-do-wells who probably took advantage of Catherine's kind heart, benevolent spirit and generosity with money. This motley band, derisively nicknamed the "bella brigata," gradually coalesced into an organization known as the "School of Mystics."

Even before her teenage years, Catharine had become possessed with the idea of penitence. As she matured, she fasted regularly and continued to wear a hair shirt under her clothing that caused her constant pain.

Though frequently suffering terrible pain, living for long intervals on practically no food, Catherine was always radiantly happy and full of practical wisdom. Despite her great suffering, her many companions praised her strength, charm, serenity and spiritual insight.

In 1366 she experienced what she described in her letters as a "Mystical Marriage" with Jesus, after which she began to tend the sick and serve the poor. Four years later, in 1370, she began to experience alarming visions of Hell, Purgatory and Heaven. These visions, combined with her "Union with Christ," probably led to her first experience with stigmata.

While in Pisa, on the fourth Sunday of Lent, 1375, Catherine received the stigmata. Embarrassed by the messy wounds, she prayed that the marks would be made invisible as long as she lived. It wasn't until after her death that the five bleeding wounds allegedly became visible.

Along with stigmata came extreme fasting—and with the fasting more visions of demons and angels. Her strength gradually waned, but for the last six years of her life she refused to eat anything except Holy Communion nourishment and water. She slept little during this time, somehow finding the strength to dictate a book called *The Dialogue of St. Catherine* and writing letters to leaders all over Europe beseeching peace.

One evening in January 1380, while dictating a letter to Urban, she suffered a stroke. Partially recovering, she lived in a mystical agony, convinced that she was wrestling physically with demons. She suffered a second stroke and died three weeks later on April 29, 1380, aged 33. She was taken to Rome for burial, but her head was afterwards removed and taken to Siena, where it is enshrined in the Dominican church.

Pope Pius II canonized Catherine in 1461. Her feast day is April 29. In 1970, Pope Paul VI bestowed on her the title of Doctor of the Church, the first woman ever to receive this high honor. In 1999 Pope John Paul II made her one of Europe's patron saints.

St. Veronica Giuliani (1660-1727)

ALL HER LIFE, Ursula Giuliani had wanted to be a nun. At the age of 17, when her wealthy father objected to her forfeiting a chance at marriage to join a convent, she willed herself to become so ill he finally relented and let his headstrong daughter have her way.

Whether she was actually ill or merely pretended to be has

never been proven. For Ursula, the important thing was that she got her way and joined a Capuchin convent known as the Poor Clares.

Sister Veronica, as she was now called, would remain a nun for the rest of her life, rising from novice to the highest rank of abbess. In time she would become well known not just for her many administrative and managerial talents, but for her many supernatural abilities, especially the stigmata.

Born into wealthy circumstances at Mercatello in the Duchy of Urbino, Italy, in 1660, Ursula revealed signs of sanctity at an early age. One story holds that, while less than a year old, she chastised a worker for trying to cheat her father, Francesco Giuliani, a superintendent for finances at Piacenza: "Do justice, God sees you," she reportedly said.

Always intensely concerned about the poor, she often setting aside food from her own portions for beggars she met on the streets of Mercatello. On several occasions she gave away her own clothes.

It wasn't until she was 37, many years after she had entered the convent, that she received her first vision of Jesus. Even before then, she complained about a "great pain" in her heart that she felt for Christ. This was real pain, not a figment of a mystic's imagination. The heat that emanated from her heart was so intense that cold compresses placed upon her heart for relief would immediately become dry.

Other sisters witnessed her suffering. One said she came into Veronica's room once and found her "suspended in midair, shedding tears of blood which stained her veil. Later she told me that God was greatly offended by sinners and that she, in a trance, had seen the wickedness of sin, and of sinners' ingratitude."

During another vision in 1694, Jesus showed Sister Veronica Hell, where the souls of unrepentant sinners chose to go to spend their eternity in its "fiery depths." Sister Veronica wrote down in her diary what she saw:

"At that moment," she wrote, "I was once again shown Hell opened, and it seems that many souls descended there, and they were so ugly and black that they struck terror in me."

During this vision in 1694 an imprint of the "Crown of Thorns" appeared on her head.

Many more miraculous events awaited this remarkable mystic. On Good Friday, 1697, Jesus appeared again. In this new vision, the "Prince of Peace" was seated on a throne next to his mother, Virgin Mary. Bathed in "rays of light" that came from Jesus' wounds, Mary told Veronica to prepare to become her son's Mystical Bride.

At that point, Veronica said, "small flames of fire" flew out of Jesus' wounds—"four in the form of great pointed nails, the fifth a spear-head of gleaming gold....

"I felt a fearful agony of pain, but with the pain I clearly saw and was conscious that I was wholly transformed into God," she wrote. "When I had been thus wounded, in my heart, in my hands and feet, the rays of light gleaming with a new radiance shot back to the Crucifix, and illuminated the gashed side, the hands and feet of Him, and gave me in charge to His Most Holy Mother for ever and ever, and bade my Guardian Angel watch over me."

She continued: "He spoke to me: 'I am Thine, I give Myself wholly unto thee. Ask whatsoever thou wilt, it shall be granted thee;' I made my reply: 'Beloved, only one thing I ask, never to be separated from Thee.' And then in a twinkling all vanished away."

It was then that Sister Veronica received the Stigmata—a form of grace granted to only a few chosen holy souls, including St. Francis of Assisi, Catherine of Sienna and Padre Pio. Those who observed this phenomenon commented on an "aromatic odor of roses" which emanated from her bleeding wounds.

Veronica would suffer greatly in the years to come, commenting often about the "fiery pain" in her heart that she endured gracefully for the rest of her life.

Sister Veronica was also known to experience other mystical phenomena, including levitation, where she would rise several feet off the ground in full view of other sisters and ecclesiastics.

Veronica's supernatural claims eventually led to an

investigation by church authorities. The local bishop eventually decided to study these phenomena himself. In the presence of several nuns, he examined the stigmata and satisfied himself that they were genuine wounds. During the investigation, he forebade Veronica from attending mass or having any contact with other nuns or lay sisters.

This prolonged study, which included a thorough medical and psychiatric examination, found no evidence of fraud or mental impairment. When the bishop sent his results to Rome, the Holy See ruled in Veronica's favor and called for an immediate halt to the grisly experiment.

The stigmata continued unabated. So did the visions. During one rapturous dream, she claimed Jesus had come again and "placed his Passion" in her heart. She drew a sketch of the cross she said Jesus had placed on her heart, marking her as His own.

Sister Veronica's long tenure at the convent was not all spent in rapture or suffering the pain of stigmata. She assumed a leadership role in management of the religious house and was credited for many improvements. In 1716, at the age of 56, she was elected abbess, an office she held for 11 years until her death from apoplexy.

An official post-mortem examination of her heart showed a number of minute objects in the right ventricle resembling those in her sketch. One of those objects was in the shape of a cross.

Interestingly, she discouraged apprentice nuns from dabbling in mysticism or reading books about supernatural phenomena. Her own experiences had shown such pursuits were not for the untrained.

This "Spouse of the Lord" was canonized in 1839 as a "woman who had scaled the heights of devotion." Her blood-stained pillowcases are still on display at the church in Citta di Castello, Italy—grim reminders, say believers, of her long life of painful suffering.

St. Lidwina of Schiedam (1385-1430)

IT WAS SUPPOSED TO BE AN AFTERNOON of fun and games on the ice for Lidwina, a pretty 15-year-old girl from the village of Schiedam in Holland.

The year was 1395, and all winter long the cold snow had blown down from the frozen north. Thick layers of ice now clogged the many lakes and canals from Scandanavia through the Low Countries. Huddled inside their cozy cottages and cabins, the children of Schiedam watched and waited for the first break in the weather so they could go outside and play.

When the sun finally came out, Lidwina—or Lydwine, as she was also known—and a group of friends grabbed their skates and darted for a nearby canal. All was going well until a companion accidentally bumped into Lidwina, causing her to fall hard on some jagged pieces of ice. The impact snapped a rib, leaving her in excruciating pain.

The accident would leave Lidwina bedridden for the rest of her life. Until her death 35 years later, Lidwina would suffer extreme pain from various illnesses and diseases. She would also experience many mystical revelations and gifts, including supernatural visions of heaven, hell and purgatory, apparitions of Christ and angels and the stigmata.

From an early age, Lidwina had yearned to be closer to God. She visited the local church every day, praying to the statue of the Blessed Mother, asking not for favors but for the privilege of serving the Lord. At the age of 7, she took a vow of virginity. Her parents, poor but descended from noble blood, were both religious and saw in their daughter the signs of something quite remarkable.

Gangrene and other severe complications set in after the accident. She suffered constantly from burning fevers and internal bruises, while ulcerated lungs caused her to vomit large quantities of blood. It was impossible to hold down any food.

Various doctors were brought in, but all seemed powerless to halt the poor girl's excruciating torment. Priests came from all over Holland to pray with her. Midwives took turns nursing her physical needs, even though she often begged them to leave her alone and tend to the poor instead.

For 19 more years, she labored in agony, not once getting out of bed and taking only minimal amounts of nourishment. Lidwina was unable to move any part of her body except her head and left arm; her mother found it necessary to bind her parts together with cloth each time she shifted her position in bed.

As the years passed, Lidwina began to have visions. Angels came to her in the dead of night. Jesus sat on her bed and talked to her. The Blessed Mother visited her often, sharing secrets and encouraging her to keep praying, to keep going because there was a special reason for her suffering.

It was ironic that Lidwina—a formalization of Lidie—comes from the Dutch word meaning "suffer." In time, as the visions came more frequently and the pain worsened, she came to find comfort in her suffering, as if it were a divine gift. To further purify her heart, she gave all of her possessions to the needy and even had her parents remove her normal bed so she could sleep on a scratchy straw mattress.

Lidwina would spend the rest of her life suffering. And while she suffered, she continued to have visions and more visions, apparitions of the saints and archangels and the whole heavenly host. These visions gave her strength, even as her health continued to fail, even as the blisters and inflamed sores and abscesses massed upon her flesh.

So pitiful was her stricken body that one witness described Lidwina as "one big sore from head to foot."

Many visitors who looked in on her were bewildered. How could anyone endure so much pain? Why had God seemingly abandoned her?

Vicious rumors spread that she might be a witch.

Through it all, Lidwina prayed constantly. She often went into trance-states of ecstasy in which she experienced many mystical gifts and supernatural visions of hell, purgatory, and heaven. During some of the raptures, she was said to enjoy two controversial miracles known as levitation and bilocation.

It was the gift of bilocation that earned her a considerable amount of fame. On several occasions, she was reportedly in two places at the same time. Once, when Jesus asked her to be with him at Golgotha, she replied, "O Savior, I am ready to accompany you to that mountain and to suffer and die there with you."

It was after this "trip" to Golgotha that Lidwina received stigmata—the marks Christ received from the nails driven through his hands and feet on the cross, the crown of thorns on his head and the spear thrust in his side.

Commenting on the wounds, one biographer noted: "He (Christ) took her with Him, and when she returned to her bed, which corporeally she had never left, they saw ulcers on her lips, wounds on her arms, the marks of thorns on her forehead and splinters on her limbs, which exhaled a very pronounced perfume of spices."

Numerous miraculous healings took place at her bedside. While praying and "laying on hands," she could heal toothaches, headaches, gastro-intestinal problems and more. A child suffering from cancer was reportedly healed after Lidwina prayed for him. That child grew up and became a priest in memory of Lidwina.

Her fame as a healer and mystic spread far and wide. Over the years, thousands of pilgrims came to be touched and healed. Others came to observe, including the celebrated preacher and seer Wermbold of Roskoop, who witnessed many phenomena that took place on a daily basis.

A few years before her death, Lidwina experienced a vision in which she was shown a rosebush with the words, "When this shall be in bloom, your suffering will be at an end."

Not many days afterward, she had another vision of Christ who came to her to administer the Sacrament of Extreme Unction. She awoke and reportedly exclaimed, "I see the rose-bush in full bloom!"

She died on Easter Day 1433 at the age of 53. Legend has it her corpse was shrouded in fragrant scents—the so-called "odor of sanctity." In her will, she instructed that her house—which she had inherited from her late father—be converted into a monastery.

The following year, a chapel was built over the marble tomb where she lay. Until Calvinists demolished the chapel and converted it into a hospital for orphans, it was a popular shrine for pilgrims. In 1615 her relics were conveyed to Brussels and enshrined in the collegiate church of St. Gudula. In 1871 they were returned to her hometown of Schiedam. It is believed her bones protected the town from bombing raids during World War II.

On Mary 14, 1890, Pope Leo XIII declared her veneration, and she was canonized. Lidwina's feast day is April 14. She is known as the patron saint of ice-skating and sports.

Theresa Neumann (1898-1962)

SHORTLY AFTER THE END of the Second World War, American soldiers stationed in Bavaria heard stories about an amazing "miracle" woman who lived with her poor parents in the tiny village of Konnersreuth near the Czechoslovakian border.

Theresa Neumann could not only heal the sick, levitate and perform other miracles, she also had regular visions of Jesus and the Immaculate Mother. The most startling thing, however, was this shy, middle-aged woman's bizarre ability to exhibit signs of stigmata—a term used to describe the intense bleeding and pain experienced by Jesus Christ after he was forcibly nailed to a wooden cross.

While startled onlookers gaped in amazement, Neumann would go into a deep state of ecstasy and utter agonizing cries while she spoke "in tongues" and conversed with angels and saints. As her anguish intensified, blood would begin to ooze from the pores of her skin, then gush from her forehead, eyes, hands and feet.

When the ordeal was over, Neumann's pain would subside and the bleeding would vanish—until the next time.

Neumann had become something of an eccentric celebrity in war-torn Europe. Since the 1920s, her modest country cottage had become a popular destination for thousands of curious visitors anxious to see with their own eyes examples of her inexplicable behavior. They were rarely disappointed.

Born in 1898, Neumann was a hard-working, normal girl who experienced her first case of stigmata after hurting her back at the age of 20. On March 4, 1926, after years of suffering from temporary blindness, convulsions, paralysis of the legs and purulent sores on the back and feet which had been brought on the injury, she had a vision where Jesus appeared in the Garden of Gethsemane.

During that first vision, Neumann felt a pain in her side and realized that blood was trickling from it. Nail wounds appeared on her hands and feet. The following November she experienced a most excruciating pain on her forehead—and realized it was the same pain felt by Christ when the crown of thorns was placed on his head.

On at least one occasion—Good Friday 1927—her eyes bled until they were swollen shut and encrusted.

Eager to cure their daughter of her terrifying affliction, Neumann's parents called in a doctor who treated her wounds with ointments and bandages. When Neumann began to shriek in agony, the parents removed the bandages and wiped off the ointment, and the wounds rapidly subsided.

Neumann continued to receive visitors until the mid-1950s. By then her ability to bear stigmata had weakened to the point where she was unable—or unwilling—to satisfy the throngs of miracle seekers. Privately she continued to suffer intermittently from one or more of the wounds until her death in 1962 at the age of 64.

Although many believed in the "miracle woman" of Bavaria and made regular pilgrimages to her house to be healed or witness the stigmata, the attitude of the church authorities remained somewhat reserved. Some years before her death, the bishop of Regensburg conducted an investigation into rumors that Neumann had eaten no food and drunk only sparing amounts of water over a 12-year period starting with Christmas 1922. Officials were shocked when examinations revealed that only wafers and wine from Holy Communion had been ingested during the entire period.

Questions about the authenticity of Neumann's mystical experiences continue to be asked, and controversy remains a hot topic of debate in the church and her hometown, even today. While many skeptics attribute her behavior to hysteria or fraud, the so-called "Friends of Konnersreuth," an organization set up to defend her honor, thinks their most famous citizen was a genuine visionary and should be considered for sainthood.

Louise Lateau (1850-1883)

THE DOCTORS were stunned.

For months they had sought—unsuccessfully—to cure a poor bedridden young peasant girl from the provincial Belgian village of Boid d'Haine who had long suffered from a variety of physical and emotional ailments, including severe neuralgia and chronic headaches.

Now, in the spring of 1867—just shy of her 17th birthday—the end seemed near for Louise Lateau, who had stopped eating food and was drinking only small amounts of water. When she started spitting up blood, the family knew it was time to bring in a priest to administer the last sacrament.

Before the rites were over, Louise sat up bed and smiled. To the amazement of everyone, the girl's health suddenly improved—so much that she was able to walk almost a mile to the parish church to attend mass the very next day.

Louise's miraculous cure was only the beginning of a remarkable transformation in Louise's life, a transformation that would soon make her one of the most famous people in Europe.

Less than three weeks after her recovery, Louise noticed blood flowing from a spot on the left side of her chest. Thinking nothing of it, she didn't mention it to anyone. The next day the bleeding started again—in the same spot—and she also observed blood on the top of each foot.

Concerned, but not frightened, the girl turned to her

parish confessor for help. The confessor examined the girl's extraordinary wounds but urged her to not tell anyone.

On the night of May 8, blood oozed from her left side again, from both feet, and, beginning the next morning, also freely from the back and palm of each hand. At this point it seemed dangerous to keep the matter a secret any longer, so the confessor called in a physician who recognized the characteristics of stigmata.

After carefully weighing every possible explanation, from hysteria to fraud, Dr. Lefebvre agreed with the church's position that Louise was suffering from a "supernatural condition" known as stigmata.

"No one with the slightest knowledge of Louise Lateau has suspected her for a single moment of a deception," Dr. Lefebvre concluded. "The integrity of her every action, her simple and unaffected piety, and, still more, the heroic and devoted charity she has so often displayed, in the eyes of all, the very antithesis of hypocrisy."

Louise continued experiencing the phenomenon every Friday. Symptoms would appear by noon Thursday, then progress steadily until full-blown bleeding occurred in all wounds shortly past noon the following day. Some 24 hours later, the bleeding would stop. The wounds then became dry and painless and remained so until the following Thursday.

"The stigmatization appears each Friday, with unbroken regularity," Dr. Lefebvre explained. "The quantity of blood that Louise loses...varies considerably, but estimated at nearly 30 ounces."

On Friday, July 17, 1868, 13 weeks after the bleeding was first noticed, Louise began experiencing weekly ecstasies. Each Friday morning, while praying the rosary or doing her daily work, her eyes would suddenly become fixed, immovable, and the trance had begun. The ecstasy lasted until about 6 or 7 in the evening.

For 12 years, Louise declined food and water other than her weekly communion and three or four glasses of water a week. She never slept, but passed her nights in contemplation and prayer, kneeling at the foot of her bed.

She also continued to serve the poor people of Bois d'Haine, something she had done since she was a young girl. She tended to the sick as well, especially cholera victims who had been abandoned by the town. During one month alone she buried all 10 patients she had nursed, then bore them to the cemetery for burial.

Over the years, a number of psychological and medical tests were conducted to verify that Louise's stigmata were real and not delusional or self-induced. One one occasion gloves were tied around her hands and blankets wrapped around her arms to prevent her from cutting herself or being able in any way to cause bleeding.

Upon removal of the gloves and blanket the next day, however, Louise's hands were found full of blood. And when this was washed off, the stigmata wounds were found just the same as on the preceding Fridays.

In 1875, the prestigious Belgian Academy of Medicine performed a thorough medical examination of Louise and could not explain the phenomenon scientifically. In the end, more than 100 professional physicians and many eminent Catholic church leaders had performed countless tests on Louise, making her one of the most thoroughly examined stigmatics in history.

St. Catherine De' Ricci (1522-1590)

THE TUMULTUOUS PERIOD of the Reformation produced many great religious leaders, both Catholic and Protestant, but none worked harder for the church or the Lord than St. Catherine de' Ricci.

Born into one of Florence, Italy's wealthiest families, Catherine—or Alessandra Lucrezia Romola, her baptized name—achieved success at an early age managing a Dominican convent of San Vincenzo at Prato. Her skills as a bookkeeper and administrator were so impressive she soon found herself advising a number of princes, bishops, cardinals and popes on a variety of topics.

But it wasn't her leadership qualities that would make

Catherine one of the most famous prioresses in the Catholic Church and lead to sainthood. It was her many mystical gifts, which included healing, stigmata (suffering the wounds of Christ in the flesh) and bilocation (the ability to be in two places at the same time),

Starting when she was 20 years of age, Catherine experienced weekly ecstasies of the Passion from noon Thursday until 4 p.m. Friday. This went on for the next 12 years. During each session, sisters observed many physical changes that came over Catherine as she acted out Christ's suffering.

Her face, for example, was said to assume many different shades and colors as she endured the different pains and agonies of Jesus as he went through his passion. While in the same trance-like state, she would unconsciously talk in a dialect and eloquence beyond her native tongue.

She also bled profusely from the mysterious wounds that appeared on her hands, feet and forehead during these stigmatic episodes. At the end of this scourging, she would always be covered with wounds. One of her shoulders was indented, as if from carrying the cross a long distance.

These periods of stigmata always left her weak and in great pain.

It was during this time that she entered into what some considered a "mystical state of marriage" to Christ. In 1542, Catherine was supposedly given a coral ring by Jesus that symbolized she was a "bride of Christ." The ring supposedly appeared on her finger during deep prayer. All who saw the ring described it differently, but she described it herself as gold set with diamond; others saw only a red lozenge and a circlet around her finger.

This "mystical marriage" to Christ was not all that unusual. Many women have claimed they were chosen as the "bride of Christ" whereby they were said to be united to Christ in mind, body and spirit, entering a spiritual union regarded as the highest mystical state possible in this earthly life.

One of Catherine's other mystical gifts was her ability to transport herself to distant places. On one occasion she visited

St. Philip Neri, who lived in Rome, a trip the saint verified himself—although he rarely gave credit to miracles and visions such as bilocation. St. Catherine was also said to have visited St. Mary Magdalen de' Pazzin in the same manner.

Catherine's supernatural activities eventually attracted large crowds to the convent of St. Vincenzo. Many came in hopes of seeing the "great lady" at work, whether healing the sick or lapsing into ecstatic visions. Skeptics and sinners flocked to her as well; many were converted.

Among the thousands of visitors who came to her for advice and prayer were three future popes—Cardinal Cervini, Pope Marcellus II; Cardinal Alexander de Medici, Pope Leo XI; and Cardinal Aldobrandini, Pope Clement VIII.

Legend says she wore a "sharp iron chain" around her neck and participated in other forms of self-punishment. Like many men and women who suffered for Christ and went on to sainthood, Catherine engaged in an extreme form of fasting, often going without food and taking in only small amounts of water for weeks at a time.

She died in 1590 after a prolonged illness, probably brought on by the severe physical punishment she endured during stigmata. She was canonized under Pope Benedict XIV in 1746. Her feast day is Feb. 13.

St. Gemma Galgani (1878-1903)

IN THE BEGINNING, Gemma Galgani had everything a girl could want—a loving family, charm, grace, intelligence, and—most noticeable of all—dazzling good looks. It was said that this petite, brown-eyed beauty from the scented Tuscan hills of Italy could "light up the heavens on a dark night."

What she wanted most, however, Gemma could never have—and that was to become a nun—a Passionate nun—to live in a convent with other sisters where she could worship and pray to God 24 hours a day.

Gemma Galgani's remarkable and brief life—she died of tuberculosis when she was only 25—was one of unspeakable pain and suffering for her faith, one that eventually led the Roman Catholic Church to honor her with its highest recognition—sainthood.

Unlike most saints, however, Gemma—whose name means "gem" in Italian—was born into a wealthy and prestigious family from Camigliano, a small town near Lucca in Tuscany, on May 12, 1878. Her childhood was devoted to reflection and prayer and helping the poor. Instead of playing with dolls and flirting with boys like the other girls, Gemma chose to spend her hours in solitude praying to the saints.

At first this kind, delicate and precocious girl seemed destined for a prominent life, just like her noble parents before her. As she blossomed into a young woman, aristocratic youths sought her favor; by the time she was in her late teens, she had already received several marriage proposals.

Throughout her brief life, Gemma was destined to have many mystical experiences and special graces. These experiences often earned her considerable ridicule and scorn from her peers, but it took more than mere words to slow the pious ambitions of this "Flower of the Saints," as she was later called.

It took a few microbes and a twisted spine.

While still in her teens, Gemma began to suffer extreme physical and spiritual anguish. After she contracted meningitis, her health quickly began to deteriorate. This would continue off and on for the rest of her life. Other ailments plagued her constantly—large abscesses on her head, a curvature of the spine, tuberculous and—most uncomfortable of all—Pott's Disease, a paralysis of the legs that left her bedridden for long periods at a time.

Doctors worked courageously to save this "magnificent virgin," as she was known, performing operation after operation in futile efforts to cure her. Finally, they told her there was no way science could save her.

But Gemma refused to give up hope.

During this time of extreme mental and physical suffering, she experienced many visions—angels, devils, long-dead saints, the Virgin Mary, even Jesus. It was during one of these visions that her "guardian angel" came to her and promised to take care of her through her suffering.

Appearing as a winged figure, this handsome apparition said he would shield her from harm, but only if she did as he instructed—starting with a vow to never wear jewelry or other fancy body ornaments.

"Remember," said the angel, "the spouses of the Crucified King should wear no ornaments, but thorns and crosses instead...."

The angel also stressed the deep need for continued obedience. "You must be a dead body," he told her. "Whatever is asked of you, you must obey quickly and joyfully....If you do not obey, I will not show myself to you again."

Gemma conversed with her guardian angel on a daily basis. They would pray together, sing hymns and recite Psalms. She often sent him on errands—the post office, the pharmacy, even to deliver a message to her confessor in Rome!

On June 8, 1899, while kneeling in a deep state of prayerful ecstasy before a crucifix, she saw another vision. Opening her eyes, she saw the Virgin Mary and Jesus standing in her room.

In her diary, Gemma describes what happened next:

"At that moment, Jesus appeared with all his wounds open, but from these wounds there no longer came forth blood, but flames of fire," she wrote. "In an instant these flames came to touch my hands, my feet and my heart. I felt as if I was dying...."

She added: "I should have fallen...had not my mother held me up....I had to remain several hours in that position."

Finally: "She kissed my forehead, all vanished, and I found myself kneeling. But I still felt great pain in my hands, feet and heart. I rose to go to bed, and became aware that blood was flowing from those parts where I felt pain. I covered them as well as I could, and then helped by my Angel, I was able to go to bed...."

So began the stigmata Gemma would suffer for the rest of her life. It always started the same way: each Thursday evening, she would fall into a rapturous state, and the same marks of the stigmata would appear. The wounds would remain, fresh and painful, until the following afternoon when the bleeding would stop and the gaping wounds would close. All that was left were inexplicable whitish marks where the deep gashes once were.

Commenting on the stigmata, Father Germano di Stanislao—Gemma's confessor, priest and later biographer— said the wounds always appeared about 8 p.m. and lasted until 3 p.m. Friday. No pain preceded their appearance, he noted, but only a "deep recollection."

In The Saints: A Concise Biographical Dictionary, Father Germano is quoted as saying: "There was seen first a discoloration on the back and palm of each hand; then a rent in the flesh under the skin which then split, and a deep laceration was observed, at least usually. The holes above and below corresponded and the perforations seemed complete, but it was hard to judge of this because they kept firing up with blood, partly flowing, partly congealing."

Father Germano measured the diameters and shapes of the wounds carefully and found "a few times a sort of fleshy swelling, like nail-head, about an inch across, covered the wounds in the hands—though not those in the feet. The deep wounds were the more usual state of Gemma's stigmata—I say, the more usual state."

He also said that "directly the Friday ecstasy was over, the flow of blood from all five wounds ceased immediately. The raw flesh healed; the lacerated tissues healed too. At least by Sunday not a vestige remained of the deep cavities. The new skin was smooth, though whitish marks remained on it...."

Besides bearing the scars of Christ's crucifixion, Gemma later received the marks of His scourging at the Pillar—described by many witnesses as "fearful to behold: great gashes...in the flesh of her body, on her legs and arms, as if they had really been torn open, in places even to the bone, by loaded whips of the soldiers, as in the case of Our Lord."

The appearance of these painful wounds always led to ecstasies, according to Father Germano, who witnessed many of the events and later declared that Gemma told him that Jesus was always corporally present.

As with St. Padre Pio and other well-known stigmatists, Gemma reportedly was attacked by the devil. On occasion, witnesses overhead the sound of these struggles and later observed bruises and lacerations on her body she claimed resulted from these supernatural assaults. She was also known to "sweat blood" and bore wounds on her left shoulder and knees that recalled those suffered by Christ as he carried his cross to Calvary.

Just shy of her 20th birthday, while on her sickbed and suffering terribly, Gemma had a vision that Gabriel Possenti, the beloved Passionate saint who died in 1862, came to her and called her "sister."

"If you wish to recover," St. Gabriel said, "then pray with faith every evening to the Sacred Heart of Jesus. I will come to you until the Novena is ended, and we will pray together to this Most Sacred Heart."

St. Gabriel did as he promised—returning to pray with her often. Finally, the pain went away. Convinced she was cured, Gemma rose from her bed and cried out with joy, believing in her heart that a miracle had taken place. For the first time in years, she was able to go to church and mass.

Gemma's experiences were widely reported throughout Italy. Through all the controversy, she remained convinced they were real and comported herself as a kind and loving servant of God. Numerous prominent people, including physicians, friends, high-ranking civic authorities and respected ecclesiastics of the Church, are on record as having witnessed many of Gemma's miracles.

One observer stated:

"Blood came from her (Gemma's) wounds in great abundance. When she was standing, it flowed to the ground, and when in bed it not only wet the sheets, but saturated the whole mattress. I measured some streams or pools of this blood, and they were from 20 to 25 inches long and about two inches wide."

Visions would continue to be a part of Gemma's life.

Witnesses commented on how she would enter a rapturous state and hear voices. When the ecstasy was over, she would resume her serene life.

In January 1903, Gemma was diagnosed with a terminal disease—probably a return of the same tuberculosis of the spine that had plagued her for years. Bedridden and vomiting blood, she died quietly in the company of the parish priest on April 11 at the age of 25. The priest noted, "She died with a smile which remained upon her lips, so that I could not convince myself that she was really dead."

Gemma was beatified in 1933 and canonized on May 2, 1940, only 37 years after her death.

Padre Pio (1887-1968)

WHEN THE ITALIAN MONK Padre Pio was canonized June 16, 2002, more than 100,000 jubilant Christians descended on Rome to hear Pope John Paul II solemnly proclaim the late friar "Saint Pio of Pietrelcina."

The celebration, which lasted for days and was attended by notables from many countries, marked the end of a long, incredible journey for Padre Pio, regarded by many in the church as greater than Francis of Assisi and more popular than Bernadette of Lourdes.

Without doubt, the miracle-working saint-to-be was seen as one of the "holiest of priests," so blessed with the power of God that just a touch of his cloak was said to be enough to cure the blind and heal the crippled.

Born to Giuseppa and Frazio Forgione, peasant farmers in the small Italian village of Pietrelcina on May 25, 1887, Padre Pio would go on to carve out one of the most unusual careers in church history. His gifts from God were as numerous as they were miraculous—the ability to heal, cast out demons, "read" souls, levitate, transport himself physically to distant locations, envision Jesus and angels and exhibit the "odor of sanctity."

He "glowed" during Communion, according to witnesses, saw angels and saints and frequently had visions of Heaven,

Hell and the Blessed Mother. His entire countenance, said one witness, "was shining with a rosy flame of light such as I had never seen before and shall, I think, never see again."

But Padre Pio's most remarkable—and controversial—miracle of all was the gift of stigmata. It was because of this last gift that most people remember the big, burly priest with twinkling eyes and bearded chin.

Stigmata, perhaps the rarest and most bizarre of all church phenomena, is a Greek word used to describe the condition experienced by someone who endures the same anguish Christ felt on the cross, including the bleeding of hands and feet, forehead and side.

Padre Pio's first experience with stigmata occurred on Sept. 20, 1918—the anniversary of Francis of Assisi's own first stigmatic encounter—while he was kneeling in front of a large crucifix in deep meditation.

He described the experience a few weeks later to his spiritual advisor: "I yielded to a drowsiness similar to a sweet sleep. All the internal and external senses and even the very faculties of my soul were immersed in indescribable stillness. Absolute silence surrounded and invaded me. I was suddenly filled with great peace and abandonment which effaced everything else."

While this was taking place, he said, "I saw before me a mysterious person….his hands and feet and side were dripping blood. The sight terrified me and what I felt at that moment is indescribable. I thought I should die and really should have died if the Lord had not intervened and strengthened my heart which was about to burst out of my chest."

As soon as the vision vanished, he said he became aware that his hands, feet and side were dripping blood. "Imagine the agony I experienced and continue to experience almost every day," he said. "The heart wound bleeds continually, especially from Thursday evening until Saturday."

News of the event spread like wildfire. Soon there began a steady caravan of pilgrims to Our Lady of Grace Church, the tiny friary where the stigmata occurred that continues to this day. Tens of thousands came each month to glimpse this remarkable priest with the wounds, to kiss his bleeding hands, to confess their sins in his presence.

But the new-found fame and frenetic schedule of hearing so many confessions and healing so many sick people took its toll on the aging priest, who had never been in good health anyway. Besides, ever since he was 5 years old, the only thing Pio wanted to do was spend his days in quiet prayer and meditation honoring God. Having come from a religious family that fasted from meat three days a week, who prayed the Rosary each night and attended Mass daily, Pio sought only to serve his Lord in quiet reflection.

Apart from the strange wounds and physiological aberrations, Pio was renowned for having another mysterious facility also attributed to saints and mystics in the past—the ability to be seen in more than one place simultaneously, a miracle known as bilocation. Many stories were told of Pio's ability to be in two places at the same time—including at least two occasions during World War II when Allied bomber pilots claimed to have actually seen the monk flying through the air over his hometown of San Giovanni Rotondo with his arms spread as if trying to protect it from bombs.

Asked once about his bilocations, Padre Pio replied that it was just "an extension of my personality."

Padre Pio is said to have suffered the painful and embarrassing stigmata for 50 years, until the time of his death at age 81 when the marks completely disappeared, leaving his skin without blemish. For all that time, the Catholic Congregation for the Doctrine of the Faith—formerly known as the Inquisition—kept Padre Pio under quiet surveillance.

Suspecting fraud, the Vatican launched a series of investigations under Pope John XXIII, including the bugging of Padre Pio's confession box, in an attempt to expose Pio as a fraud. They even accused him of having fornicated with women in his cell. The founder of Rome's Catholic University Hospital said the monk was insane, a "self-mutilating psychopath possessed of the devil who exploited people's credulity."

But legions of enraged supporters challenged the church's

persistent and barbed attacks against their favorite monk, pointing to the many cures and miracles attributed to him, as well as the scores of testimonies from doctors and surgeons who came forth to shore up the monk's character and reputation.

Some doctors who examined Padre Pio to ascertain the nature of his wounds concluded there was no evidence to indicate the wounds were self-inflicted or that he was suffering from any kind of mental disorder. Professor Francesco Di Raimondo, a surgeon who has helped the Vatican certify miracles attributed to Padre Pio, said he examined the monk's stigmata and found them to be "medically inexplicable."

Cardinal Jose Saraiva Martins, prefect of the Vatican Congregation for the Causes of Saints, explained that the essence of Padre Pio's sanctity was "the reality of the cross."

While admitting there have been many cases of false stigmata throughout church history, Dr. Nicola Silvestri, assistant director of health of the House for the Relief of Suffering, the hospital founded by Padre Pio, said of the friar's wounds: "From the medical point of view, the stigmata cannot be considered as wounds or sores, because they do not heal even when treated."

He added, "They neither become infected nor do they decompose; they do not degenerate in necrosis, and do not exude a bad odor. They bleed and remain constant and unaltered for years, against all laws of nature."

There are at least 80 saints and blessed whose stigmata have been validly documented, the doctor explained. Although the Church recognizes the phenomenon, it does not oblige the faithful to believe in it as a dogmatic or doctrinal fact.

In regard to the nature of the stigmata, he said that "a multiplicity of theories have been proposed by different schools that attempt to deny the supernatural character of the stigmata." However, he added, "none of these hypotheses can stand up to objective and scientifically rigorous criticism....the real stigmata studied to date are outside all the laws that regulate physiopathology and must be considered as phenomena of a supernatural character."

Anne Catherine Emmerich (1774-1824)

THE VENERABLE ANNE CATHERINE EMMERICH was called a lot of things—mystic, stigmatic, ecstatic, prophet and visionary. Even while alive, she was widely regarded as one of the greatest visionaries in the history of the Catholic Church.

Today, almost two centuries after her death, she continues to be revered for her many gifts from God—so much that on Oct. 3, 2004, Pope John Paul II beatified her, thereby making her forever known as "Blessed."

Born into a poor but pious farm family near the small village of Flamschen, Westphalia—a province of Germany—in 1774, Anne Catherine became aware of her spiritual gifts at an early age. Her ability to "reason" impressed everybody she came in contact with. She understood liturgical Latin before her first Mass and, most striking was her ability to go into a trance and "see" the past, present and future.

Her ability to heal sick and poor children astonished other villagers and earned her the nickname of "bright little sister." When patients came to see her, she was able to diagnose their ailments and prescribe remedies long before they arrived—and her remedies never failed.

Before she was 12, she was having regular visions of places she identified as Heaven, Hell and Purgatory. She prayed more for the salvation of those souls she had seen in Purgatory, as well as for the salvation of sinners whose miseries were known even when far away. She also had visions in which she talked with Jesus as a child.

Anne Catherine longed to become a nun, to serve Christ as his "bride." While working hard to help support her parents, she found time to prepare for the rigors of a career in the convent yet never shirked her duties and responsibilities to her parents, church leaders and employer.

Anne Catherine grew up during one of the bleakest and least glorious periods in Church history. While revolutions and counter-revolutions rocked Germany and other nations of Europe, desperate people yearned for the kind of peace, security and salvation offered only through the Church.

In 1802, just after her 28th birthday, Anne Catherine entered the Augustinian convent at Agnetenberg, Dulmen. Life was not easy for the head-strong young nun. Always in poor health, she had to struggle to win over the hearts and minds of sister nuns who looked down on her because of her impoverished background and fiery disposition. Before long, the nuns came to appreciate their fiercely independent sister's supernatural gifts.

At the end of 1811, the convent where she lived was ordered closed. The following year Anne Catherine and some of her sisters were sent back to live in Dulmen. There she spent much of her time in ecstatic prayer, especially after an injury confined her to bed for several years.

In late 1812, she received what many religious leaders say is the most precious spiritual gift of all—stigmata. From this time until her death in 1824, she bore the wounds of Christ on the cross—the crown of thorns, bleeding hands and feet, even the wound from the lance.

Embarrassed by the wounds, at first Anne Catherine tried to hide Christ's Passion on her body—but only succeeded for a short while. Soon the other sisters noticed the stigmata and informed their superiors.

An investigation followed, which concluded that the wounds were truly mystical in nature and that Anne Catherine was indeed the recipient of many supernatural gifts.

Anne Catherine's health continued to worsen. From her bed, she continued to have visions which she shared with a famous poet and biographer, Klemens Brentano, who carefully recorded on paper each miraculous occurrence. Brentano's account, published in a book called *The Dolorous Passion*, had many exaggerations and embellishments and was subsequently disregarded during the process of her beatification.

During the last 12 years of her life, Anne Catherine ate no food, except for Holy Communion, nor drank anything except small amounts of water. She also continued to bear the wounds of the stigmata until she drew her last breath on Nov. 9, 1824.

Six weeks after her death, rumors spread throughout

Germany that her body had been stolen. Concerned church officials immediately opened her grave and found the body in place—fresh as the day she was buried, without any sign of corruption.

St. Faustina (1905-1938)

THOSE WHO KNEW Mary Faustina Kowalska often commented on her cheerful attitude, her remarkable sensitivity to the poor and her childlike devotion to God.

Few were aware that, just below her sunny and loving exterior, this future saint suffered in ways they could never know, that this seemingly ordinary girl of peasant stock had been blessed with great and wondrous supernatural gifts that frequently manifested themselves in strange and disturbing ways.

Mary was a stigmatic. Like St. Francis of Assisi, St. Catherine of Sienna, Padre Pio and other noted saints before her and since, she endured painful episodes during which she received the marks of Christ on the cross—the hands and feet that bled, the pain in the side where the spear ended Christ's life, the terrible, stabbing anguish around her head where the Savior's crown of thorns had been placed.

She suffered much from this phenomenon, but she kept it to herself. Other stigmatics, from St. Francis of Assisi to Padre Pio, were well known for their affliction, but Mary quietly went about her life tending gardens, caring for the poor and seeing to her many duties as a nun and caregiver to the poor.

Born Helena Faustina Kowalska Aug. 25, 1905, in Glogowiec, Poland, to a poor religious family of peasants, Mary knew from the age of 7 that she wanted to pursue a religious vocation. Called during a vision of Christ on Aug. 1, 1925, when she was 20 years old, she entered the Congregation of the Sisters of Our Lady of Mercy and took the name of Sister Mary Faustina. She spent 13 years in the congregation, residing in Krakow, Plock and Vilnius, and other centers where she worked variously as a cook, gardener and porter.

On the outside, there seemed nothing to reveal what biographers call her "rich and mystical" interior life. She went about her daily duties with the same zest and zeal she showed for chapel and mass. Her life, noted other sisters, was rather dull and monotonous—at least compared with the extraordinary passion she held within for Christ and the church.

The years she spent in the convent were filled with extraordinary experiences. She had many visions, suffered the stigmata frequently, and—most bizarre of all—experienced the phenomenon of bilocation at least a dozen times. Bilocation has been described as the ability to transport oneself—consciously or unconsciously—across vast distances, and it is one of the supernatural gifts recognized by the church. A number of saints and holy men and women supposedly possessed this power, most notably St. Joseph of Copertino and Padre Pio.

Mary also had the gift of prophecy and spiritual healing and that rarest gift of them all—mystical espousal and marriage to Christ. "Her living relationship with God, the Blessed Mother, the angels, the saints, the souls in Purgatory—with the entire supernatural world—was as real for her as the world she perceived with the senses," said one biographer.

In her *Diary*, she wrote: "Neither graces, nor revelations, nor raptures, nor gifts granted to a soul make it perfect, but rather the intimate union of the soul with God. These gifts are merely ornaments of the soul, but constitute neither its essence nor its perfection...."

Consumed by tuberculosis and innumerable other sufferings, which she accepted as a voluntary sacrifice for sinners, Sister Mary Faustina died in Krakow at the age of 33 on Oct. 5, 1938. Even in death, her reputation for holiness grew, as did the devotion she exhibited for serving the Church during her brief sojourn on earth.

Pope John Paul II beatified Sister Faustina on April 18, 1993. Her mortal remains rest at the Shrine of the Divine Mercy in Krakow-Lagiewniki.

Marie-Julie Jahenny (1850-1941)

THE OLD WOMAN WAS BLIND, but she saw light—glorious rays of light, penetrating the darkness in flashing patterns of purest brilliance.

She smiled, even though she was dying, even as the darkness crept closer into the dazzling light. She wanted to rise, one last time, to kiss the crucifix, to mutter one last rosary, to praise God one last time. But her crippled body, frail and withered from years of abstaining from nourishment, was too weak to let her.

All those gathered around her could do was watch and wait. The end was nearing. Even they could perceive the stab of darkness pressing against the old woman's radiance.

One of those was a tall, angular man clad in a swirling mass of robes. He was Monsignor Fourier, the bishop of Nantes. It was he who wept the most, prayed the loudest for his lifelong friend whose body was now slipping away into eternity.

When the end finally came, it was the bishop who administered the final rites.

"She now rests with God," he said of Marie-Julie Jahenny, the so-called "Breton Stigmatist," recognized by many as the greatest mystic in the history of the Roman Catholic Church.

Until her death on March 4, 1941, the world had marveled at this simple woman's courageous struggle against the blindness and deafness that had plagued her most of her life. It also marveled at her many spiritual gifts, including the ability to levitate, elongate, prophesy and—last but not least—experience the wounds of Christ, a phenomenon known in the Catholic Church as stigmata.

As with most stigmatists, the gift came to her during a vision—a "vision of purest ecstasy" in which Christ manifested himself to her as he appeared on the cross, suffering and bleeding. When the apparition ended, Marie-Julie's hands, feet and chest were blotched red with blood.

The visions would return many times in the years that followed, with Jesus, Mary and a variety of angels revealing numerous "messages of divine importance." Along with the apparitions came more suffering—head wounds similar to the Crown of Thorns placed on Christ's head, and gaping sores elsewhere on her body resembling the "scourging" of Christ at the pillar and on his way to Calvary.

Over time, she endured many other wounds of a mystical nature, not all related to Christ's suffering on the cross.

She would bear these wounds for the rest of her long and remarkable life, not once complaining about her pain or the diseases rampaging through her frail and twisted body that would leave her blind, deaf, dumb and crippled during her final agonizing years.

Born on Feb. 12, 1850, in the little village of Blain on the west coast of France, Marie-Julie grew up the oldest of five children in a poor but religious family. As a child she had the uncommon ability to "recognize" true Eucharistic bread from ordinary bread; she could also pick out which objects had been blessed and which ones had not.

Before her 10th birthday, it was said she could sing hymns and utter liturgical prayers in several languages—even though she could barely read or write and had had only limited contact with other nationalities growing up.

Seeking to "work for the Lord," Marie-Julie joined the Franciscan Third Order when she was 21.

She lived most of her life in a small cottage in the hamlet of La Fraudais, not far from her hometown of Blain. It was here most of the miracles occurred, starting with the visions and stigmata.

On Dec. 28, 1875—not long after her first series of visions—Marie-Julie began to experience other phenomena. During one five-year period, while suffering in pain from the stigmata, she reportedly gave up food and drink. Except for wine and wafers and communion, the young nun ate no food and drank only small sips of water once a week.

Doctors, concerned about her failing health, examined her several times and found no traces of excretions of liquid or solid foods. They knew that if she didn't eat something soon, she would surely die.

Yet she refused to break with her fast. Instead of eating, she chanted and sang, occasionally indulging in rapturous moments during which she talked to Jesus and Mary and conversed with angels. Witnesses said she "glowed" with joy each time the heavenly spirits came upon her."

Marie-Julie spent increasing amounts of time in rapturous ecstasy. Some of these ecstasies were accompanied by levitation. Witnesses often came into her room only to see her rising from bed and floating toward the ceiling. At other times, while attending mass, she was seen floating above the altar, always in a rapturous state of ecstasy. When church leaders brought her down, they found her "exceedingly light to the touch."

It was Marie-Julie's gift of prophecy that brought so much attention to her. She's been credited with forecasting both world wars, the election of Pope St. Pius X, the various persecutions of the church and much about the future of France. Some say she even predicted a coming global holocaust.

In a vision that came to her in 1882 she predicted:

"The earth will be covered in darkness...and hell will be loosed on earth. Thunder and lightning will cause those who have no faith or My Power, to die of fear [sic]....During these... days of terrifying darkness, no windows must be opened, because no one will be able to see the earth and the terrible colour it will have in those days... .No one outside a shelter will survive....The earth will shake as at the judgment and fear will be great...."

She added: "During this darkness the devils and the wicked will take on the most hideous shapes...red clouds like blood will move across the sky. The crash of thunder will shake the earth...and the earth will shake to its foundations. The sea will rise, its roaring waves will spread over the continent...."

Finally: "The earth will become like a vast cemetery. The bodies of the wicked and the just will cover the ground...."

"For all his learning or sophistication, man still instinctively reaches toward that force beyond. Only arrogance can deny its existence, and the denial falters in the face of evidence on every hand. In every tuft of grass, in every bird, in every opening bud, there it is."
—Hal Borland

SIGNS, WONDERS & PROPHECIES

The Star of Bethlehem

"Now when Jesus was born in Bethlehem of Judea in the days of Herod the king, behold, Wise Men from the East came to Jerusalem, saying, 'Where is He who has been born king of the Jews? For we have long seen His star in the East, and have come to worship Him.'" (Matthew 2:1-2)

For 2,000 years, Matthew's story about the birth of Jesus Christ has been an everlasting source of inspiration and wonderment—not just for Christians, but for countless generations of astrologers, astronomers, historians, philosophers and theologians who have sought to fathom the mystery of the dramatic astral phenomenon that the Bible says heralded the Savior's birth.

Was the star of Bethlehem a true miracle—a divine beacon sent to guide the gift-bearing wise men to the scene of the Nativity? Or was it something else—a spectacular but natural celestial event such as an exploding star—that happened to coincide with the exact time the Scripture reckons Jesus was born?

It is worth noting that the Gospel According to Matthew is the only book of the New Testament that mentions the mysterious star. This has led some researchers to conclude that the story is nothing more than a pious legend rooted in theology rather than literal history.

Skeptics point out the fact that there is no indication in the text that any other person actually saw the star—not the shepherds in the field, not Herod, not Mary and Joseph, not even Matthew himself. Only the three Persian wise men, steadily plodding their camels across the dark desert, faithfully followed the blazing star until it appeared to stop and illuminate the place of the Christ child's birth.

One fact seems clear: the star—or whatever it was—moved. Stars don't normally move across the night sky, only in progression from east to west as the earth rotates.

So what was it? There seems to be no shortage of explanations. Some scientists speculate it was nothing more than a supernova—a very old star about to gasp its last breath of nuclear energy. However, it seems rational to assume that an exploding star would have been noticed by others on the ground besides the Persian travelers.

Others believe it was a constellation, while many suspect a comet—an object traditionally connected with important events in history, such as the birth of kings. The problem with this idea is that there are no records of comet sightings matching up with the Lord's birth. Halley's Comet, for example, was present in 11 B.C., but the first Christmas took place around 5 to 7 B.C.

John Mosley, program supervisor for the Griffith Observatory in Los Angeles, believes the Christmas star was a rare series of planetary conjunctions that took place in or during the years 3 B.C. and 2 B.C.

"The show started on the morning of June 12 in 3 B.C., when Venus could be sighted very close to Saturn in the eastern sky," says an MSNBC article about Mosley's findings. "Then there was a spectacular pairing of Venus and Jupiter on Aug.12 in the constellation Leo, which ancient astrologers associated with the destiny of the Jews."

The combined light from the lining up of the two planets could have been quite dazzling, certainly enough to give witnesses the impression that something truly extraordinary was taking place on the Judean sands below.

Meanwhile, Mark Kidger, a British astrophysicist working in Spain, argues in his book *The Star of Bethlehem: As Astronomer's View,* that the Bethlehem star was indeed a real star that can still be seen by telescopes today: a now rather dim star known as DO Acquilae.

"Back then," Kidger says, "it was a bright nova and probably the phenomenon described by ancient Chinese astronomers as an unusually bright star that appeared in the eastern sky for 70 days in 5 B.C.—the year many scholars believe Jesus was born.

While there have been other theories over the years seeking to explain the appearance of the star of Bethlehem, Kidger says ,"we will probably never know, and can never know, for certain, what the star of Bethlehem really was."

Not so fast, say the overwhelming majority of Christians who insist the celestial phenomenon was no more a fable than was the birth of their Savior. To this day, the faithful regard Matthew's account of the Star of Bethlehem as a true and accurate depiction of events that heralded Christ's arrival and guided the Magi to the house where Mary and the baby Jesus were.

As with many long-held religious traditions, believers say it's science that needs to catch up with the truth—not the other way around.

"The conclusion," according to a spokesperson for the Christian Answers Network, "is that the star of Bethlehem cannot be naturally explained by science. It was a temporary and supernatural light. After all, the first Christmas was a time of miracles."

Joan of Arc

"She was therefore right to always trust in her apparitions, for in truth Joan was liberated, as they promised, from the prison of the body by martyrdom and a great victory of patience."

> —Inquisitor Jean Brehal, the judge who established her innocence during the Rehabilitation Trial

JOAN OF ARC WAS ONLY 13 YEARS OLD when she first heard voices commanding her to "go forth and do God's command." She heard the voices again six years later, when they ordered her to lead an army against English forces surrounding the French city of Orleans.

Who were these voices that commanded a 19-year-old uneducated farm girl to strap on a suit of white armor and lead the French army to victory over the hated British?

Historians, theologians and biographers have argued that question for almost 600 years, ever since she routed the English forces from Orleans and cleared the way for Charles VII's coronation at Rehims in 1429, only to be burned at the stake as a witch six years later in 1431.

Equally unclear is whether this visionary-turned-conqueror—the most famous fighting woman in European history—was truly guided by visions or suffered from schizophrenia, hallucinations or some other mental disorder.

Joan—or Jehanne, later known as Jehanne de' Arc, or Joan of Arc—was born about 1412 in Domremy, a small village in the Champagne district of northeastern France. Raised in a poor family of sheep herders, Joan was extremely religious and spent much of her childhood praying to the statues of saints scattered around the small church in her village. It is said that when she heard the church bells ringing, she would fall to her knees wherever she might be, cover her head and pray to Jesus and the Virgin Mother.

By all accounts she was industrious, obedient and very compassionate toward the poor and needy. She focused on chores, preferring to pray rather than to go dancing and play with the other children in her village.

Joan's childhood coincided with the Hundred Years War between England and France, a time of great turmoil and anguish for France who seemed to be on the losing side of the conflict. What France needed was a miracle—a savior to ride to her rescue and turn the British back.

Both miracle and savior came in the person of Joan, this young, headstrong peasant girl who popped up out of nowhere to rally the French forces to victory after victory until treachery resulted in her capture and ultimate execution.

How did it all happen? How could an ordinary girl with absolutely no military training lead hardened veteran soldiers into victorious battle?

It began with her vision as a teenager. She would later say that St. Michael, the captain-general of the armies of Heaven, came to her in a spectacular vision and urged her to go to France's aid.

"It was St. Michael, who I saw before my eyes," she said. "He was not alone, but was accompanied by many angels from Heaven. I saw them with my bodily eyes...."

Encounters with St. Michael grew more frequent, as did visions of other saints, including Catherine and Margaret, both early Christian martyrs.

"St. Michael, when he came to me, told me that St. Catherine and St. Margaret would come to me and that I should act on their advice, that they were instructed to lead and advise me in what I had to do, and that I should believe in what they would say to me, for it was by God's order."

In 1429, after more urging from St. Michael and other saints, she met with the commander of the French army at Vancoulers to explain that God had chosen her to lead a new mission against the English. At first the commander was skeptical, but he finally sent her—dressed in a suit of soldier's clothes—to see Charles.

Joan was able to persuade Charles to let her go—but only after she assured him that God had chosen her—and her alone—for this noble and dangerous crusade. He was further convinced when Joan revealed to him secrets "known only to him and God." One revelation was the location of a sword, which had been concealed in a secret location behind the altar in the Chapel of St. Catherine de Fierbois.

Charles was greatly impressed. He outfitted Joan in a brilliant suit of white armor and gave her the sword she had located in the chapel—the same sword she would carry into battle at Orleans and beyond.

At Orleans she was wounded but fought on. Her courage

was greatly admired by her soldiers, inspiring them to press forward, eventually lifting the siege and driving the English from the city. After the victory, she became known as the Maid of Orleans.

Eventually Joan was captured by the Burgundians—allies of the English—and sold to them for 10,000 francs. After a hasty trial, she was convicted of witchcraft and heresy—the act of challenging church authority—and sentenced to death. On May 30, 1431, she was stripped of her uniform, dressed in a peasant's dress and burned at the stake in the marketplace of Rouen.

At her trial, the inquisitors had tried to get her to retract her stories about visions. She would be set free, they promised, if only she would deny that saints and angels sent her messages in apparition form.

She refused, recalling how a voice from God once told her, "Have no care for thy martyrdom; you will in the end come to the Kingdom of Paradise."

At first, most people—including the French—refused to believe Joan's wild stories about visions and miracles. It was common knowledge that God spoke only to men. Many feared it was possible she might be a witch after all. In the 15th century, anything or anyone not easily understood by the church was viewed with suspicion and could end up on the stakes.

Did Joan really hear voices? If so, were they really the voices of saints and angels? Or were they something else—perhaps the ravings and fantasies of a brave but highly delusional young girl?

In recent years, skeptics have argued that Joan suffered from a medical condition causing her to suffer delusions and hallucinations that she interpreted as being from heaven. They point to her many visionary claims as proof.

"There is not a day when my saints do not come," she once confessed. On another occasion, when describing St. Catherine and St. Margaret, she said they had "faces...adorned with beautiful crowns, very rich and precious."

At least one researcher has theorized that Joan's hallucinations might have stemmed from bovine tuberculosis, a disease that causes victims to see lights that might be confused with illuminated apparitions or visions.

The fact remains, however, that millions of people all over the world have come to accept Joan of Arc exactly as she claimed she was—a simple messenger of God gifted with the extraordinary ability to communicate with the angels.

Her tragic story would haunt the collective conscience of a shameful Europe for centuries. In 1456, a mere 25 years after her death, Pope Calixtus III declared that Joan had been not guilty and condemned the verdict against her.

In 1920, almost 500 years after her death, the Catholic Church canonized Joan of Arc.

Constantine's Sign of the Cross

ROME WAS worried.

For centuries the great empire had maintained peace and fostered prosperity throughout its sprawling realm, from the shimmering shores of the Mediterranean to the dark forests of Germany.

Now, in the third century of the Christian era, barbaric warlords and political instability threatened to topple the empire. Galloping inflation added to its woes, as did marauding bands of soldiers who ravaged the countryside, slaughtering civilians and Republican Guards who got in their way.

Unhappy people turned to magic and pagan gods in an attempt to cope with the horrific changes sweeping across the land. Some embraced strange new religions that promised salvation in the next world. Many believed that a single, all-powerful supreme god was the answer to their prayers, rather than the old Olympian deities.

To stem the growth of Christianity, Rome's rulers had resorted to harsh punishment and executions. In the name of Jupiter, Apollo, Minerva and other "immortals" who had held sway in the empire's capital for centuries, Christians were routinely beaten, tortured, mutilated, decapitated, imprisoned and thrown to the lions.

Then, all at once, the punishments stopped. Almost overnight Jupiter and his consortium of old gods were gone, replaced by Christianity as the official state religion. What happened to bring this mystifying event about?

Some scholars credit Emperor Constantine with the sudden change. According to an account written shortly after Constantine's death in 337 by Bishop Eusebius, it happened in October 312, when the emperor was marching on Rome to reclaim it from his rival, Maxentius.

As Constantine approached the city, he looked up and saw "with his own eyes the trophy of a cross of light in the heavens, above the sun, and bearing the inscription, 'In This Sign, Shalt Thou Conquer.'"

According to Bishop Eusebius, the emperor was "struck with amazement, and his whole army also, which followed him on this expedition and witnessed the miracle."

That very night Christ is said to have appeared to the emperor in a dream, carrying the same sign he had seen in the heavens and commanding him to lead his army forward to victory. At dawn the next day Constantine ordered workmen to fashion a standard made of gold, studded with precious jewels, and bearing a monogram symbolizing his fealty to Christ.

Behind the enigma—and, according to some accounts, with a special sign of the cross painted on every shield—Constantine's soldiers defeated the enemy at Milvian Bridge on the River Tiber. Constantine entered Rome victorious, and from that day on, a committed Christian.

Or was he? Some scholars suspect that Constantine never truly abandoned his pagan ways, even though he ascribed his spectacular military success to the vision of the Christian cross and much later in life was baptized into the Christian faith.

One view holds that the emperor continued to worship the sun god Mithras, the religion of his father and several emperors before him. Other scholars point to the fact that Constantine scratched pagan symbols from his coins and even removed his statues from pagan temples as proof of his conversion to Christianity.

During his long reign, Constantine saw to it that Christians were treated fairly, even though he continued to tolerate paganism as well. He enacted many laws favorable to Christians, prayed every day and enjoyed the company of Christian bishops.

The evidence, then, seems overwhelming that Emperor Constantine did believe in the Christian God. The Edict of Milan—which granted Christianity the same rights as all other legitimate religions—and his baptism seem to support this view.

Did Constantine have the experience that Eusebius describes?

Scholars have wrestled with that question for more than 1,600 years. Many skeptics want to know why—and how—such a startling revelation could have been kept secret until after the emperor's death. How, too, they wonder, was it possible to create an elaborate bejeweled standard in a single morning, almost on the very day of battle?

And why, after being converted to Christianity in such a miraculous way, was the emperor not baptized as a Christian until the last year of his life?

Historians believe that in an age of superstition, stories about divine visions were bound to gain currency. Everybody at the time, pagan and Christian, believed in miracles; and the wonder of Constantine's conversion as narrated by Eusebius had a tremendous impact not only on the bishop's contemporaries but also on many generations to come.

There can be little doubt, however, that something happened to the emperor on the eve of his entrance into Rome. Some scholars have suggested that his "vision" may have been caused by what meteorologists call the "halo phenomenon," in which ice crystals in the upper atmosphere form light rings around the sun.

Very occasionally, such rings interlock in a pattern that can suggest a cross to some viewers.

In any event, Constantine was certainly not a Christian before the battle at Milvian Bridge. But scholars say the victory convinced him of the power of the Christian faith—and he never forgot it. After unifying the Western Empire under his own rule, he moved quickly to help the poor and repressed Christians, who now suddenly saw their religion elevated to great heights of power and prestige.

And, for the rest of his life, Constantine's imperial armies marched behind the sacred labarum, the name given the banner on which Constantine's monogram of Christ was inscribed. And they never failed to emerge victorious *in hoc signo* (in this sign).

The Prophet's Bloody Revenge

ON THE MORNING OF MAY 12, 1828, a young black slave and self-appointed preacher named Nat Turner was picking corn in his master's garden when a voice "like the sound of many winds" floated down to him from heaven.

Turner, a short, powerfully built 28-year-old with clear, twinkly eyes, wasn't afraid. Nor was he really surprised as the voice whispered his name over and over, reminding him of his special purpose in life.

In fact, the soft-spoken slave had been expecting a miracle such as this for some time. Convinced since childhood that he was a prophet sent to earth on a divine mission, young Turner's eyes flashed with proud fire as he pondered the implications of that mystical vision.

There had been signs, even before God's voice came to him in the field that morning—disturbing signs that only Turner, the Almighty's Chosen One on earth, could interpret. Had he not seen in his own mind rivers of blood pouring throughout the land? Had he not heard thunder rolling through the heavens while others slept, warning of the coming clash between good and evil? Had he himself not witnessed an army of black and white angels waging spiritual warfare in the storm-scented clouds?

What were the strange lights in the sky he had watched flickering over the hilltops on several occasions if not the Savior's own redeeming glow?

That morning, standing alone in the sweeping field of corn, had not the prophet seen drops of blood staining the cornstalks? And on the leaves of bushes, had he not seen the marks of Satan—strange numbers and hieroglyphs and a blasphemous parade of stick-like men reveling in gruesome poses?

With his face uplifted toward Heaven, young Nat Turner knew he had seen and heard all those things and more. He also knew it was only a matter of time before God's mighty sword slashed down, smiting the Serpent and all the enemies of His Chosen People.

Three years later, on a warm, summer evening in 1831, Nat Turner's mystical vision would come to pass. It would come only a few months after darkness engulfed the sun in a solar eclipse—the final sign the prophet needed before springing into action.

Cross Keys, Va., was a quiet hamlet nestled in the rolling hills of Southampton County in the southwestern corner of the state. In those days, Cross Keys was populated primarily by white farmers and merchants of modest means. One of the community's most prosperous residents was a kind, gentle farmer named Joseph Travis, who happened to own several slaves.

One of those slaves was Nat Turner.

Travis was fond of his young slave, admiring him not only for his intelligence and enthusiasm for work, but also for his honesty, courage, and religious piety. He had even attended a few of Turner's sermons and, according to some records, encouraged the preacher to continue developing his oratorical talents.

What Travis didn't know—nor did any other white person living in Southampton County that unusually warm, muggy summer in 1831—was that the black preacher he had come so to admire was secretly plotting one of the bloodiest slave insurrections in American history. By the time it ended, less than a month later, at least 60 white people would be dead along with more than 100 blacks.

It is no secret that Turner, who openly called himself "The Prophet," had a mystical, almost mesmerizing influence over many people in the area, white as well as black. He was convinced of his own superiority, divinely granted by long hours of prayer and fasting in the name of Jehovah, the God of the Old Testament.

Therefore, when the time came to act, Turner had little trouble convincing a few fellow slaves that they, too, were part of his divine mission to rid the valley of whites. He told them all about his visions, about how God had spoken to him on numerous occasions, about the lights flashing over the hilltops, and about the blood-stained cornstalks, all in preparation for him to lead the glorious task that lay ahead.

In his own chilling words, Turner later wrote: "I now began to prepare them too for my purpose by telling them something was about to happen that would terminate in fulfilling the great promise that had been made to me."

That "great promise" was death.

It came quickly and mercilessly to the simple farmers and planters and tradesmen of Southampton County who lay sleeping in their beds when The Prophet and his axe-wielding band of "angels" struck.

The first white people to die were Turner's own master, Joseph Travis, and his entire family—hacked to death with axes. From the Travis farm a group of about 30 blacks armed with old muskets, knives, picks and axes surged across the countryside, stopping off at every house and cabin along the way to stab, beat, and shoot the white occupants to death.

The bloodiest carnage occurred at dawn the next morning when Turner's gang of killers broke into the home of a widow getting her 10 children off to school. The mother and nine of her children were slaughtered on the spot; the 10th child escaped by crawling inside a chimney where she hid until the murderers went away.

By eight o'clock, the enraged black rebels had hacked and bludgeoned their way halfway across the county toward the tiny town of Jerusalem. When the alarm finally sounded—sometime around nine—hundreds of white men came charging after the renegade slaves, rifles and pistols blazing. Several blacks were killed outright; others, including Nat Turner, escaped into the Great Dismal Swamp.

Almost a month later, The Prophet was seen hiding in some bushes and apprehended by a team of marshals. On Nov. 5 he was tried, found guilty, and sentenced to be hanged six days later on Nov. 11.

Throughout the ordeal—capture, trial and gallows—Turner remained calm and collected, seemingly unfazed by the angry demands for his life that swirled across the jailhouse lawn. Some say the divine mystic and rebel leader actually looked forward to his date with the hangman.

A few days before his scheduled execution, Turner set forth his thoughts and feelings about the grisly deed he had done. What emerged from his "confessions" was a rambling, sometimes incoherent outpouring of love for his fellow man. Nowhere, however, did there appear to be any signs of remorse for the tragic loss of life he had caused.

Yet Turner's confessions, shrouded in mysticism and religious symbolism, revealed the inner workings of a brilliant but deeply troubled young mind, consumed with burning visions and other Old Testament revelations about his divinely inspired mission—that of rising up against the whites and smiting them dead for having caused his people so much misery and suffering.

Commenting on his vision in the cornfield, Turner wrote: "I heard a loud noise in the Heavens, and the spirit instantly appeared to me and said the Serpent was loosened...and that I should...fight against the Serpent, for the time was fast approaching when the first would be last and the last should be first...."

Moments before the noose was placed over his neck, someone asked Turner whether he regretted what he had done or if he was afraid. In a soft voice that crackled, The Prophet described his deed as "Christ-like," concluding, "Was not Christ crucified?"

Dreams Foretell "Bewitched" Monarch's Death

A FEW WEEKS BEFORE HIS DEATH, William II, king of England, had a dream.

In that dream, he was riding through a dark forest when, suddenly, an arrow flew out of the shadows into his chest, knocking him to the ground in a welter of blood.

The king—known as William Rufus because of his red beard and florid complexion—woke up screaming. He saw the dream as a premonition of death and quickly hired more guards to protect him from "evil forces."

That same night, a nearby monk dreamed that a glowing crucifix kicked the king to the ground, where he lay breathing fire and smoke.

As news of the strange dreams spread across the land, people thought surely their monarch was bewitched. Black magic was common in those days, and not even kings and queens were immune from spells cast by witches and warlocks.

There were those who suspected their king was cursed because of his anti-Christian views. He mocked Christians, plundered their churches, stole Church property and frequently persecuted leaders of the faith.

Some loyal followers feared he would be struck down because of his open contempt for the Church and widespread rumors that he secretly worshipped pagan gods.

Then, late one afternoon in August 1100, the monarch went on a stag hunt in the New Forest, a royal game preserve in southern England. Accompanying him were his brother, Henry, and a number of attendants—including close adviser Walter Tirel.

Not long into the hunt, Tirel spotted a stag and let loose an arrow. The arrow sailed wide of its mark but struck William. Mortally wounded, the king fell forward, driving the arrow deep into his chest as he hit the ground.

Terrified, Tirel fled the forest and escaped to France. Henry and the rest of the hunting party galloped off to the nearby city of Winchester, where the royal treasure was housed, leaving brother William's body where it lay.

After seizing the treasure, Henry hurried to London where he was crowned Henry I on the third day after his brother's death.

Henry's hasty actions have led some historians to suspect he might have engineered William's death. After all, it was common knowledge that the youngest son of William the Conqueror resented his two brothers—William and Robert of Normandy—because their famous father had left them all the territory.

In the weeks prior to William's death, Henry had even hatched a scheme to capture Normandy while Robert was away fighting a Crusade in the Holy Land. With William out of the way and Robert in a distant land, the road lay open to Normandy.

Another point linking Henry to William's death was the fact that Walter Tirel was never prosecuted, nor were his lands seized. Was that Tirel's payoff for assassinating the king?

Defenders say it was not in Henry's nature to organize such an odious crime. They say he deeply loved his older brother and vowed to bring his murderer to justice. Critics, however, point to the fact that Henry was despotic and cruel. On occasion, he blinded state prisoners and frequently castrated criminals.

But while his was a reign of calculated terror, few believe he was capable of outright murder. Moreover, what had Tirel to gain by collaborating with an enemy of William Rufus, his friend and patron?

As for Tirel, he went to his grave maintaining his innocence.

Some scholars have suggested there might have been a second arrow—fired not by Tirel but by an unidentified member of the hunting party. Others insist it was not murder at all, only a freak accident. Hunting in those days was a dangerous sport.

One more theory holds that William Rufus ordered Tirel to kill him because he had outlived his usefulness as a monarch. With his power waning, the king feared he would be ritually sacrificed in accordance with pagan law.

Skeptics like to point out that those who consider Henry

incapable of fratricide can hardly praise him as a model of fraternal love. During the 35 years of his reign as Henry I, he wrested Normandy from his only remaining brother and kept him imprisoned in England until Robert's death at the age of 80.

Soothsayer with the Divine Pen

IN AN AGE WHEN SOOTHSAYERS and witches were routinely burned at the stake, it is somewhat amazing that a figure with the reputation of Michel de Nostradame survived to become one of the most famous—and beloved—men in all of Europe.

Part prophet and part witch doctor, the French-born scholar credited with saving thousands of lives during outbreaks of bubonic plague during the 16th century achieved almost saint-like status among the masses and went on to become a close consort to queens and kings throughout Europe.

Some saw his uncanny ability to heal and foretell future events as the work of the devil. Others, however, regarded his strange powers as a special gift and sought to take advantage of it.

Nostradame—or Nostradamus, as he was better known— did not start out on such a favorable footing. Born in St. Remy, France, on Dec. 14, 1503, he encountered considerable prejudice early on because of his Jewish ancestry. At Avignon he learned philosophy, classical literature, history, medicine and grammar. His special interests were herbal and folk medicine and astrology—then generally regarded as a legitimate science.

He also published almanacs, which were popular items in 16th-century Europe. Nostradamus's almanacs became bestsellers, filled with the usual predictions about weather and crop conditions, but also containing "secret" prophecies that made them wildly popular throughout France and much of Europe.

When the plague struck France in the early 16th century, he stopped publishing almanacs and went to work treating patients by administering his special concoction—"Rose Pills," which consisted of ground rose petals, sawdust, iris, cloves, calamus and lignaloes. He refused to "bleed" patients, the customary treatment for everything from minor colds to the Black Death.

In 1537, plague struck the city of Agen where the famed physician, poet, philosopher and publisher lived with his wife and two children. Although he managed to save hundreds of lives, his own family perished in the epidemic. Devastated, the great healer spent the next six years wandering Europe, questioning his abilities and the meaning of life.

It was during this period of "dark torment" that Nostradamus became aware of another special gift—the power of prophecy. Retreating to his study in the dead of night, he would consult magic mirrors, divining rods, a brass bowl and other "magical instruments" to conjure up visions of future events.

In 1550, he published his first almanac of prophecies. *The Prophecies*, written in a curious blend of French, Greek, Latin and Italian, made Nostradamus a household name in Europe. Nearly a thousand prophetic verses were written, each containing four lines, or quatrains. These were arranged in 10 books, called *Centuries*.

The *Centuries* contain prophecies covering nearly 2,250 years, until the year 3797.

Nostradamus did not reveal how he arrived at his prophecies. The best guess is that he wrote primarily by inspiration—that is, he wrote down whatever verses came to him while working alone in his study late at night.

Like most prophetic writing, Nostradamus's *Centuries* are couched in obscure, archaic, almost unfathomable riddles, puns, anagrams and epigrams.

His most famous early prophecy, contained in stanza 35 of *Century 1*, apparently concerned King Henry II, though the king's name is never stated. It reads as follows:

"The Young lion will overcome the old one
On the field of battle in a single combat;
He will put out his eyes in a cage of gold:
Two fleets one, then to die a cruel death."

On July 1, 1559, English King Henry was riding in a tournament against young Gabriel de Lorges, Comte de Montgomery, Captain of the Scottish Guard. The lances of the two riders met and splintered. Montgomery dropped his shaft a second too late and the jagged point pierced the king's gleaming gold visor and entered his left eye, killing him.

Other quatrains predicted the coming of three Antichrists. Some scholars have detected references to Napoleon, Hitler and a third "harmful world leader" not yet identified. The verse also has been said to refer to the overthrow of the Shah of Iran and the rise of Saddam Hussein of Iraq.

Some contemporaries saw Nostradamus's prophecies as a curse and burned him in effigy. The Catholic Church also took a dim view of the prophecies—especially when they turned out to be bad—and threatened to burn him at the stake.

But one of the prophet's most powerful fans was Queen Catherine de Medici, who not only protected him from enemies but also required regular forecasts of her children's future. Nostradamus was said to have conjured up an angel who showed Catherine a bright and promising future for her children by looking in a mirror.

The prophet fell ill in mid-1556. On July 1, he told friends gathered at his bedside: "You will not find me alive at sunrise."

True to form, he died that night. In his will, Nostradamus expressed the curious wish to be buried standing upright, supposedly so that "boorish" people would not step on his body.

His body was placed within the walls of the Church of the Cordeliers of Salon. The Latin inscription on his tomb reads: "Here rest the bones of the illustrious Michel Nostradamus, alone of all mortals, judged worthy to record with his near divine pen, under the influence of the stars, the future events of the entire world…"

"Cursed" Lance Guided Conquerors

ONCE A WEEK, the huge double doors of Vienna's Hofburg

Museum would open and a pale, shabbily dressed young man would step through and head straight for a special exhibit featuring the treasures of the House of Hapsburg.

There, transfixed by the glittering crowns and other jeweled displays behind the glass cases, he would often stand for hours, not moving or speaking until ushered away at closing time.

Of special interest to the young visitor was one particular object, the remains of a spear, dull and blackened with age. According to legend, the spear point was none other than the one used by a Roman centurion named Longinus to kill Jesus as he hung on the cross. For his bloody sin, Longinus was cursed to walk the earth forever—or at least until the time of the Apocalypse.

Another legend holds that Longinus converted to Christianity after his failing eyesight had been healed by Christ's blood flowing down the spear. Longinus quit the army, became a monk and eventually was tortured to death for his faith.

The year was 1909. The visitor was a struggling young Austrian artist named Adolf Hitler. For the next three decades, until his death in 1945, the fanatical leader of Germany's Third Reich sought to possess the famous spear, not so much for its historical and religious value, but because of its purported mystical properties.

Tradition held that the owner of the Spear of Longinus— also called the Spear of Destiny, the Spear of Hofburg, the Spear of the Holy Grail and occasionally the Spear of Christ—would possess the power to conquer the world. But the relic also carried a terrible curse—whoever controlled the relic and then lost it would suffer defeat and death.

Some said Alaric carried the holy lance when he sacked Rome. King Heinrich of Saxony had it in his possession when he defeated the Magyars. Pope John XII is thought to have used it to christen Heinrich's son, Otto the Great, as Holy Roman Emperor. Otto later used the spear when he defeated the Mongolian Hordes in the Battle of Leck.

Constantine the Great claimed that he was guided by divine providence via the spear in his victory at Milvian Bridge, which established Christianity as the official religion of the Holy Roman Empire. Charlemagne later acquired the spear, followed by Charles Martel, Frederick Barbarossa and a long list of other great generals, emperors and statesmen who profited politically and militarily.

Some lost the lance and paid the price—Charlemagne died after accidentally dropping it; Barbarossa drowned while crossing a river after letting the lance slip from his hands into the water. Even Napoleon sought the lance but failed in his attempt to acquire the relic when enemies beat him to it following the battle of Austerlitz.

The spear finally wound up in the possession of the House of the Hapsburgs, and by the early 1900s was part of the collection stored in Hofburg Musuem. It was there that Hitler, a young painter living in Vienna, learned about the lance and its mystical reputation.

Dr. Walter Stein, who accompanied Hitler on one visit, said, "When we first stood side by side in front of the Spear of Destiny, it appeared to me that Hitler was in so deep a condition of trance that he was suffering almost complete sense-denudation and a total lack of self-consciousness."

Later, Hitler reportedly said: "I stood there quietly gazing upon it for several minutes, quite oblivious to the scene around me. It seemed to carry some hidden inner meaning which evaded me, a meaning which I felt inwardly I knew, yet could not bring to consciousness. I felt as though I myself had held it before in some earlier century of history. That I myself had once claimed it as my talisman of power and held the destiny of the world in my hands."

Some historians say that Hitler saw the lance as his "mystical connection with generations of conquering Germanic leaders that had come before him." Others say his interest probably originated with his fascination with Richard Wagner's opera *Parsifal* in which the Spear of Destiny plays a predominant role.

Soon after rising to power as chancellor of Germany, Hitler moved quickly to annex Austria into his Third Reich. One of his first actions was to claim his "Spear of Destiny" from the Hofburg Museum.

On Oct. 13, 1938, the lance was loaded onto an armored train and sent to Nuremberg, heart of the Nazi movement. There it was kept in a sealed vault at St. Catherine's Church throughout most of the war. To protect it from Allied bombing raids, Hitler had the mystical relic moved to another specially constructed vault beneath Nuremberg Castle.

Finally, on April 30, 1945, U.S. troops who had fought their way into Nuremberg in the face of fierce resistance entered the vault and came upon the spear. Completely unaware that his treasured artifact had fallen into enemy hands, Hitler committed suicide in his Berlin bunker—just 80 minutes after Lt. Walter William Horn had seized the spear in the name of the United States of America.

Some historians saw Hitler's obsession with the spear as proof that Nazism was more than just a political system aimed at world conquest.

"Nazism," wrote Jean-Michel Angebert, a French historian and author of *The Occult and The Third Reich*, was "only the most recent outcropping of a militant neo-paganism locked in a death struggle with its arch enemy, traditional Christianity, a struggle which will go on to the end of time."

Hitler's own words, uttered in 1944, hinted at the darker side of Nazism: "He who has seen in National Socialism only a political movement has seen nothing."

Today the spear is back in Hofburg Museum, an ancient relic with a notorious past. The shaft is long gone, but the spearhead— held together by gold, silver and bronze thread and containing a nail from the crucifix—remains a favorite attraction, drawing thousands of visitors from around the world each year.

The Man in White

FOR CENTURIES, men and women of all faiths and nationalities have reported startling encounters with a radiant "man in white" they thought—or knew—to be Jesus Christ. The

New Testament offers many such accounts, as do the Holy Men and Women of the Middle Ages, from St. Francis of Assisi to St. Catherine of Sienna.

While these alleged sightings more often than not occur amid the sacred settings of priests, nuns and other church leaders, an increasing number of these "miracles" are now being reported among ordinary, even homeless, people.

Alejandro Diaz, a 67-year-old Miami man who had been diagnosed with terminal cancer, told a local newspaper that a "soft-spoken man" dressed in a white shirt and pants approached him one night while he was digging through garbage cans for food.

Thinking the "stranger in white" was just another homeless man, Diaz offered him a chunk of his bread. It was at that point that Diaz knew there was something special—something quite otherworldly—about the strange man with the soft smile and twinkling eyes.

Then something quite remarkable happened. The stranger took Diaz's hand and asked him to kneel down with him and pray.

"He took my hand, and it was a feeling like none other," Diaz said, as they knelt and prayed amid the cockroaches and rotting food. "A comforting warmth oozed through my body. For the first time in years I felt happy to be alive."

Diaz knew—without being told—that the man was Jesus.

He wasn't surprised to learn a few days later that his cancer had been completely cured.

On both sides of the Atlantic and throughout many other regions of the world, stories about a mysterious "stranger in white" similar to Diaz's continue to crop up. In almost every case, he appears as a homeless man, sometimes in rags, but always described as soft-spoken and seemingly shrouded in a soft, radiant glow.

In Birmingham, England, an off-duty policeman crashed his motorcycle on a lonely road late one night and broke both of his legs. Death seemed certain, until a man dressed in a white coat walked in out of the fog, knelt down beside him and prayed.

"He stayed with me and talked to me about how I should treat people better and what it's like in Heaven," the officer said.

Minutes later an ambulance appeared, gathered the injured officer up and whisked him away to a nearby hospital where doctors saved both of his legs. Before pulling away, the officer looked around for the gentle stranger—but he was nowhere to be found.

What were the odds of an ambulance showing up on that road, at that time of night? The policeman, now fully recovered and back on the force, says it was a miracle.

He also knows it was Jesus who took care of him until the ambulance arrived.

A Cairo woman whose back had been crushed by a five-ton block of stone told a Dutch television reporter that a "strange man in white" came to her out of nowhere, touched her back and she was healed.

"The man looked like Jesus," she said. "He told me to live a good life and pray to God daily."

Apparently Christians aren't the only ones having visions of Jesus or the "Man in White." Muslims reportedly see him in visions and dreams and even have a name for him—"Aisa," the Muslim Arabic name for Jesus.

"Whole villages are visited by the 'man in white robes,'" one television producer was quoted as saying. "People see him and recognize him...."

Historian and author Lance Lambert, a Messianic Jew, believes that many Jews "for the first time are discovering that Jeshua (Jesus) is the Messiah for Israel." He adds, "The larger number of Messianic Jews that I know all have visitations or a supernatural revelation of the person of the Messiah."

In February 1932, the figure of Christ appeared on a sanctuary wall at St. Bartholomew's Church in New York City. The rector, the Rev. Dr. Robert Norwood, had just concluded a talk on "The Mystery of Incarnation" when the miraculous image was spotted.

"I happened to glance at the sanctuary wall and was amazed

to see this lovely figure of Christ in the marble," he said. "I had never noticed it before....I consider it a curious and beautiful happening."

News of the Christ-figure appeared in New York papers on Feb. 23, and crowds of curiosity-seekers pressed into the church to glimpse the image. In an interview with the *New York Times*, Dr. Norwood commented: "I have a weird theory that the force of thought, a dominant thought, may be strong and powerful enough to be somehow transferred to stone in its receptive state. How this Christ-like figure came to be there, I don't know. It is an illusion that grows before the vision. Has thought the power of life? People can scoff at it, but the figure is there."

*"For the truly faithful, no miracle is necessary.
For those who doubt, no miracle is sufficient."*
—Nancy Gibbs

PORTALS TO THE HEREAFTER

Each year, thousands of people the world over experience deathbed visions. Some recall vivid images of an afterlife—including tunnels of light, peaceful meadows and angelic figures clad in white that "guide" them along their journey.

One man recalled meeting a "being of light" who forgave him for a lifetime of violence. Another survivor said she traveled down a long tunnel to "a place filled with love and a beautiful bright white light" where Elvis Presley took her gently by the hand.

In almost every case lives are dramatically altered.

Some scientists who study these "near-death-experiences" theorize that they may be "peep-holes" into a world beyond. Bruce Greyson, a psychiatrist at the University of Virginia Medical School, says that those who have had such experiences "become enamored with the spiritual part of life, and less so with possessions, power and prestige."

Nancy Evans, president emeritus of the International Society for Near-Death Experiences, said, "Most near-death experience survivors say they don't think there is a God….They know."

Such revelatory experiences are nothing new. Writing in *The Republic*, Plato told the story of how a wounded solder journeyed toward "a straight, light-like pillar, most nearly resembling a rainbow, but brighter and purer."

Art and literature of the Middle Ages is replete with the borderland between life and death. One 13th-century monk recounted tales of people who supposedly returned from the edge and reported "corridors of fire" and "icy" paths to the afterlife.

Skeptics insist these experiences are nothing more than hallucinations, usually brought on by drugs, sleep deprivation or other natural causes. Daniel Alkon, chief of the Neural Systems Laboratory at the National Institutes of Health, says oxygen deprivation in the brain lies at the root of near-death experiences.

"When death appears certain, the body will often shut down and play dead as a last course of action," he said. "I think that the mind is just trying to save itself from the horror of unbelievable trauma."

But the medical community's perception of these reports began to change in 1975, when Raymond Moody published *Life After Life*, a book that coined the term "near-death experience" to describe this phenomenon. Nowadays the study of NDEs has become a serious academic pursuit at many universities and clinics from Moscow to New York City.

"Near-death experiences, while still rather remarkable, are no longer relegated to the mumbo-jumbo realm of the miraculous," commented one researcher. "We are learning a lot more about this phenomenon and its causes—whether from disease-induced hallucinations, oxygen deprivation to the brain, wish-fulfillment or other cause."

But specialists who have studied the phenomenon maintain that medical factors alone do not necessarily generate true deathbed experiences. According to Rosemary Ellen Guiley, a respected author and journalist who has studied the subject, such visions are sometimes shared by those near the dying person.

"As the person dies," Ms. Guiley said, "clouds of silvery energy are sometimes reported floating over the body. In some cases, the energy is seen to clearly form into the astral body of the dying one, connected by a silvery cord which severs at the moment of death."

Ms. Guiley said deathbed visions have been found in all cultures throughout history.

Studies show that deathbed visions typically occur to individuals who die gradually, such as from terminal illness, rather than those who die suddenly, such as from heart attacks.

214 IN THE REALM OF

214 IN THE REALM OF

The majority of visions are of apparitions of the dead, usually described as "glowing" and dressed in white.

Sometimes mythical and religious beings are perceived, including angels, Jesus, the Virgin Mary, Krishna, Yama (the Hindu god of death) or similar figures. Apparitions invariably are close family members, such as parents, children, siblings or spouses.

One study suggested that the purpose of these apparitions is to beckon or command the dying to accompany them.

"They appear to assist in the transition to death," Ms. Guiley noted. "The descriptions most frequently given are of endless gardens of great beauty...gates, bridges, rivers, boats and other symbols of transition."

The response is usually one of happiness and willingness to go, especially if the individual believes in an afterlife.

An Angel Takes Flight

ALL HER LIFE FRANCIS TIPPINS had been a kind, caring woman who rarely complained about anything.

Her friendly smile was legendary.

"She was one of the happiest, brightest, and most cheerful persons I've ever known," a neighbor recalled. "She was like a saint—always doing things for the church, local school, and community, always smiling and never asking for anything in return."

When she retired from the Baxley, Ga., school system, Mrs. Tippins remained active in her small south Georgia hometown, promoting community events and festivals and helping out the needy.

She never stopped.

Then one day she felt a sharp pain in her lower chest. When her husband, Dennard, offered to take her to a doctor, she declined, assuring him she'd be better in a few days.

The pain got worse.

Still, she refused to see a doctor—or to slow down. For months she courageously kept the pain to herself, not wishing to bother her busy husband, a prominent local businessman and farmer.

Finally, unable to endure the suffering any longer, she spoke up, and the alarmed Mr. Tippins got her to a doctor.

It was cancer.

"We were shocked," a friend related. "This brave woman had been suffering all these months, yet she went on about her business without anybody knowing, helping others and going to church. It was amazing."

The cancer continued to spread in spite of treatment at several regional hospitals. Doctors told Mr. Tippins there was nothing more they could do.

So it went for another dozen years. Some days the spirited ex-schoolteacher felt fine and looked for forward to full recovery; at other times the pain became so intense that she had to be sedated.

Through it all, however, Francis Tippins continued to smile, never once complaining.

"That woman suffered so much," her friend noted. "God surely had a purpose for all that pain."

Although Dennard Tippins went to church, he was never one to believe in magic or miracles. But he prayed. For 12 long years he prayed that the disease sapping the life out of his beloved wife would go away, that she could get back on her feet and one day be whole again.

But, as he later admitted to friends, "God must have had other plans for Francis."

In the early 1980s, Mrs. Tippins was hospitalized in Brunswick. Specialists worked around the clock to ease their saintly patient's suffering, but to no avail. As he watched and waited, Mr. Tippins knew the end was near.

To be closer to his wife, Mr. Tippins gave up his business and went to Brunswick, Ga. He bought a motor home which he kept parked in the hospital parking lot. By day he stayed by Mrs. Tippins' side; by night he slept in the RV.

"He never left her side," a nurse recalled. "He stayed with her until the staff had to shoo him out to his RV at night."

Then one morning, as a gray and windswept sky hovered over Brunswick, Mr. Tippins was summoned to his wife's bedside. For several minutes he stood over his sick wife, listening to her final gasps for breath.

"I could see death all over her face," Mr. Tippins was later quoted as saying. "But there was no sadness in her eyes. Only a strange happiness."

About eleven o'clock in the morning, her condition deteriorated. At that point a nurse suggested that Mr. Tippins go out to his motor home and get some rest. Since there was nothing he could do—he had been by his wife's side for six straight hours, watching her gracefully but futilely struggle for life—the grieving husband agreed.

As he started across the parking lot, a light rain began to fall. Mr. Tippins had never felt so lonely, so sad, so utterly helpless. His lifelong companion—his wife and the mother of his children—was dying, and there was not one thing he could do about it.

He went inside his motor home and prayed.

Sleep came softly, almost like an uninvited whisper. He dreamed he and his wife were back home, and they were young and she was well again. It was a sad, sweet dream and when he awoke to the rain, he was crying.

Outside a strong wind had picked up, gusting across the parking lot and blowing the rain about the lonely motor home. Then a strange thing happened—the rain suddenly stopped and the sun came out.

"It was raining and windy one second, then sunny and calm the next," Mr. Tippins recalled.

He sat up in bed, thankful for the calm.

That's when he heard the sound, a "whooshing, swishing" noise that sounded like the wind. He looked out the window. Not a leaf or branch was stirring.

That's odd, he thought, heading for the door. The whooshing, swishing sound continued.

He opened the door and looked outside.

His mouth dropped open.

Above the motor home, arching slowly across the sky toward him like a flaming meteor, was Francis.

"She was like an angel, flying overhead straight toward me," the astonished husband explained. "She had wings and there was a glow all around her. She was smiling."

Then, as suddenly as it had appeared, the apparition vanished.

"I knew what had happened," he said.

After collecting himself, Mr. Tippins walked over to the hospital. He saw the nurses standing outside his wife's door and waked straight toward them.

They told him what he already knew—his wife was dead.

Until his death a few years later, Dennard Tippins continued to believe that he had witnessed a miracle that morning in the parking lot of a Georgia hospital.

"I Was Dead...Cold, Drifting Down..."

BOB SMITH CLEARLY REMEMBERS that hot, hazy afternoon in the early 1980s when he climbed onto the roof of his house to install a short-wave radio antenna and was electrocuted.

"There was a blinding flash—then everything was black," he recalled on a nationwide radio show. "I was dead—cold, drifting down into what seemed to be a dark pit."

Then an incredible thing happened.

"I saw a bright light coming straight toward me," he recalled. "It was like a tunnel of light, and it was natural as sunlight coming in through my window. I felt glorious, completely at peace."

He remembers one other thing.

"Even though I didn't understand what was happening to me at the time, I was aware that I had to make a choice—either to go on or return to life."

He chose to come back.

Smith had apparently experienced what some investigators call a near-death-experience, or NDE. According to parapsychologists and others who study the phenomenon, tens of thousands of Americans experience near-death episodes every year. One source estimated that as many as 23 million people in the United States have died and come back to talk about their experiences.

Many of these "survivors" were pronounced clinically dead at the time but revived to provide detailed—and often startling—accounts of leaving their bodies, passing into a light, and, in some cases at least, visiting "heavenly" realms.

P.M.H. Atwater, author of the best-selling book, *Coming Back to Life: The After-Effects of the Near-Death Experience*, insists that NDEs occur frequently.

"It's been shown that 40 percent of all resuscitated patients have near-death-experiences," said Atwater, a Charlottesville, Va., writer who claims to be an NDE survivor herself.

How does one know if he or she has had an NDE?

"There is the sensation of floating out of one's body," Atwater explained. "There is also a feeling of passing through a dark tunnel or black hole, then ascending toward a light at the end of darkness.

"Also, many people hear greetings from friendly voices, people or beings they recognize. Some also say they are provided a panoramic review of the life just lived from birth to death in reverse order."

Atwater added that victims are usually reluctant to return to what she called the "earth plane." There is also a warped sense of time and space and disappointment at being revived, she added.

Studies show that people all over the world, from every culture and religion, have experienced NDEs. While adults—especially the very old—are more likely to experience the same basic phenomena, the percentage of children is quite remarkable. One Hungarian university study showed that three out of 10 teenagers who had experienced traumatic, life-threatening injuries had experienced at least one episode.

Most survivors have trouble recalling how long they were "dead." Atwater, who has interviewed hundreds of people who claim to have died and come back, said the average time is about five minutes, though some experiences last for more than an hour.

Bob Smith said he had no idea how long he was out. But it was to be "quite a while," he noted, because when he finally woke he was in a hospital operating room.

When he related his experience to attending physicians, they dismissed it as "hallucination...brought on by the electrical shock...."

Like most survivors, Mr. Smith said he rarely talks about his NDE anymore for fear of ridicule. In fact, he added, men are more reluctant to talk about their sensation than are women.

The vast majority of NDE survivors are likely to experience waves of euphoria—often described as incredible and overwhelming. They discover new plateaus of love, peace, and complete compassion for others. One survivor said he felt "totally accepted by angels...and in the presence of God."

Many survivors relate encounters with "beings of light" on the other side, while others saw images that appeared to be human and clad in either modern or old-fashioned clothes. In almost every case, these images were described as "angel-like" in shape.

Atwater explained that most survivors no longer fear death.

"These people usually become more loving, more peaceful, and much more content with a less materialistic lifestyle," she noted.

> *"Miracles are contrary to nature, but only contrary to what we know about nature."*
> —St. Augustine

MINDS & HANDS THAT HEAL

In the right hands, the power to heal is said to be a gift from God. In the wrong hands, this incredible gift is often seen as the work of the devil.

The Bible talks of divine healing—the kind manifested by Jesus when he cured lepers and raised Lazarus from the dead. It also talks about a pernicious desire among the angels of darkness to pretend to heal and cure in order to mock and deceive the true teachings of the church. Such was the case, it appears, with the power possessed by Simon Magus.

In *City of God*, St. Augustine tells the story about a Carthaginian woman named Innocentia, a devout woman who had been diagnosed with terminal breast cancer. Distraught, the woman sought relief in prayer. In a dream, a woman in white appears to her and says she will be healed if she makes the sign of the cross on the breast of the first woman she sees coming out of baptism.

Innocentia did as she was told—and the cancer went away.

Sometimes healing power manifests itself in other forms— crystals, tea leaves, playing cards, even dirt. Author Ann Hood credits a handful of dirt from a sacred place in New Mexico as curing her father of cancer. It was "completely…100 percent gone," Ms. Hood says. "When the doctor walked in, he said the words we had been hoping for, 'it's a miracle.'"

Following are several noteworthy cases of bizarre healing power that modern science has yet to explain.

Cajun Country Angel

IN LIFE, Charlene Richard was an ordinary little girl who liked dolls and went to church every Sunday.

It was only after her death of cancer in the mid-1960s that the 12-year-old girl became famous.

Today Charlene's name is revered in southeastern Louisiana's Cajun country, where many folks believe the girl still lives—even after death—as an angel sent to Earth to help heal the sick and lame and to perform other miracles.

Each year, thousands flock to Charlene's grave at St. Edward's Church in Richard, La., to meditate and pray and seek divine guidance. Hundreds of miracles have been reported, many of them verified by authorities.

In 1979, for example, Lucy and Roger Courville's 5-year-old daughter was diagnosed with terminal cancer. They took the girl to Charlene's grave and spent all day praying for a miracle.

A few days later doctors reported that the little girl's cancer was in remission. The girl, now grown, is completely recovered.

"We think it was a miracle from Charlene," insisted one family member.

The Rev. Floyd Calais also believes in Charlene. Shortly after her death, Calais was the chaplain at a state hospital in Lafayette, in the heart of Cajun country. For months he had hoped for an opportunity to move to a small parish. When he heard about Charlene, he went to her grave and prayed that she would inspire the bishop to reassign him.

He was soon appointed pastor of the church where the girl was buried.

"When I found out which church I had, the hair on the back of my neck stood on end," said the preacher.

On the night of Aug. 11, 1989—Charlene's birthday—a crowd of about 4,000 Catholics gathered at her grave to pay homage to their young candidate for sainthood. Those present that night sincerely believed in the departed girl's ability to reach beyond the walls of the spiritual world and touch the lives of those in the physical.

One such man was Paul Olivier, a retired state policeman.

"We had a child who was a year old and diagnosed as having

cancer of the larynx," Mr. Olivier said. "The doctors said it was very rare, but it was a killer. They put her life span at 3,4,5 months at most."

Then Mr. Olivier heard about Charlene. At first, he was skeptical. He was a deeply religious man, but he still didn't know what to think about miracles, prophets or divine intervention in earthly life. Desperate for help, however, Mr. Olivier took his sick daughter to the dead Cajun girl's grave.

"We asked her to help us," Mr. Olivier explained.

That was in 1970. Angela Olivier survived her bout with cancer and went on to graduate from the University of Southeastern Louisiana and become a housewife and mother.

"I would say that is a sign of a miracle," her father said. "A prayer was answered."

Mr. Olivier's story is similar to hundreds of others that started cropping up shortly after Charlene's death. Talk of the girl's miraculous healing powers spread like wildfire though the region, and soon network television and national newspapers and magazines began to report on some of the more spectacular events.

Although many accounts were dismissed as hallucinations or hoaxes, a number of puzzling cases remain a mystery—except to those who believe.

Today there is a box on Charlene's grave where visitors hoping for miracles can drop their requests. The grave itself is simple, marked with a marble headstone and two elevated tables. A steady stream of visitors come and go, mainly curiosity seekers anxious for a glimpse of the famous grave, and at night a candle burns to light the way.

Even though she isn't convinced herself about her daughter's miracles, Mary Alice Richard, Charlene's mother, still reportedly visits the grave every day.

"Charlene was not a remarkable child,." Mrs. Richard told one reporter. "She was full of life. She liked sports and was always busy with something. She went to church and said her rosary, but she was just a normal little girl."

Charlene's miracles have prompted many Roman Catholics

to petition for her sainthood. One of her biggest backers is the Rev. Joseph Brennan, a former pastor of St. Edward's Church, who said it was the girl's death that made her a saint.

"Charlene taught the world not how to live, but how to die," Brennan said. "Thirty years ago they didn't have the pain medicine they have now, and she died in excruciating pain but in perfect grace. She became great at that time."

Although the United States has produced only three saints, the diocese of Lafayette has begun the slow process of sainthood for Charlene. Local church officials are still involved with the first step of canonization process, collecting sworn testimonies from people who say Charlene performed miracles on their behalf.

It will be up to the Vatican to determine whether Charlene is suitable for sainthood. Veneration would come first, then beatification and finally canonization, according to a church spokesman.

"None of that really matters," explained the Rev. Calais. "I'm sure she is in heaven."

For those who have seen the miracles, the canonization of Charlene is only a formality.

"For us, she is already a saint," said Wilson Daigle, who credits Charlene's intercession with helping his wife recover from a mental illness. "We talk to her, and she understands us."

The "Miracle-Maker" of Paris

WHEN FRANCOIS DE PARIS, the Deacon of Paris, died of heart failure in the summer of 1727, thousands of mourners flocked to his funeral in the little churchyard of Saint-Medard.

One of the mourners, a crippled boy, laid a rose on the deacon's coffin. Suddenly, the child went into convulsions and had to be taken away. When he recovered, he was no longer crippled.

Word spread of this apparent miracle.

Within hours, cripples, lepers, hunchbacks and blind men rushed to the church. Like the boy, they, too, appeared to be healed by merely touching the deacon's coffin.

Deformed limbs were straightened. Hideous growths and cancers disappeared without a trace. Horrible sores and wounds healed.

Even powerful magistrates, Jesuit priests and theologians were drawn to the Parisian churchyard to observe miracles taking place daily.

One of those who investigated the happenings was an attorney, Louis Adrien de Paige. Mr. Paige asked one of his friends, the magistrate Louis-Basile Carre de Montgeron, one of the most powerful men in Paris, to accompany him to the church.

According to author Colin Wilson who researched the case, what the pair of skeptics saw when they entered the churchyard was "a number of women writhing on the ground, twisting themselves into the most startling shapes, sometimes bending backward until the back of their heads touched their heels."

Mr. Wilson said that "an incredible number of them were cured of deformities or diseases by this violent treatment."

One of the most startling sights was that of a young girl eating filth. The girl had come to the churchyard to be cured of a neurosis—washing her hands hundreds of times a day.

"Such cases might not be remarkable in asylums," Wilson wrote. "But what was more extraordinary—indeed, preposterous—was that after one of these meals she opened her mouth as if to be sick, and milk came pouring out. Monsieur Paige had collected a cupful; it was apparently perfectly ordinary cow's milk."

Montgeron and Paige wandered the churchyard, watching young girls being bitten, impaled with spears and pounded with heavy rocks—all with no visible harm done. In fact, Montgeron later noted, the girls "sang and were cheerful throughout their ordeal, and walking away smiling and looking very healthy."

King Louis XV was so shocked at Montgeron's official investigation of the incident at Saint-Medard that he had the magistrate thrown into prison. Paris authorities eventually closed the churchyard.

But the incidents continued when women who believed they had been cured at Saint-Medard discovered they could perform their miracles anywhere, and they continued for many years.

In 1759, scientist La Condamine watched as Sister Francois was crucified on a wooden cross. The girl later walked away unharmed, even though she had been nailed through the hands and feet and stabbed in the side with a spear.

Most investigators attribute the bizarre events at Saint-Medard to some kind of self-hypnosis. But Colin Wilson concludes: "What seems to be at work here is some power of mind over matter, something deeper than mere hypnosis."

Sai Baba: "Man of Miracles"

ON AN EARLY MORNING in midsummer, Sai Baba sits in his tiny hut on the outskirts of Dehra Dun, a village in northern India, calmly awaiting visitors.

Outside, long lines of men, women and children have been forming for hours. Many are near death. Others cannot walk and have to be carried.

All are anxious to see the "Man of Miracles"—as Sai Baba is known throughout India—to let him pray for them and touch them with his powers.

The first visitor is Khare, a civil servant who had recently gone blind.

"You will see again soon if you do exactly as I tell you," Sai Baba said in his soft voice.

Then Sai Baba produced sacred wood ash out of thin air and told Khare to take it home with him.

"Rub it on your eyelids for one week," he explained.

Khare did as he was told, and one week later his vision was back to normal. Even the eye specialists who had examined his eyes a short time before were amazed.

Tens of thousands of people around the world claim to have witnessed Sai Baba's extraordinary powers. Skeptical scientists and journalists have observed him at close range but have yet to find an explanation for his feats.

Australian journalist Howard Murphet set out to expose him as a fraud. Things changed, however, during an interview with Sai Baba.

"Sai Baba asked me to tell him the year of my birth," Murphet said. "Then he told me he would get me an American gold coin minted that year."

The guru circled his empty hand in front of Murphet and dropped a coin into the journalist's palm.

"When the coin dropped from his hand into mind, I noted first that it was heavy and golden," Murphet noted. "On closer examination I found to my delight, that it was a genuine minted American $10 coin, with the year of my birth stamped beneath a profile head of the Statue of Liberty."

But perhaps the most astounding display of Sai Baba's powers took place in 1953, when a 60-year-old man asked him to heal a painful stomach ulcer. Sai Baba was busy at the time and had to turn the visitor away.

The man died the next week.

Three days later, according to one account, Sai Baba walked into the room where the body lay cold and stiff. Minutes later, relatives saw the "dead man" get up and walk out, flush with life.

An examination showed that his stomach ulcer had vanished.

Although Sai Baba claims that his miracles are "tinsel" compared with his religious message, he performs them readily, often before huge audiences. Many witnesses claim that Sai Baba produces objects on demand; he asks people what they would like then plucks it from the air.

There are many accounts, too, of Sai Baba asking a number of people in a crowd to name their favorite fruit, then pointing to a single tree from which are hanging all the fruits that they have named.

Sai Baba, who has been demonstrating his extraordinary power for more than half a century, refuses to submit to rigorous scientific testing. He insists that he will use his powers only for religious purposes, such as inspiring faith or helping followers in need.

"No one can understand my mystery," he said.

Edgar Cayce: America's "Most Mysterious Man"

ON THE NIGHT OF APRIL 18, 1900, a young Kentucky photographer named Edgar Cayce suddenly lost his voice. His condition was diagnosed as "paralysis of the vocal organs," and it was doubtful he would ever speak again.

Unwilling to accept such a fate, Cayce turned desperately to hypnosis for relief. At the time, hypnosis was still a relatively new branch of science and very few doctors were trained in its application. Of those trained, fewer still were willing to use it.

But Cayce finally found a physician who agreed to take the chance. After 10 months of hypnotic therapy, the 23-year-old photographer's voice finally returned. It seemed a miracle at the time, but the truly amazing thing is what happened to him during those long hours of treatment each day.

Whenever he went into a trance, this shy, sensitive, deeply religious man who dropped out of school in the seventh grade would talk about things far beyond his range of knowledge and expertise. In fact, he would often discuss complex medical matters, drawing upon principles, theories and terminologies unknown outside the medical and scientific community.

In no time, Cayce was astounding the academic world with his pinpoint diagnoses and recommended remedies for other patients, some of whom were hospitalized hundreds of miles away. Cayce was even credited for having identified and prescribed the treatment that eventually led to his own cure.

It didn't take long for news of this amazing "miracle healer" to spread across the country. Newspapers and magazines were quick to pick up on the Cayce story, and soon banner headlines were proclaiming him "America's Most Mysterious Man." One paper wrote: "Edgar Cayce Startles Medical Men With His Trances."

As for himself, Cayce was startled by all the hoopla. Even more confounding, he couldn't remember any of the things he

228 IN THE REALM OF

was credited with having said while under hypnosis! It was as if somebody else would step inside his body and speak for him, some highly trained doctor of medicine whose authoritative voice rumbled with confidence and wisdom.

Gradually, Cayce came to appreciate his unusual, seemingly miraculous powers. Shortly after his remarkable recovery, he discovered that by lying down, thoroughly relaxing, and taking a deep breath, he could duplicate the trances on his own. In such self-induced states, Cayce's voice would boom across the room, diagnosing problems and prescribing remedies for patients and visitors who flocked to him from over the world.

There now had merged two Cayces—a "waking" Cayce, the reclusive, soft-spoken photographer, and the "sleeping" Cayce, the psychic healer the media were now calling the "miracle man" and the "sleeping prophet."

It was this second Cayce, the psychic healer who dabbled in reincarnation, astrology and other occult arts, that earned him a reputation among some church-goers that Cayce was a concerned and demonically inspired prophet whose influence among New Agers helped pave the way for the popularity of "channeling."

According to Louis D. Whitworh, affiliated with Christian Information Ministries, Cayce came by his occult talents naturally.

"His family was ordinary in most ways, except for a current of demonic dabbling and occultism among the males," Whitworth wrote in an article for Probe Ministries entitled "Edgar Cayce: The Sleeping (False) Prophet." "His grandfather was a water witch and unerringly accurate in dousing for water with the forked limb of a witch hazel tree. Many of his acquaintances held that he was also able to make tables and brooms dance."

He added, "Edgar's father was an unwitting Pied Piper of snakes. Apparently snakes loved him and followed him around and even wrapped their bodies around his hat brim if he put his hat down while working the fields."

As a boy, Edgar attended the Christian church and wanted to be a minister. He read the Bible often—and had his first vision at the age of 13 when a "woman in brilliant white clothing wings" came to him in the woods and told him his prayers would be answered.

He also is said to have exhibited occultic tendencies to see and hear things that others couldn't—"little playmates," for example, who disappeared when others came around. Cayce began his readings in 1901. Over the next several decades the young "healer" would delight and astonish the world with his accurate and often reassuring predictions about future events. But most people came to his office for "healing" purposes—about 16,000 between 1901 and 1944, with maladies ranging from eye problems to cancer, multiple sclerosis, diabetes, arthritis, gall stones, kidney stones, hay fever, mental and psychological problems, digestive problems, epilepsy, hemorrhoids, ulcers and psoriasis.

Copies of most of his readings are still on file in the archives of the Association for Research and Enlightenment, an institute set up at Virginia Beach, Va, to study Cayce's unique powers.

In all that time, there was never an indication that Cayce was conscious of a single word he uttered while in the self-imposed hypnotic state. Even though Cayce couldn't account for this himself, he theorized that the thousands of readings and predictions apparently came through or out of his unconscious mind.

By 1913, Cayce's fame as the "miracle man" had reached international proportions. Hundreds of people visited his office each year, some from as far away as Europe and Asia. Each day his office was flooded with requests for special readings that usually involved healing, although a few preferred "psychic readings."

Cayce, a self-taught preacher of the strictest integrity and character, rarely charged for his psychic services. But his conditions were strict: an appointment would have to be set up for 11 a.m. or 3 p.m., on a specific day. The applicant did not have to be present, but it was necessary that Cayce be given the person's real name and address—and where that individual would be at the specified time of reading.

Cayce's own routine never varied. He would come in from the garden or from fishing, loosen his tie, shoelaces, cuffs and belt, then lie down on a couch. His hands would be placed first palm-up on his forehead, then across his abdomen. Drawing in deep gulps of air several times, he would close his eyes and relax. When his eyelids began to flutter, the reading would begin.

Afterwards, he might sleep for a couple of hours or more. He would awaken—refreshed—without remembering a single thing about the reading.

In the early 1920s, the "sleeping prophet" became obsessed with reincarnation. Often, when tracking patients' previous lives, Cayce would take them hundreds of thousands of years into the past. Occasionally, he would link them to the lost continent of Atlantis, where he proclaimed some of their "spiritual entities" had been born.

Some of Cayce's readings about Atlantis received special attention from the press. Not since Plato had anyone spoken with so much authority about the fabled landmass that supposedly sank beneath the waves during a cataclysmic upheaval some 12,000 years ago. According to Cayce, who "visited" Atlantis hundreds of times during his trances, runaway technology was the cause for its demise.

In 1936 he wrote:

"In Atlantean land just after the second breaking up on the land owing to misapplication of divine laws upon those things of nature or of the earth; when there were the eruptions from the second using of those influences that were for man's own development, yet becoming destructive forces to flesh when misapplied [sic]."

Before their land was destroyed, Atlanteans had developed a kind of nuclear energy superior to modern-day technology. "Rays...invisible to the eye" propelled vehicles through the air and beneath the sea, Cayce revealed.

Upon waking, Cayce was sometimes startled, even embarrassed, at some of his revelations. A religious man who read the Bible every day, the last thing he wanted was for anybody to accuse him of being un-Christian. He was especially troubled about his comments on reincarnation, though day after day, reading after reading, his sleeping self always kept coming back to the subject.

Cayce's biographers often attribute his healing powers to an ability to tap into what they called the "Universal Mind" or "Universal Consciousness." Whitworth sees this as more "evidence of demonic activity in his life."

Until 1923, says Whitworth, there were two sides to Cayce—the Cayce who was orthodox: "a church-going, Bible reading, Sunday School teaching man who would have steadfastly defended Christ as the unique Son of God, the Bible as the Word of God, the reality of heaven and hell, and so on."

Then there was "the Cayce who had a family heritage of psychic abilities, a person who saw visions, heard voices, and who performed trance-style medical readings that looked suspiciously like what mediums do."

Although Cayce's "life readings" on reincarnation and Atlantis deviated from his normal "healing" sessions, he would remain fascinated with those subjects for the rest of his life. In fact, Cayce's peculiar work in the field has been quoted numerous times by scientists, theologians, spiritualists and other investigators in the field of paranormal research.

In 1945, Cayce went to his grave still unaware of his miraculous gifts and unique contributions to the field of paranormal science.

The Amazing "Doctor" Fritz

JUSCELINO KUBITSCHEK, the brilliant mathematician who engineered the construction of Brazil's capital city of Brasilia, had lost hope of saving his sick daughter's life.

"She's dying," the doctors told him. "It's only a matter of time."

Then one day a friend suggested he take her to see "Dr. Fritz," an illiterate Brazilian peasant known for his ability to heal the sick and wounded through psychic surgery. Some said he was capable of predicting the future and could even communicate with the dead.

Kubitschek agonized over the decision. What would his colleagues and sophisticated friends say if he took his dying daughter to see a "psychic surgeon"?

He decided to take her anyway. If the doctors couldn't heal her, perhaps the quaint jungle peasant could come up with something.

Two weeks later Kubitschek and his daughter were huddled in the shadows of a tarpaper shack in Congohas do Campo, a village some 250 miles from Rio de Janeiro. After some preliminary questions about the girl's ailment, Dr. Fritz placed his hands on her stomach and nodded.

"It is here," he announced in a strange, faraway voice, then withdrew a small, rusty pocketknife and cut out a small cyst from the girl's abdomen—without benefit of anesthesia. Kubitshek's daughter was cured.

Just who was this Dr. Fritz? How was it he was able to perform such a miracle?

Dr. Fritz's real name was Jose Arigo. His uncanny surgical powers had been with him since early childhood, but it was not until the 1950s and 1960s that his fame began to spread. From Rio de Janeiro to the jungles, the unorthodox and unlicensed physician reportedly cured thousands.

One year, Mr. Arigo was said to have healed 10,000 people of ailments ranging from broken bones to malaria, tuberculosis, leukemia and cancer. Arigo supposedly performed the feats under the guidance of "Dr. Fritz," the spirit of a long-dead German surgeon who died while tending injured soldiers during World War I.

According to Arigo, who had no schooling beyond the third grade, Dr. Fritz's spirit told him what was wrong with each patient and guided his hands during delicate surgical procedures.

On numerous occasions, newspaper reporters and physicians watched Arigo perform miracles. His tools were mainly pocketknives, nail scissors, tweezers and other ordinary instruments. He used them to remove cancerous stomach tumors and life-threatening cysts, to mend broken bones and restore vision.

Arigo used no antiseptic. Some said he could make blood stop flowing with a spoken command.

The soft-spoken man also could diagnose patients without examining them—sometimes from many miles away. While similar operations in a modern medical facility would have taken hours involving a team of highly trained specialists, most of Dr. Fritz's operations were completed in less than five minutes.

While there are many skeptics, Dr. Fritz's miracles were investigated and witnessed by trained physicians from both Brazil and the United States, by sleight-of-hand stage magicians and by experienced parapsychologists. Physicians from some of Brazil's leading hospitals confirmed his healings on patients they themselves had treated unsuccessfully.

Curiously, Jose Arigo could not treat himself or members of his own immediate family. He did predict his own death, however, which came on Jan. 11, 1971, a few days after he started telling friends that his "time on earth" was coming to an end.

The Miracles of Jesus

MILLIONS OF PEOPLE THE WORLD OVER believe that Jesus of Nazareth, the simple carpenter son of Joseph and the Virgin Mary, was the greatest maker of miracles the world has ever seen. The Gospel writers—Matthew, Mark, Luke and John—describe some 37 miracles said to have been performed by Jesus before his death on the cross.

Every Sunday School child knows the stories about how Jesus—called the Christ by Christians—resurrected Lazarus, cast out demons, healed the sick and lame, fed the multitudes, walked on water, changed water into wine, calmed the stormy seas and returned from the dead himself.

These miracles were not performed for entertainment or in secret, but out in the open, in full view of others, to support his claim that he was the Son of God, the long-awaited Messiah known in Aramaic as Yeshua.

234 IN THE REALM OF

Why did Jesus perform miracles? Like most holy men throughout history, Jesus is said to have performed various "wonders" in the course of his controversial public ministry. These mostly consisted of cures and exorcisms, but some other miracles displayed the power of absolute dominion over nature—a supernatural gift from his Father, according to Christian belief.

Until recent years, people generally accepted without question the Bible's portrayal of Jesus as a miracle worker. But in recent decades, the Gospel accounts have come under fire from critics. In his book *Deceptions and Myths of the Bible*, Lloyd Graham blasts the biblical account of Jesus walking on water, saying, "It takes a lot of ignorance to believe this literally, as, millions do."

It seems that in today's increasingly complex and busy world, people rarely have time for stories about miraculous works and divine wonders. While some scholars see these accounts as myths and allegorical in nature, others say the miracles of Jesus are "nothing more than marketing devices" to propagate Christianity.

Not all criticism is new. According to Justin Martyr, the second century Christian apologist, detractors in his day called Jesus a magician and "deceiver of the people," saying he did not perform his miracles as Jewish prophet but as a magician.

Today's critics are more likely to say miracles—even those associated with Jesus Christ—are the product of superstitious and ignorant minds. The 18th-century Scottish philosopher David Hume called miracles "a violation of the laws of nature."

When skeptics look at many of the miracles attributed to Jesus—such as exorcisms—they tend to dismiss them as the result of psychological disturbances and mental illness. Their conclusions are generally based on what they consider the lack of "empirical evidence" for demonic possession, even though belief in supernatural creatures was very common in Jesus' time.

The World Book Encyclopedia calls a miracle "an event that cannot be explained through the known laws of nature." But is that an accurate definition? A century ago people would have been hard-pressed to accept the existence of laptop computers, cell phones, space travel, wireless communications and laser surgery.

Surely, argue the faithful, it is unwise to assert that miracles are impossible simply because they cannot be explained based on present knowledge.

The Bible claims that Jesus' miracles were a manifestation of "the majesty power of God." They stand in stark contrast to the work of professional illusionists, magicians and faith healers such as those whose powdered, anguished faces dominate Sunday television broadcasts. Unlike those of modern faith healers, Jesus' miracles were always performed out in the open, with no stage tricks and always in full view of numerous eyewitnesses.

Arthur Pierson, author of *Many Infallible Proofs: The Evidence of Christianity*, says of Christ's miracles: "Their number, the instantaneous and complete character of the cures he wrought, and the absence of one failure in the attempt even to raise the dead, put infinite distance between these miracles and the pretended wonders of this or any other age."

He adds: "No confirmation of the miracles of scripture is more remarkable than the silence of the enemies."

In the fourth century, Eusebius writes in T*he History of the Church From Christ to Constantine*: "Our Savior's works were always there to see, for they were true—the people who had been cured and those raised from the dead, who had not merely been seen at the moment when they were cured or raised, but were always there to see, not only when the Savior was among us, but for a long time after His departure."

According to John, Jesus' powerful works always glorified God—free of emotional rituals, magic incantations, showy displays, trickery and hypnotism. When Jesus encountered a blind beggar named Bartimaeus who cried out for help, Jesus simply said to him, "Go, your faith has made you well."

Perhaps the greatest miracle of them all was Christ's own resurrection. According to the Gospels, Jesus rose from his tomb and met various people in various places over a period of 40 days before "ascending into heaven."

His promise to return stands to be an even greater miraculous event.

"A miracle is an event which creates faith.
That is the purpose and nature of miracles. Frauds deceive.
An event which creates faith does not deceive;
Therefore it is not a fraud, but a miracle."
—George Bernard Shaw

SOME MODERN MIRACLES

The primary focus of this book has been sacred miracles—not the tabloid variety where Joe Cool blows his last buck on the lottery and wins the big banana or Oral Roberts reaches out through the TV and heals Aunt Betty's lumbago.

Most of the miracles presented in these pages deal with much bigger and broader events—the kind of miracles that are everlasting, the kind that have touched millions of lives and, in some cases, altered the course of history. Yet, for all the mystical attraction of levitating saints, sacred oils, holy fires and bleeding icons, most people remain fascinated by less dazzling miraculous events.

Following are samples of some miracles closer to home that have made news in recent years.

Autistic Basketball Star

JASON MCELWAIN HAD WAITED a long time to show his team what he could do.

His big moment came on Feb. 23, 2006, when Coach Jim Johnson asked the 17-year-old senior to "get in the game" with only four minutes left on the clock.

Nobody expected much because Jason had never played a game in his four-year career at Athena High School in Greece, N.Y. As manager of the team, his job was to keep stats, hand out water bottles and run the clock.

"Go get 'em," the coach urged his young player.

Jason got the ball and nailed a three-point basket. Then, with the clock ticking down, he got the ball again, fired and hit another three-pointer—then another and another. He finished with 20 points and was carried off the court on his teammates' shoulders.

The crowd went wild. "He's a hero," one teammate said.

What most people didn't know was that Jason was autistic. His incredible and inspiring story made headline news around the world.

"This is the first moment Jason has ever succeeded," reflected Debbie McElwain, Jason's mom." I look at autism as the Berlin Wall and he cracked it."

Seven-story Fall

ONE MOMENT, 5-year-old Paul Rosen was playing near the open window of his parents' seventh-floor apartment on New York's Upper East Side.

The next he was gone.

"Paul is a strong, brave boy who thought he could fly," was how the child's mother, Christine Rose, summarized the near-tragedy that occurred in 1993 when the child leaped out the window.

Medical officials are still puzzled about how Paul could have survived the accident. Other than a few bruises, the child was unharmed.

One attending physician speculated there is a "less than 50 percent survival rate" for a person who falls more than five stories. What makes Paul's case even more unusual is that he fell onto concrete with no apparent cushion to break his fall.

Was it a miracle? Many people think so, including Dr. Roger Yurt, director of Cornell Medical Center where Paul was treated.

"It's very surprising—I would say miraculous—that he was able to fall from that height and have so little injury," he said.

Christmas Miracle

IT WAS CHRISTMAS EVE, and the 400 or so Christians from Meulaboh, a tiny village on the Indonesian island of Aceh, were gathered on a remote hilltop to celebrate the birth of their Lord and Savior, Jesus Christ.

They had arrived on the high hill hours earlier because the town fathers, who were mostly Muslim, had refused to let them honor Christ inside the city limits.

Huddled on the hillside three miles outside of town, they prayed and sang throughout the night.

Early the next morning, a powerful earthquake struck a nearby coastline, resulting in a powerful tsunami that swept across Indonesia and killed tens of thousands of people. The town of Meulaboh was wiped off the map, along with most of its inhabitants.

The band of Christians gathered on the nearby hilltop escaped without a single injury. Had they been allowed to celebrate Christmas down below in the village, many would have certainly died.

Some Muslims who survived blamed the "God of the Christians" for the disaster, saying they were singled out for punishment because they refused to allow the Christians to celebrate Christmas in town.

Rescued from a Well

ON THE AFTERNOON OF NOV. 1, 2004, 2-year-old Da'jour McMillian was playing with his older brother and sister in their grandparents' backyard near Mobile, Ala., when he disappeared.

After a frantic search, the toddler's mother came across an old abandoned well. Her worst fears were realized when she peered down inside the deep hole and heard her child crying some 20 feet straight down.

It took rescue workers more than 13 hours to drill a side shaft through to the bottom of the well and haul the boy to safety. More than 100 people who had gathered to watch the spectacle wept and shouted "Praise the Lord!" when the child was reunited with his mother.

"When he came out of that hole and saw his mama, it was a miracle," said Tammy Howard, a cousin.

Frisco City Mayor Jim Cave is one of those who agrees the outcome was nothing short of miraculous. "It wouldn't have taken but a little dirt on that child to suffocate him," he said.

Terror Two Miles Down

RANDAL MCCLOY'S OPTIONS in life were limited. Without a college education, it was either join the army or go to work in the coal mines. Like many boys in his blue collar hometown of Simpson, W. Va., he decided to become a miner. Mining was hard work, but the pay was better than average.

It was also one of the most dangerous jobs in America.

The 26-year-old father of two had always known of the dangers. He had thought about quitting many times, but a steady paycheck and two children to feed had kept him going back down into the mine day after day for more than three years.

On the morning of Jan. 2, 2006, while working at the Sago mine near Morgantown with a dozen other miners, tragedy struck when an explosion of still-undetermined origin trapped all 13 men more than two miles inside.

At first news reports indicated all miners were still alive, but those reports turned out to be horribly wrong.

It wasn't until more than 40 hours after the initial blast that rescuers finally reached the trapped miners, who had barricaded themselves behind a makeshift barrier of plastic. Only one was alive—Randal McCloy, who had somehow survived in the dark without food, water and clean air while his fellow miners had slowly succumbed to carbon monoxide poisoning as they awaited rescue.

Randal was carried out with kidney, lung, liver and heart damage and remained in a coma for weeks. Three months later, he was eating and breathing on his own and was even looking forward to taking his family to Disney World in Orlando, Fla. There has been much speculation about why Randal survived while the 12 other miners perished. One unsubstantiated theory is that older miners kept feeding him their supplies of oxygen until it ran out. Some doctors suspected that Randal's youth might have helped him survive. Most of the other miners were older, overweight, many were in their 50s.

While specialists have been unable to account for Randal's remarkable survival, some in this coal mining community have a pretty good idea.

"You could call it a miracle," said Russ Biundo, medical director at HealthSouth Mountain View Regional Hospital where Randal received treatment. "I never would have expected him to get so far along in such a short period of time."

Wife Anna McCloy says her husband's recovery has been "like a resurrection."

Randal agrees. "I'm a miracle," he said.

Lost at Sea

NATHAN NEESMITH KNEW HE and his three partners were goners the moment their boat started taking on water.

It was night, and they were more than 67 miles out at sea with no radio, food, water or lifesaving equipment. To make matters worse, a thick blanket of fog had settled over the dark Atlantic, making it nearly impossible to see more than a few feet in any direction.

Their only hope was a couple of flares which Neesmith, a 32-year-old commercial fisherman from Darien, Ga., kept in a tackle box. About an hour earlier, they had passed an oil rig. With any luck, someone on board the rig would spot the flares and come to the rescue.

Working quickly, Neesmith unwrapped the flares and set off the first charge. Minutes passed. Then, growing more desperate as the cold water continued to pour into the fiberglass hull, he fired the second flare.

Neesmith remembered thinking: "They've got to see it, they've got to!"

The four fishermen looked at each other, wondering what to do next. All they could do was sit and wait—and pray that someone saw the flares.

Fifteen minutes went by.

Half an hour later they began to panic.

"There's no way they couldn't have seen those flares," Neesmith later said about the occupants of the oil rig. "It was right there in their faces."

Then, as the thin hull of the 34-foot Casis Nichole began to dip below the water line, Neesmith and his companions prepared to do what every fisherman and sailor has dreaded since the beginning of time—abandon ship. It seemed like the only thing left to do. It was either that or drown on the spot.

Neesmith doesn't remember what happened next.

"All I know is that water came in, and it came in fast," he told reporters later. "We didn't have much time to do anything but jump."

Neesmith grabbed an open box and clung to it for dear life. His companions, brother Billy Joe Neesmith, 23, Keith Wilkes, 18, and Franklin Brantley, 23, all of Darien, drifted away, in the darkness.

That was the last he ever saw of them.

All night long he called out their names. He figured they must have either drowned right away or the current scattered them quickly in all directions.

For four days and nights, Neesmith drifted upon the open sea, alone and without food or water. He splashed his face continually to stay awake, hopeful that a rescue ship or airplane would soon reach him.

Several times he thought he felt sharks brush against his legs. One night he saw a tall dorsal fin slowly circling him. On another occasion he became entangled in a jellyfish colony but, fortunately, suffered no stings.

If help did not arrive soon, he knew he would die. He was growing weaker by the hour and did not know how much longer he could hold onto the box. The temptation to drink saltwater was almost overwhelming, but the burly, mustachioed fisherman resisted.

Only a miracle could save him.

Sometime during the second or third day, he heard voices—voices calling out his name, voices telling him to keep going, not to give up.

"I heard people talking to me," Neesmith recalled. "I heard people yelling out, 'Nathan!' I thought sure somebody was there. I'd look around, but nobody was there."

Sometimes the voices were so clear they sounded only a few feet away. Neesmith said he'd "jump up and look around," half expecting to see somebody behind him.

At first he felt afraid of the voices. All his life he had heard tales about mariners who also heard voices before they died at sea. Neesmith thought they might be demons or angels, he did not know which, coming to claim his soul.

As the days passed, however, and his strength waned, he concluded that "it was only the good Lord keeping me awake so I could survive."

Late on the afternoon of the fourth day, a Coast Guard craft spotted Neesmith and the bobbing box about 20 miles off the South Carolina coast near Hilton Head. The currents had taken him more than 150 miles away.

He was flown to Memorial Medical Center in Savannah where he was treated for hypothermia and dehydration.

Later that night, a Coast Guard C-130 aircraft found debris from Neesmith's boat—but no sign of the other crewmen. The search was called off a week later.

Neesmith's ordeal, which made national headlines, left the veteran fisherman badly scarred but not defeated. Grateful to be alive, he attributes divine intervention to saving his life.

"It was the good Lord," he said.

He continues to fish for a living, but now he carries a ship-to-shore radio, cell phone and plenty of lifesaving equipment whenever he goes out to sea.

Fall from the Sky

ON A CLEAR, cold night in the spring of 1944, British Royal Air Force Sgt. Nicholas Alkemade climbed into the tiny "gunner bubble" at the rear of the Lancaster bomber and settled back for the long, dangerous flight to Berlin.

He was a little nervous, since this was his 13th bombing raid over Germany.

As he hunkered down behind the pair of Browning machine guns, he couldn't stop thinking that this was the loneliest, most dangerous job in Bomber Command.

With any luck, the mission would be over in a few hours. Then it was back to England, where the 21-year-old airman was looking forward to spending a much-needed leave of absence with his girlfriend, Pearl.

Everything was going fine until a German Junker 88 aircraft raced up to meet them over Frankfurt. There was a loud explosion, followed by a blinding flash—then screams from the front of the plane.

The Lancaster was on fire and going down.

"Bail out! Bail out!" the captain shouted over the headsets.

But the young flight sergeant couldn't bail out. His parachute, which was stowed outside the gunner's turret in the fuselage, was in flaming shreds.

"My stomach seemed to drop out of my body when I realized my parachute was useless," he later recalled.

His choices were clear: stay inside the plane and die—or jump and take his chances on surviving a fall of more than 18,000 feet.

Thinking it was better to die a quick, clean death than to fry, he jumped.

"It was perfectly quiet and cool, like resting on a cloud," he recalled. "It was as though I was lowered onto a super-soft mattress. There was no sensation of falling….I thought, 'Well, if this is dying, it's not so bad.'"

Indeed, he felt so peaceful that he was able to calculate that from 18,000 feet it would take him 90 seconds to reach the ground.

Then he blacked out.

Three hours later, Sgt. Alkemade awoke. Staring up at the stars, he wondered if he was in Heaven. He shouldn't be alive, that much was clear. By all accounts, he should be dead, his body broken into pieces on the hard, German ground. "It was a miracle," he said. "I was in one piece.—hardly hurt, in fact."

Somehow the trees had broken his fall. Eighteen inches of fresh-fallen snow made a final cushion that saved his life. The only damage were a couple of cuts on his face and a badly twisted right knee.

A few minutes later German soldiers arrived and took him to a hospital. There he tried to explain what had happened. Predictably, his incredible story fell on deaf ears. The airman had to be a spy; no one could have survived an 18,000-foot fall without a parachute.

Then news reached the hospital that a Lancaster had crashed nearby during the night. When investigators sifting through the ruins of the downed British bomber found items in the gunner bubble that belonged to the young airman, they were convinced he was telling the truth.

Sgt. Alkemade survived his 13th bombing mission and continued to live a "charmed" life, working in a chemical factory. Once a steel girder fell on him. Hauled out for dead, he walked away with a bruised scalp.

He narrowly escaped death several years later when he was drenched with sulfuric acid. He also survived an electric shock that threw him into a hole, where he lay breathing chlorine gas for 15 minutes.

His luck finally ran out in 1988, when he died of a heart attack at the age of 65.

*"And I saw three unclean spirits like frogs come out
of the mouth of the dragon, and out of the mouth of the beast,
and out of the mouth of the false prophet. For they are the
spirits of devils, working miracles, which go forth unto the
kings of the earth and of the whole world, to gather them to the
battle of that great day of God Almighty."*
—Revelation 16:13-15

ARE MIRACLES THE WORK OF EVIL?

*"...Satan himself
is transformed into an angel of light."*
—2 Corinthians 11:14

Turn on the television almost anytime of day or night
and you're bound to see one—a honey-tongued, fast-
talking hunk or babe, usually garbed in a glittering
gown or silk suit, spouting hellfire and salvation to a packed
crowd of tearful, hand-waving spectators.

Long before Jim and Tammy Faye Bakker, back before
Elmer Gantry and the Rev. Jonas Nightengale, charlatans in the
church were a common problem for true believers trying to get
right with the Lord. Early Christian writers warned of "evil-
doers" masquerading as men of God, at least since the 1600s
when a Portuguese nun painted nail wounds on her hands, feet,
side and forehead to fake stigmata, the wounds Christ received
on the cross.

The Bible, too, warns of "false prophets" in the church who
offer counterfeit miracles in their efforts to deceive the righteous
in the name of Satan.

In the early days of America, circuit-riding preachers
galloped across the land promising visions and signs to isolated
communities of settlers who prayed and paid for these services—

sometimes to great disappointment. Many a backwoods preacher rode into town preaching messages of fire and brimstone, only to ride out on a rail after being found lacking in certain fundamental virtues.

In the 19th century, the whole séance-oriented spiritualist movement in Europe and America fizzled and sputtered after client "victims" wised up and discovered hidden wires, microphones and other equipment. When radio came on line in the early 20th century, unscrupulous hucksters took to the airwaves to bellow the gospel and plead for donations.

That tradition continued, when the magic of television allowed a new breed of sweet-talking, sweat-stained evangelists such as Oral Roberts and Jimmy Swaggart to saunter onto the scene. While not all televangelists are outright crooks, many have been forced out of the pulpit after confessing to great misdeeds.

Such shenanigans might seem innocent, almost harmless, by today's standards. With the dawning of Aquarius in the 1960s, a new age in mysticism was launched in places like Sedona, Ariz., and Santa Fe, N.M. Amid the deserts and wild mountains of California, Oregon and elsewhere, beaded, self-professed pagans struck up a hew harmony with nature, unlike anything since the great mystic cults that flourished in the early centuries after Christ.

Crystals, channeling, divining and even witches are all part of this New Age of Enlightenment. Trends such as these are gaining new popularity, especially among the disaffected young, fueled by popular television shows and ladies magazines that explore psychic frontiers, parallel universes and the inner sanctum of consciousness. Many who embrace this form of entertainment seek radical spiritual methods of reaching out to the cosmos, new alternatives to help explain life's age-old mysteries.

Not lost amid these novel and profound movements, a new generation of Christians—mostly Roman Catholics—has emerged to claim mystical experiences and miracles that challenge established traditions. Visions of the Virgin Mary are on the increase; so are sightings of strange "crosses of light," speaking in tongues and other mystical phenomena associated with Catholic traditions.

Some of these miracles are honest mistakes due to natural causes—lighting conditions, optical illusions, hallucinations, delusions, even mass hypnosis or hysteria. Some scientists speculate that a "spinning" or "pulsating" sun, as seen accompanying many Marian visions, can be the result of involuntary eye movements caused by staring at a fixed, brilliant object for long periods of time. As for rosaries that turn from silver to gold, metallurgists say that color changes can result from tarnishing or rust.

Amid all the confusion, what is the Church to make of all this pseudo-mysticism? Some religious leaders see Satan behind much of the miracle-mania. Their conclusion: it's the devil's way of deceiving Christians and destroying the church.

"Beware of false prophets and phony miracles, is all I can say," one Baptist pastor warned. "They are the work of the Devil and his evil partners."

Writing for *Catholic Culture*, Kevin Orlin Johnson says, "People claim to see apparitions just to get in the spotlight."

He adds, "The minute you see self-proclaimed visionaries giving interviews to the press, dashing off reams of prophecies, asserting that they've seen Mary and that they have an urgent message that can save the world...certainly as soon as you see a reported visionary routinely blessing people, curing pilgrims, you can safely assume that person is a fraud, or, if you want to be particularly charitable, that the person is deluded."

Many religious leaders acknowledge that miracles come in two ways—through God and through Satan. Satan, theologians rush to point out, is forever trying to duplicate God's power to perform miracles and occasionally resorts to his own trickery.

In the Book of Exodus, for example, we learn that Satan mimicked God's power to enable Egyptian magicians to turn wooden staffs into serpents and water into blood and to perform other miracles.

"Demons can and do perform miraculous signs," says Dan

Corner of an online Christian group called Evangelical Outreach. "Satan has in the past, is now and will continue in the future to use miracles to deceive."

Christians are also taught that the number of "miracles and visions" will increase at the approach of the "last days"—the end of time. Many of these miracles and visions will be rendered in the name of Christ—something preachers have been warning about for a long time.

It was the Apostle Paul who warned that evil powers were already at work in his day. He prophesied that prior to the return of the Messiah, the "restraining power of the Holy Spirit" would be removed to allow the power of Satan and his associates full sway to deceive the world—by means of miracles and lying wonders.

"And then shall that Wicked be revealed," Paul says, "whom the Lord shall consume with the spirit of his mouth, and shall destroy with the brightness of his coming: Even him, whose coming is after the working of Satan with all power and signs and lying wonders, and with all deceivableness of unrighteousness in them that perish; because they received not the love of the truth, that they might be saved. And for this cause God shall send them strong delusion, that they should believe a lie: That they all might be damned who believed not the truth, but had pleasure in unrighteousness" (2 Thessalonians 2:7-12).

As people move away from the "true church" and embrace New Age religions, some religious leaders complain they're leaving open the door for Satan and his "evil host" to creep through and spread confusion and fear with miracles and wonders.

"One should be very careful in accepting miracles as a proof of Jesus Christ or God the Father," says Ernest L. Martin, author of *The History and Prophecy of Miracles (and their Failure)*. "Only if the signs and wonders are manifested within the righteous standards shown in the Holy Bible can any credence be afforded them."

He adds, "Simply because a miracle is performed in the name of God or Christ is no guarantee that the source is the true

God."

In Matthew 7:21-23, it is written:

"Not every one that says unto me, 'Lord, Lord,' shall enter into the kingdom of heaven; but he that does the will of my Father, which is in heaven. Many will say to me in that day, 'Lord, Lord, have we not prophesied in your name? and in our name have cast out devils? And in your name done many wonderful works?' And then will I profess unto them, I never knew you, depart from me, you that work iniquity."

When we read newspaper accounts of porcelain statues that wink or bleed or shed milk; when we see thousands of worshipers gathered on a hillside to try to see the Virgin Mother in clouds; when we see stories about images of Christ in a bowl of cornflakes or on the side of a barn; when we witness ordinary people walking barefoot across a bed of hot coals; when we hear someone speaking in tongues or handling poisonous serpents in a religious ceremony—what are we to think?

Mainstream religious leaders insist that many of these so-called miracles are performed by the "prince of darkness," saying that the adoration of statues, objects, pictures or the like is strictly forbidden in the Scripture and originates with the "great imitator, Satan." They seem to be saying: "The more one believes in these things, the more power he receives from the devil.

In 2 Thessalonians 2: 9-12, Paul writes: "The coming of the lawless one will be in accordance with the work of Satan displayed in all kinds of counterfeit miracles, signs and wonders, and in every sort of evil that deceives those who are perishing. They perish because they refused to love the truth and so be saved. For this reason God sends them a powerful delusion so that they will believe the lie and so that all will be condemned who have not believed the truth but have delighted in wickedness."

The Roman Catholic Church, while taking great pains to carefully investigate each miraculous claim, maintains a super-cautious attitude before recognizing or endorsing any miraculous event, whether weeping Madonnas, Marian apparitions or other phenomena.

Some fundamentalists see the world as being in its last days, a time when miracle-working abounds in the churches, synagogues and temples around the world. They remind us of the biblical warning that we will see strange sights in the heavens, false prophets and counterfeit miracles, and that "even the very elect might be deceived."

"Those today who wish to adopt the attitude of emphasizing signs, wonders, tongues, prophecies, healings, etc., should look at their desires and re-evaluate them in the light of biblical history and prophecy," says Martin.

How can we determine if a miracle is divine—or simply the work of the devil?

"The criterion is God's word," says Corner. "If God's word isn't considered as final authority when testing a miracle, vision, dream, prophecy, teaching, etc., one will probably be deceived and could possibly lose his soul."

SOURCES & ADDITIONAL READING

ABC News. "Surviving Miner Fighting for His Life." 2006.

About.com. "Biography of Saint Padre Pio." 2006.

"All About God." *Speaking in Tongues: The Biblical Record.* 2006.

"All About God." *Speaking in Tongues 2: Christian Viewpoints.* 2006.

"All About Jesus Christ: Why did He Perform Miracles?" Allaboutjesuschrist.org. 2002.

Alnor, Jackie. "Offer it Up: Stigmatas. Suffering and the Catholic Church." *Catholic Answers*, 2003.

Alnor, Jackie. "Stigmatas, Suffering and the Catholic Church." *Catholic Answers*, 2003.

Anderson, Joan Wester. *The Power of Miracles.* Ballantine, 1998.

Ang, Roseline. *Miracles in Naju.* Korea. 1997.

"Apparitions of the Virgin Mary." *A History of Marian Appearances.* 1998.

Arthur, Bob. "Images of the Madonna in Texas." mcn.org/Miracles. 1998.

Associated Press. "Autistic teen's 20-point night touches all." ESPN.com. 2006.

Associated Press. "Public to be Barred from Site of Visions of Mary." 1999.

Associated Press. "Survivor of W. Va. Mine disaster McCloy learning to walk and talk again." *The Pittsburgh Tribune-Review*, 2006.

Aveni, Anthony F. "The Star of Bethlehem." Archaeological Institute of America. 1998.

Baker, Jane. "Storey Images of Madonna." *Eyewitness Report.*

Balaban, Victor. "The Marian Apparition Site at Conyers. Georgia. Religions of Atlanta: Religious Diversity in the Centennial Olympic City." Scholars Press, 1996.

Barron, Tracy. "Priest Receiving Treatment." *Evening Telegram*, 1998.

BBC-Radio4. *The Miracle Men.* 2002.

Blackbourn, David. "Visionaries: Seeing Was Believing." *The New York Times Book Review.*

Blackbourn, David. *Marpingen: Apparitions of the Virgin Mary in Nineteenth-Century Germany.* Knopf, 1994.

"Blood Brother." *Fortean Times*, 2006.

"Blood, Sweat and Tears." *Fortean Times*, 2002.

Bradley-Steck, Tara. "Miracle Attracts Crowds." Associated Press. 1997.

Bread of Heaven. "The Stigmata: True and False Prophets."

Brown, Tom. "Speaking in Tongues." Tom Brown Ministries. 2006.

Butler. Rev. Alban. *The Lives of the Fathers. Martyrs and Other Principal Saints.* Sadlier, 1864.

Caesarius of Heisterbach. *Dialogue on Miracles.* Routledge, 1929.

Campbell, Glenn. "*Blessed Virgin Mary Sightings in Mojave Desert.*" Campbell@ufomind.com. 1997.

Capua, Raymond. *The Life of Catherine of Siena.*

Carroll, Susan S. *The Star of Bethlehem: An Astronomical and Historical Perspective.* 2006.
"The Case of the Weeping Madonna." *U.S. News & World Report*, 1993.
"Catherine del Ricci." *Patron Saints Index.* 2006.
Catholic Encyclopedia. "Imposition of Hands." 2003.
Catholic Encyclopedia. "St. Joseph of Cupertino." 2003.
Catholic Encyclopedia. "St. Lidwina." 2006.
Catholic Encyclopedia. "St. Veronica Giuliani." 2006.
Catholic Encyclopedia. "Ven. Anne Catherine Emmerich." 2005.
Catholic Online. "All About Saints." 2006.
Catholic Online. "Mystical Stigmata." 2006.
Catholic Online. "St. Bernadette Soubirous." 2006.
Catholic Online. "St. Elizabeth of Hungary." 2006.
Catholic Online. "St. Gemma Galgani." 2003.
Catholic Online. "St. Pio of Pietrelcina." 2006.
Catholic Web Services. "Father Pio's Celestial Perfumes." 2006.
Catholicity. "St. Lidwina." 2006.
Catholicpages.com. "Medjugorje." 2005.
Cavendish. *Man, Myth and Magic.* Vol. 59.
"Charlatans in the Church." *U.S. News & World Report.*
Christian Apologetics & Research Ministry. *What is Speaking in Tongues?* 2006.
Christian, William A. *The Spanish Republic and the Reign of Christ.* University of California Press, 2000.
ChristianAnswers.net. "What was the Star of Bethlehem?" Eden Communications, 1997.
Christopher, Milbourne. *ESP, Seers & Psychics.* Crowell, 1970.
Committee for the Scientific Investigation of Claims of the Paranormal (CSICOP). *FOX's Miracles and Visions*, by Joe Nickell. 2006.
Concernedcatholics.org. "Eucharistic Miracles." 2006
"Conyers Apparitions of the Virgin Mary." *New Georgia Encyclopedia.*
Corner, Dan. *Miracles: Two Sources.* 2006.
creativespirit.net. "Aromas Carry the Awareness of Spirit." *Books in Brief.* 2006.
Crystallinks. *Crosses of Light.* 2006.
Crystallinks.com. "Stigmata." 2001.
Daczynsky, Vince. "Self-Levitation." *Unexplained Mysteries.* 2006.
Daily Bible Study. "Laying on of Hands." 2006.
"Daniel Dunglas Home." Survivalafterdeath.org. 2004.
Danis, Jim. "Apparitions in the News." The Marian Library/International Marian Research Institute. 2001.
Daughters of St. Paul. "The Apparitions at Banneux." 2003.
Daughters of St. Paul. "Our Lady of the Poor." 2006.
De Giorgio, Dr. Laura. "Levitating Saint." www.deeptrancenow.com. 2005.
De Oliveira, Prof. Plinio Correa. *St. Joseph of Cupertino: Tradition in Action.* 2005.
Deliriumsrealm.com. "Witches & Sorcerers of Antiquity: Simon Magus." 2003.

DePalma. Anthony. "Let the Heavens Fall. Mexicans Will Revere Virgin."
  The New York Times, 1996.
Deutsche Welle. "Virgin Mary Gets an Excused Absence in Germany." 1999.
Dewhurst. Kenneth, and A.W. Beard. "Sudden religious conversions in
  temporal lobe epilepsy." *Science Direct*, 1970.
Easton, Kary. "Levitating Saints." Paranormality.com. 2002.
Educational Broadcasting Corporation. "Miracles." 2000.
Edwards, Harry. "Incorruptibility: Miracle or Myth?" www.adam.com.
  au/bsteee/. 1995.
Edwards, Harry. *Skeptoon: An Illustrated Look at Some New Age Beliefs.*
  1994.
Edwards, Harry. *Stigmata.* Skeptics SA. 2005.
Encyclopedia Britannica. "Saint Bernadette of Lourdes." 2006.
Encyclopedia Britannica. "Simon Magus." 2006.
Eternal World Television Network. "Lidwina." 2006.
Eternal World Television Network. "Joseph of Copertino." *The Saints: A
  Concise Biographical Dictionary.* Ed. John Coulson. Hawthorn Books,
  1960.
"Firewalking." *Skeptics Dictionary.* 2006
"Firewalking." Spiritweavers.com. 2006.
Floyd, E. Randall. "Barnwell Springs deeded to God." *Augusta Chronicle*,
  1990.
Floyd, E. Randall. "Unexplained Mysteries: Deathbed Visions a Common
  Thread." 2004.
Floyd, E. Randall. "Unexplained Mysteries: Near-death encounters have long
  history." 1998.
The Franciscans. *St. Francis Receives the Stigmata.* Felix Timmermans,
  2006.
Friary of Our Lady of Grace. "Voice of Padre Pio." 1998.
Geissinger, Steve. "Pilgrims Crowd California Town to See Image."
  Associated Press.
"Gemma Galgani." *The Saints: A Concise Biographical Dictionary.* Ed. John
  Coulson.
"Gemma Galgani." www.frenchpress.com. 2002.
Great Miracle Given by God." "Light at the Holy Sepulchre." *The Christian
  Life.* 1999.
Griffin, Stan. "Stigmata." *Workers for Jesus.* 2005.
Gubanov, Vladimir. "Holy Fire: Miracles on Holy Sepulchre." 2002.
Hanley, Robert. "Struggling with Those Who Seek the Virgin Mary." *The
  New York Times*, 1998.
Hansen, John-Erik Stig. *The Nature of Miracles.* Afdelingsleder, 1999.
Herbert, Thurston. *The Physical Phenomena of Mysticism.*
"Hindu Milk Miracle." *Empower.* 2006.
Holt, Jim. "The Bloody Truth: Are Stigmatics Neurotics?" *Lingua Franca*,
  1999.
"Holy Visions: Mystical Experience of Brain Malfunction." www.
  religioustolerance.org. 2006.
Homewithgod.com. "Saint Lidwina of Schiedam." 1923.

Homewithgod.com. "Venerable Anne Catherine Emmerich."
Hvidt, Christian. "The Miracle of the Holy Fire." cytanet.com. 2003.
"Incorruptibles." www.protestanterrors.com. 2006.
Jackson, Wayne. "Can Christians Speak in Tongues?" *Today*, 2003.
"Jesus's Miracles—History or Myth?" *The Watchtower*, 1995.
Johnson, Bob. "Toddler OK After Being Rescued From Well." Associated
    Press. 2004.
Johnson, Kevin Orlin. "Apparitions: Mystic Phenomena and What They
    Mean." Trinity Communications, 2006.
Ken Collins Web Site. "The Star of Bethlehem." 2006.
Kennedy, Allison. "Visions attract visitors to farm." *Augusta Chronicle*,
    1992.
Knight-Ridder. "Weeping Painting Seen as a Miracle."
Kselman, Thomas. "Miracles and Prophecies: Popular Religion and the
    Church in Nineteenth-Century France." Unpublished Ph.D thesis.
    University of Michigan. 1978.
"Laying on of Hands." *The Latter Rain*. 2006.
Leach, Monte. "Manifestations from Medjugorje." 2006.
Leikind, Bernard J., and William J. McCarthy. "An Investigation of
    Firewalking." *The Hundredth Monkey and Other Paradigms of the
    Paranormal*. Ed. Kendrick Frazier. Prometheus Books, 1991.
"A Light History of Levitation." www.goldendome.org/levitation/index.
    2006.
Lindsey, David Michael. *The Woman and the Dragon: Apparitions of Mary*.
    Pelican, 2000.
Livingmiracles.com. "Eucharistic Miracles." Wonders Unlimited. 2005.
Livingmiracles.com. "Incorruptibles." Wonders Unlimited. 1999.
Livingmiracles.com. "Miraculous Images." Wonders Unlimited. 2005.
Livingmiracles.com. "Tears of Blood." Wonders Unlimited. 1999.
Livingmiracles.net. "Apparitions." 2005.
Livingmiracles.net. "Holy Oils." 2005.
Livingmiracles.net. "Holy Relics." 2005.
Livingmiracles.net. "Miracle of the Holy Fire." 2005.
Livingmiracles.net. "Stigmata." 2005.
Martin, Ernest L. *The History and Prophecy of Miracles (and their Failure)*.
    Associates for Scriptural Knowledge. 1983.
Marypages.com. "Our Lady of Beauraing." 2006.
McClory, Robert. "Sightings, Signs and Wonder." *America: the National
    Catholic Weekly*. 2004.
McGregor. *The Spirituality of Padre Pio*. The National Center for Padre Pio.
    2005.
"Melanie of La Salette." www.churchijnhistory.org. 2005.
Michael. *Saint Padre Pio: The Priest with the Stigmata*. 2002.
"Milk Drinking Statue." *The Supernatural World*. 2006.
"Miracle." *The Skeptics Dictionary*. 2002.
"Miracle of Lourdes." www.olrl.org/stories. 2006.
"Miraculously Cured by St. Gabriel of the Sorrows." www.stgemma.com/
    eng. 2006.

Mizrach, Steve. "Miracles examined from a Fortean perspective." 2006.

Modern Day Saints. "Saint Gemma Galgani." *The Defender*, 2001.

Modern Stigmatics. *Blood on their Hands*. 2002.

Morris, Linda. "Priest offers $5000 to disprove miracles of Lourdes." FaifaxDigital, 2004.

"Mother Mary Apparitions: The Hidden Dark Side." www.biblestudysite. com. 2006.

"Mother Mary Comes to Me." *Fortean Times*, 1999.

MSNBC.com. "Miracle child survivors of the tsunami." 2005.

National Center for Padre Pio. *The Life of Saint Pio*. 2005.

New Advent. *Mystical Stigmata*. 2006.

News24.com. "Lourdes miracle is official." 2005.

Nickell, Joe. *The Encyclopedia of the Paranormal: Miraculous Phenomena*. Prometheus Books, 1996.

Nickell, Joe. "Examining Miracle Claims." Deolog. 1996.

Nickell, Joe. *Looking for a Miracle: Weeping Icons, Relics, Stigmata, Visions and Healing Cures*. Prometheus Books, 1993.

Nicozisin, Fr. George. "Speaking in Tongues: An Orthodox Perspective." Greek Orthodox Archdiocese of America. 2003.

O'Connell, John. "Our Lady of Guadalupe." Catholicnet. 1998.

Ojito, Mirta. "The Power of St. Irene's Hand." *The New York Times*, 1996.

Orthodox Wiki. "Church of the Holy Sepulchre." 1999.

"Padre Pio's Stigmata Analyzed by Scientist." *Signs and Prophets of God*. 2002.

Peterson, Daniel C., and William J. Hamblin. "The Descent of the Holy Fire in Jerusalem." *Meridian Magazine*, 1999.

Peterson, Iver. "Diocese Finds Virgin Visions Aren't Miracle." *The New York Times*, 1995.

Peterson, Wayne. *The Visions of Children: Messages From Medjugorje*. 2006.

Pilcher, James. "Virgin Mary Message Draws Crowd." Associated Press. 2002.

"The Plain Truth about Protestantism." www.protestanterrors.com/miracles. 2006.

Podles, Leon J. *There's No Smell Like Home*. Touchstone, 2003.

Preston, June. "Mary Apparitions on the 13th." 2002.

Prichard, Rebecca Button. "What Presbyterians Believe." Presbyterians Today Online. 1999.

Radkowsky, Alvin. *Manifest Wonders*. 2006.

Reeves, Thomas C. *Miracles and History*. History News Network. 2005.

Report of General Information and Complaints Department. *Messages From Heaven: Apparitions of the Virgin Mary*. Zeitun, Egypt. 1996.

Rotten.com. "Firewalking." 2006.

Rotten.com. "Marian Apparitions." 2006.

Rotten.com. "Miracles." 2006.

Ruoppolo, Germano. *Blessed Gemma Galgani: The Holy Maid of Lucca*. 1913.

Sack, Kevin. "Miracle Farm's Flocks are Pilgrims." *The New York Times*, 1995.

"St. Catherine of Sienna." *The Saints: A Concise Biographical Dictionary*. Ed. John Coulson. 2006.

"St. Januarius." *Old and Sold Antiques Digest*, 1883.

"St. Januarius." www.catholicity.com. 2006.

"St. Veronica Giuliana." www.americancatholic.org. 2006.

Saints Alive. "St. Catherine de' Ricci." St. Thomas The Apostle Church. 1984.

Saints Alive. "St. Gabriel Possenti." St. Thomas the Apostle Church. 2006.

Saints Alive. "St. Januarius of the Miracle." St. Thomas the Apostle Church. 2006.

Saints Alive. "St. Veronica Giuliani." St. Thomas the Apostle Church. 2004.

Saunders, Fr. William. "What is the Stigmata?: Straight Answers." *Arlington Catholic Herald*, 1999.

Schwebel, Lisa J. *Madonnas: Christianity and the Paranormal*. Paulist Press, 2004.

Sermon Notes. "Miracles." 2001.

SHARE International. "Crosses of Light." 2005.

SHARE International. "Healing Water and the Science of Light." 2005.

SHARE International. "Healing Water Found in Germany." 2005.

SHARE International. "Magical Water Found Near Delhi." 1993.

SHARE International. "Signs and Miracles." 2006.

Sheehan, James J. "A Figure in White: How a Vision of the Virgin Mary a Century Ago Rocked a Small German Village." *New York Times*, 1994.

Sheler, Jeffery. "What's in a Vision?" *U.S. News & World Report*, 1990.

Sheler, Jeffery L. "A Gift to the Magi." *U.S. News & World Report*, 1999.

Shelley, Bruce L. "Signs & Wonders: Miracles Ended Long Ago—or Did They?" *Christianity Today*, 2006.

Shermer, Michael. "Miracle on Probability Street." *Skeptic*. 2004.

"Sign of the Cross Crosses Appear in the Windows of a Norfolk Church." *The Virginian-Pilot*, 1996.

Smith, Dr. Arthur. "Relics." Noetic Health Center.

Smith, Marie. "The Visions of Saint Gemma Galgani." 2006.

Smith, Marie. "The Visions of Saint Veronica Giuoian." 2006.

Steinfels, Peter. "The Vision That Wasn't. Or Was It?" *The New York Times*, 1992.

"Stigmata." *Skeptics Dictionary*. 2005.

Stockbauer, Bette. "The Heart of Tlacote." *Miracles*. 2006.

Straus, Rabbi Andrew. "Everyday Miracles Are All Around Us." *Jewish News*, 2006.

Sullivan, Randall. "The Miracle Detective." *Atlantic Monthly Press*, 2004.

"Temples full after reports of miracles." *The New York Times*, 1995.

A Treasury of Catholic Reading. Ed. John Chapin. Farrar, Straus, 1957.

Trexler, Frank. "Visions: Miracles or Spiritual Messages?" *The Knoxville Journal*, 1988.

Tucker, Liz. "God on the Brain." *BBC News*. 2003.

Villoldo, Alberto. *Healing States.*
"Visions of the Virgin." www.jeremiahproject.com. 2006.
Wagner, Stephen. "The Star of Bethlehem: Paranormal Event?" 2006.
Whitworth, Lou. "Edgar Cayce: The Sleeping (False) Prophet." Probe
    Ministries. 1996.
Wikipedia. "Bernadette Soubirous." 2006.
Wikipedia. "Catherine of Siena." 2006.
Wikipedia. "Fire-Walking." 2006.
Wikipedia. "Glossolalia." 2006.
Wikipedia. "Incorruptibility." 2006.
Wikipedia. "Januarius." 2006.
Wikipedia. "Laying on of Hands." 2006.
Wikipedia. "Levitation." 2006.
Wikipedia. "Miracle." 2006.
Wikipedia. "Simon Magus." 2006.
Wikipedia. "Star of Bethlehem." 2006.
Wikipedia. "Teleportation." 2006.
Wikipedia. "Stigmata." 2006.
Williams, Daniel. "In Italy, Where Statues Weep, Scientists Test the
    Miraculous." *Washington Post*, 2005.
Wilson, Ian. *The Bleeding Mind: An Investigation into the Mysterious
    Phenomenon of Stigmata.* Weidenfeld and Nicholson, 1988.
Wooden, Cindy. "Woman whose healing is 67th Lourdes miracle tells her
    story." Catholic News Service. 2005.
Woodward, Kenneth. "Should You Believe in Miracles?" *Reader's Digest*,
    2000.
Woodward, Kenneth. *The Book of Miracles: The Meaning of the Miracle
    Stores in Christianity.* Simon & Schuster, 2000.
Workers of Our Lady of Mount Carmel del Garabandal. *What is
    Garabandal?* 1997.
"Yesterday and Today." *Ice Skating Magazine.* 2006.
Zurl, Carmen. "The Madonna of Medugorje." 2006.

ABOUT THE AUTHOR

E. RANDALL FLOYD is a motion picture screenwriter and best-selling author of several books, including *Deep in the Heart, The Good, the Bad and the Mad: Weird People in American History* and *100 of the World's Greatest Mysteries: Strange Secrets of the Past Revealed.* His latest book is *In the Realm of Ghosts and Hauntings.*

A former European correspondent for United Press International, he worked for *The Florida Times-Union* and the *Atlanta Journal-Constitution.* He later lectured at Georgia Southern University and Augusta State University. He is also a former nationally syndicated newspaper columnist.

Mr. Floyd has appeared on hundreds of national television and radio talk shows, including Art Bell's *Coast-to-Coast, Strange Universe,* the *Barry Farber Show, ManCow,* the *X-Zone, Good Day, USA* and others. He lectures on a number of topics, ranging from strange and unusual aspects of Civil War history to historical oddities and the paranormal. He lives in Augusta, Ga., with his wife, Anne, and their son, Rand.

To contact Mr. Floyd to arrange lectures, guest appearances and autograph signings, or to order books, please call the Augusta office, 706-738-0354, write Harbor House, 111 Tenth Street, Augusta, GA 30901 or e-mail: rfloyd@ harborhousebooks.com.